MARESFIELD LIBRARY

# TRAUMA, GROWTH, AND PERSONALITY

PHYLLIS GREENACRE, M.D.

*Introduction by*
*ERNST KRIS, Ph.D.*

**MARESFIELD LIBRARY**
LONDON

Reprinted 1987 with permission
of Hogarth Press Ltd, by
H. Karnac (Books) Ltd,
58 Gloucester Road,
London SW7
England

ISBN 0 946439 37 0

Printed and bound in Great Britain by
A. Wheaton & Co. Ltd, Exeter

# PREFACE

THIS volume consists of a selection of related studies made during the past decade, all but one of which have appeared as contributions to various journals. Their publication in the present form was stimulated by the desire of numerous students and colleagues to have the studies made more easily accessible.

Although these studies were not planned to form a book originally, there is, I believe, a kind of organic connection each with the next, starting with birth and neonatal influences and continuing through the fateful first five years of life to the oedipal period. Obviously there are many areas of early personality development which have not been investigated or where the investigation has been along certain lines, undoubtedly representing special interests, namely the interaction of maturation phases and special traumas in the first few years of life and the probable effect of these early patterns on the structure of the later personality.

The investigations are clinical in origin, *i.e.*, have arisen almost exclusively from therapeutic work with patients to whom I have a deep debt of gratitude for all they have taught me. I wish to thank the Editors of *The Psychoanalytic Quarterly*, of *The American Journal of Orthopsychiatry*, and of *The Psychoanalytic Study of the Child* for their co-operation. Especially would I thank my many friends and colleagues who have encouraged, discussed, and criticized my work, and Miss Mary Elizabeth Killiam for her secretarial help in the preparation of the manuscript.

PHYLLIS GREENACRE

# CONTENTS

|  |  | Page |
|---|---|---|
| Preface | | v |
| Introduction by Ernst Kris, Ph.D. | | ix |

*Chapter*

| I | The Biological Economy of Birth | 3 |
| II | The Predisposition to Anxiety, Part I and Part II | 25 |
| III | Infant Reactions to Restraint: Problems in the Fate of Infantile Aggression | 78 |
| IV | Urination and Weeping | 99 |
| V | Pathological Weeping | 111 |
| VI | Vision, Headache, and the Halo | 122 |
| VII | Anatomical Structure and Superego Development | 138 |
| VIII | Conscience in the Psychopath | 153 |
| IX | A Contribution to the Study of Screen Memories | 174 |
| X | The Prepuberty Trauma in Girls | 189 |
| XI | General Problems of Acting Out | 208 |
| XII | Special Problems of Early Female Sexual Development | 220 |
| XIII | Respiratory Incorporation and the Phallic Phase | 240 |
| XIV | Some Factors Producing Different Types of Genital and Pregenital Organization | 272 |
| | References | 283 |
| | Index | 297 |

# INTRODUCTION

PUBLISHED during the course of only one decade, the
studies collected in this volume draw on insight gained
from many years of psychoanalytic practice combined with a
lifetime's experience in teaching and in investigative work in
clinical psychiatry. Many issues in psychoanalysis are touched
upon and many of the shortcomings of current psychoanalytic
writings are here redeemed. There is the complaint that the
art of case presentation has been lost, and this is attributed by
some to a widening cleavage between the descriptive and the
explanatory, *i.e.*, the psychoanalytic approach to psychiatry.
In Dr. Greenacre's writing we find enthralling clinical descriptions, sometimes sketched in a few strokes next to detailed case
histories condensed in a few poignant pages. There is no cleavage here; all is of one piece since it all is seen from one angle.

The quest for a rationale in psychotherapy and, simultaneously, the expanding range of psychoanalytic therapy itself
have in recent years stimulated interest in varied types of discussions of psychoanalytic technique. But where generalities
tend to predominate, Dr. Greenacre excels by directness and
simplicity, the hallmark of assuredness. We are told in detail
how certain types of resistance are best handled and with
what approach even severe cases can be made amenable to
psychoanalytic therapy. One hears the analyst's voice as she
addresses the patient. The freedom of these interventions
becomes possible since all that happens in the therapeutic
situation is clearly structured by theoretical expectations and
presented to the reader with one dominant question in mind:
How did it all originate?

Once more this is the point where controversy is frequent;
much is being made of the danger that an understanding of the
defensive surface of behaviour should be neglected for the sake
of the ' depth ' of unconscious and instinctual strivings or that
the patient's involvement into current reality should be
neglected for the sake of his infantile past. The reader of this
book is tempted to consider such dichotomies as spurious.
Minute and subtle links lead from defence to instinctual drive,

from surface and present and even from the appearance of the
adult to early childhood. They are interconnected by what at
one occasion Dr. Greenacre called the telescopic manner in
which earliest experiences of the organism are registered and
gradually merge with later ones in the structure of human
memory.

Though the essays here collected were written without the
full awareness of the closeness of their internal cohesion, they
follow each other more closely than many a time the chapters
of a book planned as a unit. Several years ago, when only the
first of these studies had been published, I noticed that here was
the nucleus of a large contribution, which would lead the
author into an already determined direction, and enable her to
revitalize an avenue of psychoanalytic thinking. To this early
—however distant—participation in the development of Dr.
Greenacre's thought I owe the privilege of introducing this
volume.

The preoccupation with ontogenetic problems, with the
reconstruction of life history, is a part of and the differential
characteristic of any truly psychoanalytic approach. Early in
his work Freud postulated the co-operation of reconstructions
of infant and child. A step in this direction was made when in
the 1920s child analysis came into its own.

The lesson was great and data and insight were rapidly
expanding. And yet child analysts soon had to realize that a
relevant part of their work was on another level once more
reconstructive; even they had to look through the telescope.

It is the mastery of the reconstructive method that gives to
these studies their place in psychoanalytic writings. But the
power of intuitive understanding follows the lead of the most
careful and detailed study of all available data on sequences of
maturational and developmental processes. Dr. Greenacre
succeeds in bringing to life the findings of observers and investigators who started from premises very divergent from her own,
in placing them into the wide framework of clinical material.
The development of isolated ego functions, the maturation of
libidinal and aggressive proclivities are viewed not only as interconnected but also in their relation to modifying external circumstances. It is in this sense that Freud's concept of the

trauma, implicit as it is in some of these chapters, gains its central importance as a point of integration. It enables Dr. Greenacre to enlarge her vista beyond the range of psychological events, and to re-emphasize the continuity that links earliest physiological reactions of the organism to its gradually differentiating psychological experiences.

The question of what distance from each other physiological and psychological processes are usefully viewed has been with psychoanalysis since the time when it presented itself to Freud in the earliest phases of his work. At the present stage of our knowledge no prescription can be given when the fruitful approach becomes too speculative. No guarantee exists against the fantastic except the rare combination of courageous vision tempered by what one might call scientific tact. The present volume is, I believe, witness to their happy and productive fusion.

However great the contribution made by these studies, even greater seems to me the promise they hold. The careful reader will find himself over and over again wandering off from problems that are presented to others that are only outlined, sometimes as it were in an 'aside,' half-unintentionally and yet full of meaning. Many of Dr. Greenacre's hypotheses seem to lead into a definite direction of research: they lend themselves to empirical validation by further and systematic investigations by others, who will be able to build on the foundations which Dr. Greenacre has laid.

ERNST KRIS

*Trauma, Growth,*
*and Personality*

## CHAPTER I

# THE BIOLOGICAL ECONOMY OF BIRTH*

## *I*

IN this chapter a number of questions are asked regarding the biological economy of birth. It is my intention to bring together as much evidence as possible bearing on the answers and to indicate certain lines of research emanating from them. In what way does the process of birth subserve the new individual, and through him the race? It is my belief that it exerts definite influences on the future psychic and physical patterns of the child, especially on these larger patterns of the distribution of energy and the intensity of drives rather than on the specific smaller patterns which characterize one neurosis or another. These influences are accomplished, I believe, mainly by the degree and shape of the organization of antenatal narcissism to meet postnatal needs, such organization resulting largely from the process of birth.

This study concerns itself with the effect of normal birth—whatever that is—or of usual average abnormal birth, on the infant. It is much easier to establish criteria for definitely abnormal births than to define normal birth. In fact some obstetricians will question whether human birth among civilized people is ever normal; and pregnancy has been defined by one as a disease of nine months' duration.

The lines of inquiry are as follows: the general implications of pain; the question of painful birth from the child's rather than from the mother's angle; an examination of the sensory-motor balance of stimulation and response possible in the infant just before, during, and after birth; the possible relation of this sensory-motor ratio to patterns of normal tension potential established at birth; and, finally, the effect of such patterns on the primary narcissism of the infant and on the energy distribution.

Physical pain is regarded as a signal to the individual that

* Reprinted from *The Psychoanalytic Study of the Child*, Vol. I. New York, International Universities Press, 1945.

something is wrong with the body. Pain may differ greatly in quality, varying from the sharp, shooting character of neuritic pain to the dull ache associated generally with visceral disease. Cannon (1)* in his book, *The Wisdom of the Body*, states: 'As a rule pain is associated with the action of injurious agents, a fact well-illustrated in cuts, burns and bruises. There are, to be sure, instances of very serious damage being done to the body—for example in tuberculosis of the lungs—without any pain whatsoever; and there are instances, also of severe pain, as in neuralgia, without corresponding danger to the integrity of the organism. These are exceptions, however, and the rule holds that pain is a sign of harm and injury.'

Pain occurs in varying combinations with pleasure, as for example in the itch and, especially, in its paler relative the tickle. But in all these forms it is either a herald or a memory of danger and appears as one of the organism's self-protective devices. It resembles in this respect anxiety, the signal of hidden (future or inner) danger, and fear, the reaction to outer danger. Indeed in some states pain, anxiety, and fear are not readily distinguishable one from another, and, in a larger sense, all are varieties of pain, if we consider this as distress, or the opposite of pleasure. The derivation of the word itself from the same root as is found in *penalty* indicates directly its relation to *wrongness* in some form.

It does not seem very important at this point to differentiate clearly between the general category of pain as distress and the specific definition of pain as a sensory perception in the strictly neurological sense. It appears that pain in the perceptive sense is probably an evolutionary refinement accompanying the development of the nervous system and that in the lower animals without developed nervous tissue there exist, nonetheless, indications of organismic distress. Indeed it may seem from the fact that 'pain is a primitive sensory modality and the free nerve endings are the least differentiated of possible cutaneous receptors' (2) that the ability to feel pain in any degree in this perceptive sense is one of the most important landmarks in evolutionary development, and

* Numbers in parentheses refer to the bibliography at the end of this book.

marks the inception of the differentiation of the nervous system.

The one situation in which pain seems conspicuously to appear as part of an ordinary physiological function is in child-birth. It seems best not to become involved here in the questions of the nature, degree, and inevitability of maternal pain. The obstetricians DeLee and Greenhill (3) consider that human birth is always painful and cannot be regarded as a normal physiological process for the mother. That the sensory perception of pain is readily influenced even by the factor of attention is a common experience and can be measured in the laboratory (4). Pyschoanalysts (5, 6) have been impressed especially by the importance of unconscious attitudes of un-willingness and apprehension as contributors to the maternal pain of labour.

While the birth of a baby may be likened to a loss of a part of the body by the mother, as is seen in so exaggerated and special a form in certain neurotic patients, this is hardly true in the same way from the infant's angle. Further, the special pain to the human mother caused by the birth of her baby seems due in some degree to the large size of the infant head, *i.e.*, the pain of the mother may be in part the penalty for the large cerebral development of our species as represented by her off-spring. There is, too, the question of the pain or distress suffered by the infant in the process of being born. It does seem strange, however, that the head, containing the most precious heritage, the well-developed cerebrum, should be not only the cause of much of the stress of birth, but especially that it is, at the same time, the very part of the infant most endangered during birth.

One might inquire why does Nature arrange for the infant to 'lead with its head' in the struggle of being born? The head, being used in the majority of cases as the tool of dilata-tion of the cervix, is given a rhythmic pounding by the periodic uterine contractions. It is protected, to be sure, by the bag of waters during the first stage of labour, but even this protection is generally lost when the head is actually passing through the birth canal; and the effect of the pressure pounding is readily evident in the *caput succedaneum* with which many infants are born, or the moulding where the pressure has been more severe and prolonged. It can readily be seen that it is a natural advantage for the baby to come head first in order to get its nose out quickly and its respiration stimulated. The dangers of breech presentation because of premature respiration are part of general knowledge. It is not the face of the infant, however, that generally presents at birth, but the top of the head, that portion exactly enclosing the cerebrum.

There is evidence that the trauma of birth may cause considerable damage to the infant (7, 8) and that blood is found in the cerebrospinal fluid of the newborn in a surprising number of instances even when there has been no clearly detectable clinical evidence of damage and sometimes when the birth itself has not been conspicuously long or hard. Looked at from a long biological range, it might be expected that this organ, the cerebrum, would be the most protected part of the newborn rather than the most endangered. If the damage of ordinary birth were permanently and appreciably destructive to the cerebrum it would negate the development of that organ. The question then arises whether ordinary uncomplicated birth, even with its considerable degree of trauma to the infant, is not of some advantage, whether in some way this particular workout, rough as it is, serves as a good introduction to life, a bridge between the greater protected dependence of intrauterine life and the incipient increasing extramural independence.

The question of the relation of birth to anxiety is discussed at some length in Chapter II, which deals essentially with the possible effects of difficult abnormal births or poor antenatal or neonatal conditions in producing a state of excessive chronic tension or susceptibility to excitation, which I have characterized as a state of predisposition to anxiety (9). The rather tentative statements made in that chapter are based on my clinical observations, supplemented especially by laboratory experiments, and observations of infants carried on by various investigators. Subsequent clinical experience has reinforced these impressions, but there has not yet been the opportunity to carry out the systematic clinical and experimental investigation necessary to validate more thoroughly or to discard the theory stated.

The problem of the relation of normal birth to anxiety

is touched upon in that study but not adequately dealt with. To recapitulate and redefine now: While anxiety as such cannot exist until there is some dawning ego sense and therefore some individual psychological content, the forerunner of anxiety exists in a condition of irritable responsiveness of the organism, at first appearing in a number of loosely organized reflex responses. The experience of birth is considered by Freud as a prototype of the anxiety reaction (10) but is conceived of as operating through the assimilation into the constitutional make-up (*i.e.*, genetically) of all the births of the ancestors. Freud tended to discard the possibility that the individual birth was of any great importance in determining the strength of the later anxiety reaction. It appears to me, however, that there is little evidence that birth has changed in such a way as to have become less important or more incidental in the life of the organism and that it continues to be the period of organization and patterning of the somatic components of the anxiety response which have previously consisted of loosely constellated and relatively superficial defence movements. It marks, also, the time of the more definite participation of the respiratory and cardiovascular systems in the defence activities of the infant, these very components forming so characteristically the integral part of the commonest somatic pattern of anxiety responses later in life. I conceive of a situation in which the antenatal, natal and neonatal experiences have very slight or no true (differentiated) psychological content at the time of their occurrence, but do nonetheless leave some individual and unique somatic memory traces which amalgamate with later experiences and may thereby increase later psychological pressures. It is in fact extremely difficult to say exactly at what time the human organism develops from a biological to a psychobiological organization.

A general condition, omitted in Chapter II, which I now believe to be important in the development of anxiety potentials in any human being, is the degree of tension existent, dependent on the sensory-motor balance, *i.e.*, the ratio between the sensory stimulation and the capacity (development and opportunity) to effect some sort of motor discharge. Where there has been considerable disproportion between an increased sensory stimulation and a limited motor discharge over a period of time, such tension may conceivably be incorporated into the working balance of the individual, and may become temporarily or permanently, a characteristic of his make-up. Where this is true, a sudden increase or decrease in the established tension level of the individual contributes to symptoms of anxiety. There is, however, in each individual a unique primary organization and level of tension which is determined, in some measure, by the birth experience, furnishing an important element in the patterning of the drive and energy distribution of that individual.

To examine the effect of the process of birth more specifically, one must inquire into the sensory-motor state of the fetus, of the infant during the course of birth, and of the infant immediately after birth; and then consider the relations between these three states, which differ so very markedly. An imposing mass of literature dealing with the ante-natal and neonatal states has grown up. The older investigators, being largely morphologically oriented, were concerned mostly with the presence or absence of various responses in the fetus and in the newborn infant. Later attention focused more on the significance of such behaviour responses. Among all the investigations, the observations and experiments of Preyer (11), Minkowski (26), Langworthy (35), and Windle (15, 21, 23) stand out as most significant.

## II

In antenatal life, the fetus is surrounded by a fluid medium which supports it and protects it against the fullest severity of external impacts. That considerable stimulation may reach the fetus both from the outside and through unfavourable metabolic changes in the mother is definitely established. By and large, however, in a relatively good pregnancy the fetus appears to live a life of comparative ease, relaxation and passivity, even receiving its nutrition in an effortless fashion through the blood stream. Thus its capacity for and rate of growth is enormous and will never again be approximated throughout its life.

When an attempt is made to examine the embryonic development of sensation and of motor activities, an interesting dilemma arises as to which capacity—to receive stimulus or to move—comes first, and it is easy to drift here into a kind of bio-philosophizing. Preyer (11) in his extraordinarily fine classical monograph on embryonic motility and sensitivity, published as far back as 1885, concluded that the sensitivity of the embryo begins later than the motility, and described early movements as both passive and irritative in type. The original passive movement of the fetus depends on the change of position of the mother, e.g., from standing to lying or in the movements of walking or even of breathing, as well as on such impacts of the maternal abdomen with external objects as might cause a change of position or dislocation of the embryo within the uterus. He notes that such passive movement merges over into clear reflex responsive movements, and that, for example, in the twisting of the umbilical cord which may occur quite early, it is not easy to determine whether this has been caused by the purely passive movement of the embryo or by some kind of irritative response to the movement of the mother. Preyer seems in his statement about the late development of sensitivity to be considering this in its stricter sense of a function of differentiated nervous tissue, rather than in its more general biological sense of tissue irritability. The more recent work (1939) of Hooker (12) indicates a response to tactile stimulation with a hair at a little after the eight-week embryonic stage, and he noticed spontaneous movement of a 'total pattern' type at nine and a half weeks, in which the local specific response to tactile stimulation could be superimposed. Preyer (11, p. 40) deals with this problem in the following way: 'I must agree with Griesinger and C. Wernicke, the latter of whom explains that the first movements of our body, the changes in the musculature, give rise to sensations, memory patterns of which remain in the cortex of the cerebrum. These memory pictures of *motion sensations*, motion pictures or ideas[1] of movement, persist alongside of the memory pictures of the sensations of senses.' This is a

[1] One notes how hard it is to avoid the terminology really belonging to a later development. It is obvious from the context that Preyer does not mean *an idea* but only some sort of organic imprint which may later be a factor in an idea.

particularly interesting statement, however, because it implies the possible participation of the cerebral cortex as a kind of repository of experience very early in fetal life, even though we know that its very presence is not essential for the existence of the infant even immediately after birth, as is so grimly demonstrated in the cases of monsters, who move, nurse, and cry even with the complete absence of a cerebrum. Certainly it is known (13) that the 'fetuses of three months have the gray substance arranged in what is essentially the permanent form.' [1] While there is an ontogenetic indication of past changes in the cortex in response to varying needs in the course of phylogenesis, the functional relationship of the cortex to the experiences of the individual fetus remains as yet unclear and still assigned to the realm of speculation. According to some workers (16, 17) on the histological evidence of maturation in brains in newborn babies, there is no indication that at birth the cortex is functioning to any *appreciable* degree as a *mechanism for controlling behaviour*, which appears rather to be mediated through the subcortical nuclei (18). This does not absolutely preclude the possibility, however, that the cortex might be a passive repository as Preyer suggested.

Investigations carried on in recent years seem to substantiate Preyer's observations that the nervous mechanism for motor discharge functions before that for sensory perception. In the very earliest stages the cellular protoplasm has the property of irritable response which is later to be allocated to nervous tissue. During embryonic life, *i.e.*, during the period before the body has taken on the specific form characteristic of its species, little movement occurs spontaneously but it may be elicited by stimulation of the embryo. These investigations in the human have been reported by Hooker (12). Such motion is at first a massive

---

[1] The description of the phenomenon of *neurobiotaxis* by Kappers (14) and Windle (15) gives one a glimpse of the possible participation of the cerebral cortex in the early embryonic life, and the realization that it is conceivable at least that it may be affected by the experiences of the fetus. This phenomenon consists of the mass migration to new locations of nuclear cells, in response to special needs of the organism. This has been noted from one group to another among vertebrates, but more importantly for our purposes, is the fact that it has been observed in the development of individual embryos, and is thought to be a shift to an area closer to the source from which they receive most of their messages, *i.e.*, it is an example of the economizing tendency of nature.

organismic response; later myogenic responses occur, and finally reflex neuromotor responses are established. There are two trends of thought concerning the origin of these reflexes. One group of observers (18, 19, 20) thought that reflexes developed by individuation from the mass or 'total pattern' responses. The other school believed that the early behaviour consisted for the most part in a number of relatively simple reflex responses (21, 22). All this is concisely summarized in Windle's book, *The Physiology of the Fetus* (23).

It appears that the nerve endings which will later serve as receptors of pain are the most primitive of all sensory nerve endings and mark the beginning development of the peripheral sensory system. Further, the fact that neuromotor functioning precedes neurosensory functioning even slightly would tend to establish a favourable situation for the fetus, *i.e.*, that incoming stimuli would be effectively discharged without any degree of tension being established under ordinary conditions. Thus the passivity and protection of the fetus is furthered. This is stated in another way by Windle (23, p. 165). 'The relative quiescences of the normal fetus in utero is somewhat surprising when one considers all of the activities of which the growing specimen is capable when removed from the uterus. The reasons seem to be twofold: lack of adequate stimulation and high thresholds in the fetal central nervous system.'

The same differences of viewpoint as to relation between reflex behaviour and 'total pattern' response in the fetus are carried over to interpretations of the behaviour of the newborn. As has already been mentioned, an anencephalic infant may survive birth for a short time with essential behaviour carried on at a special reflex level. This does not indicate, however, that the normal newborn does necessarily function at this level. Irwin and Weiss (24) believe that the diffuse activity of the newborn is of a thalamic type of organization.[1] Although the fetus has been found by Minkowski (26) and Hooker to respond to tactile stimuli from a quite early period in its life, many

[1] This is of some interest inasmuch as it appears that certain types of head sensations or headaches occurring in states of chronic or severe anxiety later in life may be determined by the sensory patterns set up during birth and integrated at a thalamic level (25), either with or without projections into the cortex.

observers have noted the relative insensibility of the newborn to cutaneous stimulation. McGraw (27, p. 102) remarks: 'When only a few hours or days old some infants exhibit no overt response to cutaneous irritation such as pinprick. It is impossible to know whether such absence of response should be attributed to an undeveloped sensory mechanism or to lack of connection between sensory and somatic centres, or between receptor centres and those mechanisms governing crying. Such infants usually do respond to deep pressure stimulation. In any event, this period of hypaesthesia is brief; by the end of the first week or ten days most infants respond to cutaneous irritation.' Gesell (28) speaks of the newborn infant as being 'quasidormant' and as showing an apparent 'instability' in his reactions. Both authors emphasize the change that occurs at about four to six weeks, when the cortex begins definitely to take hold, as it were. Because of the organization of C. Bühler's (29) observations according to the supposed functional meaning of the behaviour, it is difficult to get from her accounts a good composite picture of the newborn's activities. She mentions the extreme amount of sleeping or napping during the first day or two, the onset of hunger crying generally only on the second day, the twitching at the moment of falling asleep and the irregular twitchings which may occur at other times. In general she considers that 'the sensitive and helpless bodies of newborn children encounter decidedly more situations from which to flee than to seek and probably also encounter much more displeasure than pleasure.' One gets the impression that she found considerable individual differences in the behaviour immediately after birth. Dewey (30) considers that it is practically impossible to investigate pain due to proprioceptive stimuli in the newborn; and sums up the literature up to 1935 with the statement that it is the general opinion that infants at birth do not react to these stimuli in ways that give evidence of much discomfort.[1] Canestrini (32) reported little reaction to pain

[1] She quotes Carmichael (22) who accepts an earlier opinion of Genzmer (31) that the fetus has a poorly developed pain sense. This is based on the observations of the first postnatal day of a premature infant, who could be pricked until blood came without giving any response. This would seem to me hardly a reliable conclusion since it appears to ignore the trauma to an ill-prepared fetus of the impact both of birth and of external conditions.

stimuli, but like other authors found that the lips were the most sensitive. Koffka (33) states simply that the infant's pain sensitivity is subnormal. The Shermans (34) attempted a more extensive investigation of the reaction of the newborn to pain, and seemed to find that pain could be elicited in the first day if stimuli were repeated frequently enough, but that the reaction to the *first* pinprick was generally established only after the seventy-sixth hour. From all these observations it appears that there is some reduction of cutaneous sensitivity during the early neonatal period.

It is interesting that practically all of these investigators ignore the possible effect of birth in producing this change in the newborn. Dewey alone mentions that birth may give a spurt to the sensory development, referring especially to the special senses; but she does not seem to consider that sensory fatigue in some infants may be the cause of apparent regression of some functioning immediately after birth. Among the neurologists, Langworthy (35) makes the important observation that in the human infant birth serves as a great stimulus to the deposit of myelin in the nervous system. 'In the first few weeks after birth, the optic and olfactory systems acquire myelin sheaths, and myelinated projection fibers from the thalamus extend to many areas of the cerebral cortex. The question arises as to the changes at birth that account for this increase in the deposit of myelin. Probably it is the *result of increased stimulation of the sensory organs.*' He believes that human sensory pathways are myelinated at the time when sensory endings receive adequate stimuli. It is not quite clear whether Langworthy considers such stimulation to occur during the course of birth or in the period soon after; probably both. This question of the state of functioning of the central nervous system, especially the possible participation of the cortex, will be again referred to later.

### III

In the review of the literature on fetal and neonatal conditions, it is apparent that the great chiasma is that of birth. It is striking how little attention has been paid to the effect of this process on the development of the organism itself. It seems that serious scientific students following the development of the fetus, make meticulous inquiries into its life and activities right up to the time of birth; pick them up again with the infant after birth and start afresh, without daring to look at the effect of birth itself unless the damage had been so gross as unavoidably to rivet attention upon itself. Perhaps birth is inevitably too close to death in our feelings; perhaps the struggle of birth is at once too terrifying and too inspiring for us to regard it readily with scientific dispassion. Perhaps men have too much exclusion anxiety and women too much direct anxiety.

The fact remains that studies, even thought, concerning any of the subtler effects of birth on the newborn are very scant. Birth seems in the scientific world to be tacitly regarded almost as a rebirth or a reconception. This point can hardly be overemphasized, for among the hundreds of otherwise careful studies of the newborn as to its motor activities, its sensory responses, the state of its rudimentary psyche, and even electroencephalographic studies immediately after birth, references as to the type of birth experience or its effect are conspicuously lacking.[1] Langworthy in his study of myelinization (35, p. 52), makes the suggestion: 'Tracts in the nervous system become myelinated at the time when they become functional.' Later he makes clear that the sensory tracts must function to some degree before myelinization, and that the increase in sensory stimuli, as for example during and immediately after birth, determines the further maturation including the myelinization of the nerve fibre. Thus the myelinization in a premature infant exceeds that of an infant born at term of the same age, if age be considered from the time of conception; and preventing the opening of an eye at the proper time

---

[1] In this connection it is interestingly reported that Erasmus Darwin (grandfather of Charles) in a biological system of medicine published in 1796, under the title of *Zoonomia* describes fear as originating in each individual from the experiences at birth, a description which is said to have suggested Freud's concept of the organization of anxiety by birth. If one reads the original of Darwin, however, it is apparent that his conception was that fear was established by the onrushing multiple stimuli of the world immediately after birth. He, too, could not, or at any rate did not, consider the process of birth. In fact, he gives little more than a paragraph to the business of birth itself, stating somewhat summarily that healthy women should not feel pain but that London ladies were spoiled by tight clothing and city air.

delays the process of medullation in the corresponding optic
tract. Langworthy further states that conditioning reflexes
may occur at subcortical levels. Windle (23, p. 163), too, states
that 'there can be a great deal of well-organized activity in the
brain before any nerve fibers become myelinated' and considers
the possibility (p. 164) that with increasing fetal size, distances
between points in the nervous system become greater and
myelin may be laid down to compensate by increasing the
conduction speed of the fibres. All this is important because it
contributes to the idea stated sixty years ago by Preyer, that
there may possibly be some traces of fetal experience deposited
even at a cortical level but even more assuredly at a thalamic
level. It seems, further, not only possible but a reasonable
expectation that birth itself may contribute to the patterning of
the organic integration.

In the psychoanalytic field, Rank made a contribution in
his visionary theory in regard to the birth trauma, after which
the subject was dropped. There have recently been a few
articles attempting to penetrate into the intrauterine psychology. While these may contain a nucleus of good observation, the specific interpretations appear as fantasies of patient
and author, in which psychic constellations belonging to considerably later periods of development are projected backward
and make it appear as though the fetus lived a full and thoughtful life. The effect then is slightly wild and unconvincing.

Recently there has been some renewal of interest in the
psychology of birth and the effects of different forms of birth
experience on the offspring. Some very important work of
this nature is being carried on in animal experiments by Windle
and his co-workers, observing the effects of asphyxia and other
deleterious conditions at birth.

Let us dare to look at the process of birth and its effects on
the infant—or rather on transforming the fetus into the infant.
In the majority of cases (approximately 96 per cent) (3, p. 198),
the child is born head first.[1] It is not clearly known whether
there is any sort of forerunner of consciousness *in utero*; whether

[1] The distribution of presentations at birth is cephalic approximately 96–
97 per cent.; breech between 3 per cent. and 4 per cent.; transverse generally
less than ½ per cent. Of the cephalic presentations approximately 94 per

from the neurological point of view, there is even slight relatively passive participation of the cortex in fetal life. All we can say is that it is not absolutely impossible. There are some workers who believe that there is a forerunner of consciousness, basing their conclusions on the periodic activities of the fetus which appear as though the fetus had times of something akin to sleep alternating with times of wakefulness.[1] I myself incline somewhat to this point of view not so much from these observations on the fetus about which I do not have the background for a discriminatingly critical attitude, but rather from observations on the newborn with which I am more familiar and especially from certain observations on psychoanalytic patients. Whatever the state of the fetal psyche, we do know that in the process of birth the fetal head is generally subjected to extreme pressure, sufficient to mould it and sometimes to produce hemorrhage, and that, likewise, too quick birth (precipitate or Caesarian) is also associated with increased tendency to cerebral hemorrhage. It would appear, therefore, that even if there were some sort of fetal rudimentary consciousness, the process of birth would be in most instances, and perhaps always, a self-narcotizing or anesthetizing experience to the infant—something akin to a pressure-concussion. It is necessary to concede, however, that there would be some threshold early in labour at which that rudimentary preconsciousness would be lost. Further, one is confronted with the problem whether during birth the extreme sensory stimulation to the infant is such that it leaves some sort of central record, whether at cortical, thalamic or spinal level, or in combinations of these. These considerations cannot be dismissed lightly.

It seems likely that there is some sort of rudimentary

cent. of the 96 per cent. are vertex presentations. It is of special interest that pediatricians have made the general observation that there is a high degree of pathology (injuries to the neck, disorders of breathing, and many other disturbances) among babies born by breech presentation, but this subject has not been carefully studied. (Personal communication from Dr. Milton J. E. Senn.)

[1] The anencephalic monster also has periods of 'sleep' and 'wakefulness' after birth, so that some degree of variation in consciousness must be conceded either at a spinal level or working through the total functioning of the organism. It would be a subject for investigation to determine the differences or similarities between this type of sleep and the sleep of the normal newborn.

consciousness or at least variations in degrees of unconsciousness, for in spite of the enormous sensory stimulation of birth and its probable self-narcotizing effect during birth, and the sensory fatigue immediately afterward, and in spite of the fact that the neonate may live at a spinal level (like an anencephalic monster) after birth until the cortex recovers, develops, and participates in functioning, yet the newborn who has not been subjected to especially severe traumas of birth recovers more promptly from its immediate post-birth sluggishness and its variations between sleep and wakefulness soon become qualitatively different from those of the anencephalic. Its 'recovery' generally occurs around the second or third day. Further, the recent electroencephalographic studies of Smith (36) on the newborn extending through the first ten days of neonatal life indicate the presence of certain rhythmic waves that occur over the sensory-motor area during the sleeping periods of the infant but disappear on his awakening. It has been suggested that these waves are due to developing cortical function. Reasoning from Langworthy's (35) and Windle's (23) formulations (already quoted), this area may be dormant in the fetus although capable of some degree of activity if specifically stimulated. It seems probable that such stimulation does occur at some stage during birth and immediately afterward and thus promotes myelinization and increases efficiency and capacity of functioning.

The work of Stirnimann (37) on the reaction of the newborn to thermal stimulation is also of interest. Working on 50 to 100 babies, he found that they reacted to thermal stimuli as early as 10 minutes after birth, that the most sensitive area was the cheek and that throughout the first day of life this response to thermal stimulation was clearly greater when the infant was awake than when it was asleep. He concluded that some slight degree of consciousness participated in the response. Again, neither of these authors makes any attempt to correlate the findings with types of birth preceding. Perhaps the findings in themselves are not sufficiently intense or the observations made on a sufficient number of infants to warrant such attempt at correlation. Another observation along this same line is that of Wagner (38) who studied the sleep of 40 newborns beginning

8 hours after birth and extending through the first 10 days. Using a polygraph, and classifying his records according to the depth of sleep, he noted great variations between infants and in the same infant at different times, but a general decrease in individual variability during the first 10 days. (As Gesell has remarked, the newborn is 'unstable.') But especially he noted that yawning, sneezing and regurgitation were most likely to occur during complete waking and never occurred spontaneously during the three deepest stages of sleep. Even though these reactions may be provoked from the anencephalic monster it seems to me that these experimental findings, if confirmed, strongly suggest a general participation to some extent of nervous organization above a spinal level relatively soon after birth.

What do we see in this, in its effect on the rudimentary psyche, especially from a psychoanalytic point of view? We may concern ourselves at present with three general categories of inquiry: the effect on patterning of the sensory-motor tension level and its relation to anxiety; the effect on the organization of the narcissism of the fetus/infant; and the effect on the later sexuality of the individual especially in relation to masochism. While these are interrelated subjects, this study touches only upon the first two, leaving the subject of masochism for a further research.

Birth seems to organize the anxiety pattern, setting in motion the genetically determined elements fused with those individually determined ones resulting from the special or unique birth experiences of the given infant. The commonest somatic elements are the cardiorespiratory ones, and the ever-present psychic element of later stages of development is the anxious attitude itself—the sense that something unpleasant or positively painful will happen. But there are a great variety of individual variations: one person feels his anxiety with creepy sensations in the skin, another in weakness in the legs, a third with headache, a fourth with diarrhoea. One could go on to many more examples. From a careful scrutiny of reconstructed material from analytic patients, it seems that such patterning of the anxiety reaction always represents the genetic constitutional elements fused with birth experiences and further mediated through and increased by the traumata of the early years, with which we are so used to dealing in our analytic work. These traumata may in themselves be the predominantly determining experiences for later forms of anxious expression, but in any event never occur without some of the earlier elements. If the anxiety is extreme, these deeper elements always become more conspicuous. The psychic part of anxiety, the quality of anxious expectation, is generally considered to occur after the ego has developed somewhat. That anxious expectation occurs very early, however, in some rudimentary form can readily be directly observed in babies, e.g., a 7-month-old infant gasped and puckered its face with the appearance of frightened anticipation when a large inflated ball rolled silently toward it on the bed. In fact every new experience of the infant may have some tinge of this anxious reaction which is allayed when the experience is repeated or is related to some pleasantly tinged earlier experience. It is a further observation that this early attitude varies greatly from infant to infant in the matter of what stimuli will provoke it. But the whole subject, and especially the questions of the time and stimulations of susceptibility to anxiety-like reactions in the first year require much more thorough systematic study.

While the establishment of the anxiety pattern is a protection against danger, the organization of the narcissism forms an instrument of positive attack, a propulsive aggressive drive. What is narcissism? Freud's deepening conception of it may be followed by consulting his early papers. In 1911, writing concerning the Schreber case (39), he described it as the stage between autoerotism and object love, 'the individual . . . unifies his sexual instincts (which have hitherto been engaged in autoerotic activities) in order to obtain a love object, and he begins by taking himself, his own body and only subsequently proceeds to the choice of some person other than himself as his object.' This description reminds one of the vivid slang taunt among adolescents, 'I love myself, who do you love?' In 1914, Freud (40) wrote, 'Narcissism in this sense would not be a perversion [referring to the original use of the word by Havelock Ellis in 1899 to refer to the specific perversion of self-admiration and love of one's own body] but the libidinal complement to the egoism of the instinct of self-preservation, a measure of which may justifiably be attributed to every living creature,' and later in the same article he states, 'We form a conception of an original libidinal cathexis of the ego, part of which cathexis is later yielded up to objects but which fundamentally persists and is related to the object cathexis much as the body of a protoplasmic animalcule is related to pseudopods it puts out' (p. 33), *i.e.*, primary narcissism is partly given up to object love, but may be withdrawn again and appear in a secondary form. In his choice of this particular analogy, Freud approached a concept of the deepest and simplest form of narcissism, the biological. From a biological viewpoint, narcissism may be defined as the libidinal component of growth which may, however, become turned one way or another by the vicissitudes of experience at any time in the course of life. It is this fundamental biological concept which I am especially considering.

What are the properties or characteristics of narcissism? How does it act in times of stress and in times of plenty? Freud's own simile of the animalcule is extremely helpful. I shall use it not just as a simile but as the fundamental biological conception which it is. In times of organismic distress, trauma, or deprivation, there is at first an increase in the narcissism. It is the libidinal charge of the impulse to conquer, to survive, to attack or to defend. In more elaborated forms of life we see it operating in good and bad forms of attack and defence—in humans in the increase in the wish for omnipotence, for magic, for shortcuts to successful survival as well as in realistic ambition, the drive to hard work, zestful interest, etc. In the amoeba it appears as part of the capacity of the organism to send out a pseudopod to engulf its food. It would seem then to be somehow the force of the cellular protoplasm flowing out through a lessened peripheral cellular tension, some essence of the quality of life.

But what is the characteristic of fetal narcissism? Of the narcissism of the neonatal period of infancy? What does the process of birth do in furnishing a bridge from the one to the other? Is birth a chiasma, or is it a hiatus—a kind of blackout, very closely resembling death? How much of its appearance as a hiatus is due fundamentally to the scotoma even of the scientist? The process of human birth actually does combine some of these opposites: it probably does involve something of a blackout, an apparent almost complete interruption in the life of the organism, but one through which a new arrangement of organismic energy is effected. Perhaps the idea of birth as a rebirth is not so fantastic after all, even though it may be used in quite fantastic ways under stresses in our later life. In dreams and neurotic symptoms, the symbolism of birth is always invested somewhat with death, as for example in the impulses and phobias of jumping. Perhaps suicide always has lurking somewhere the hope of rebirth.

During fetal life under optimum conditions, the neuro-motor maturation preceding slightly the neurosensory, the piling up of tension due to external stimuli is lessened. The libidinal charge, the primary fetal narcissism, would appear to be distributed variously throughout the fetal structure, its patterning determined almost entirely by the phylogenetic history of the species, i.e., any special accumulations would accompany the maturation processes which were quickening at a given time.[1] Probably even during a 'good' pregnancy there is some slight infiltration of stimuli from the extramural world, with corresponding temporary effects upon the fetal narcissism, but these are generally negligible.

Birth itself is an enormous experience, with a sudden increase in the total sensory stimulation in the setting of limited opportunity for motor response, probably proceeding to some degree of sensory fatigue. There is in this way some sort of organismic tension established with a transformation of the relaxed relatively sleepy narcissistic state of the fetus to a neonatal condition with a beginning propulsive psychic drive, the condition of primary infantile narcissism which has previously been considered.

It is apparent, however, that in the process of birth, the amount of stimulation is uneven. Commonly there is an

---

[1] It is obvious that such maturation processes may be affected by internal stimuli arising, e.g., from metabolic products received from the mother. Just how these may produce fetal distress and influence endogenously tensions of the organism is extremely complicated and embraces the field of fetal pathology. In a normal pregnancy these tensions would presumably be minimal.

especially strong stimulation of the head, producing not only an effect upon the scalp and its underlying structures, but especially even a kind of cerebral massage. Under good conditions this acts as a marked stimulation to the nervous system, but especially to the cortex, and according to Langworthy's work, there is thereby a stimulation of myelinization and a preparation for the development of cortical control which will begin to be apparent in a few weeks' time. Under too severe birth conditions, it is obvious that the stimulation proceeds to a stage of destruction and gross damage. In addition to this stimulation of the head, there is obviously a considerable stimulation of the entire body of the infant, with marked internal changes, and a toning up of the skin and muscular systems. Here, indeed, in skin and muscles together with the mouth areas (this latter probably largely genetically determined) is the first libidinal concentration. Rado (41) has referred to this as the 'narcissistic rind of the ego.'

This birth stimulation probably produces a rudimentary erogenization of different body parts, at a level of development when erotism and aggression cannot be separated, but appear identical. Under normal good birth conditions there is sufficient cerebral stimulation to make for good functioning, but not enough to make a vulnerable focus for the later castration anxiety. In the study of psychotics, however, and of certain severe neurotic states, too great erotization of thinking with resultant overactivity and then blocking on a castration basis, is quite apparent. In a number of cases I have been able to recover sufficient material from adult dreams and from the interpretation of adult symptoms to give some idea of the special birth experiences of the given individual; and in the few cases in which it has been possible to check against objective birth records, subsequently obtained, my reconstructions have sometimes proved rather surprisingly correct.

These effects of birth may also be noted in regard to other body parts. For example a dry labour produces, among other things, a subsequent increase in skin erotization and seems the earliest determinant in certain instances, of a body-phallus identification. (I do not wish to imply, however, that this may not develop also in the absence of a dry labour if later conditions are such as generally to overerotize the skin and kinesthetic functions.) When a dry labour has occurred, the later special skin erotization and its corresponding narcissistic investment never disappears in the life of the individual but remains a part of his acquired 'constitutional' equipment. It may be heightened by later experiences, to be sure, but is not lost.

Another example, which I have had the opportunity to study considerably in the course of analytic work, is the production of certain types of head sensations or headaches, which occur in states of marked anxiety. While these can be most easily studied in schizophrenic patients in whom they appear commonly, they may occur also, if the anxiety is marked, in neurotic and even in severe reactive states. In my experience the type of head sensation may often be correlated quite definitely with the form of birth experience of the individual and appears under *any* conditions of very severe anxiety, but especially in later life situations in which the subject of birth is being stirred in the unconscious of the patient. M. Chadwick (42) has also made some valuable suggestions regarding the connections between birth experience and forms of headache but has not presented much clinical material. It is a subject that requires a detailed presentation in order to be in the least convincing, and one that I hope to develop in a more careful study. Another special problem is suggested by Bak (43) who emphasizes the disturbed thermal orientation of the schizophrenic and relates this possibly to the thermal experiences, the too sudden cooling or near 'freezing' of the baby immediately after delivery. He raises other interesting questions regarding the changes of libidinal cathexis of the skin determined at birth, and by the contrast between the antenatal and neonatal states. Jones (44) has hinted at similar questions in an earlier paper on 'Cold, Disease, and Birth.' This paper is only intended to lay the ground work for certain other studies, especially the one on masochism.

Jones obviously makes use of the concept of memory traces that exist in the organization of the individual—organic memories determined by experiences from the very beginning of the life of the individual. Certain neurological aspects of this point of view were stated quite clearly by Preyer (11, p. 40) in the passage already quoted in which he in turn gave credit to Griesinger and Wernicke. In the psychoanalytic literature there are many references to conceptions of such memory traces as they appear in the behaviour of the individual or of his organs, but the subject has not been very thoroughly presented. Ferenczi left a rather specific note (1932) on this subject, stressing that psychological events of the remote past may have left their hardly recoverable traces only in the 'organophysical mimes of the individual.' It should be further emphasized that such traces are generally amalgamated with and often almost concealed by the effects of later events. As has been stated, the focus in this study has been only on certain essentially normal patterning.

In summary, it seems that the general effect of birth is, by its enormous sensory stimulation, to organize and convert the fetal narcissism, producing or promoting a propulsive narcissistic drive over and above the type of more relaxed fetal maturation process that has been existent *in utero*. There is ordinarily a patterning of the aggressive libidinization of certain body parts according to the areas of special stimulation. Specifically, birth stimulates the cerebrum to a degree promoting its development so that it may soon begin to take effective control of body affairs; it contributes to the organization of the anxiety pattern, thereby increasing the defence of the infant, and it leaves unique individual traces that are superimposed on the genetically determined anxiety and libidinal patterns of the given infant.

## CHAPTER II

# THE PREDISPOSITION TO ANXIETY

## PART I *

THE considerations which are presented here have to do chiefly with the predisposition to anxiety and its relation to increased narcissism, especially in severe neuroses. These considerations are largely in the form of questions rather than conclusions. The stages by which I arrived at these questions are given here in order to present the background of this study: (1) the analysis of particularly severe neuroses in adults, (2) the searching for supportive or related data in the medical, psychiatric and psychoanalytic clinical experience of myself and others, (3) a supplementary review of some experimental work and observations, (4) a review of Freud's later publications concerning anxiety, especially *The Problem of Anxiety*, and finally (5) a return to my own case material which I reviewed in the light of my questioning. For the sake of consolidating this presentation, however, this circle of search is taken in a little different order. I shall reserve the presentation of the case material for the second part of this chapter, in which will be discussed also some special considerations of treatment. I have chosen this order because I believe that the clinical material in itself is inevitably so detailed as to be possibly confusing unless the reader is already aware of the underlying thesis. In my work, however, the clinical material came first and the thesis was the result of my observations. I shall first discuss Freud's later statements concerning anxiety, then present factual observations and the results of experiments of some significance in the problem of basic anxiety.

### I

In *The Problem of Anxiety*, Freud (1) says:

'Anxiety is the reaction to danger. . . . But the dangers in question are those common to all mankind; they are the same

* Reprinted from *The Psychoanalytic Quarterly*, Vol. X, No. 1, January, 1941.

for everybody; so that what we need and do not have at our disposal is some factor which shall enable us to understand the basis of selection of those individuals who are able to subject the affect of anxiety, despite its singularity, to normal psychic control, or which on the other hand determines those who must prove unequal to this task' (p. 121).

Then after commenting briefly on the inadequacy of Adler's organ inferiority explanation, Freud turns to a critique of Rank's birth trauma theories. What Freud says here is of importance in regard to his own evaluation of the role of the birth trauma and is in no sense an endorsement of Rank's somewhat mystical therapeutic aggrandizement of it.

'The process of birth constitutes the first danger situation, the economic upheaval which birth entails becomes the prototype of the anxiety reaction; we have already followed out the line of development which connects this first danger, this first anxiety-occasioning situation with all subsequent ones; and in so doing we saw that they all retain something in common in that they all signify a separation from the mother, first only in a biological aspect, then in the sense of a direct object loss, and later of an object loss mediated in indirect ways' (p. 122).

Then, in objecting to Rank's emphasis on the severity of the birth trauma as a determinant—the main determinant—in producing varying degrees of intensity of the anxiety reaction in different individuals, Freud says:

'The emphasis on the varying severity of the birth trauma leaves no room for the legitimate aetiological claim of constitutional factors. This severity is an organic factor, certainly, one which compared with constitution is a chance factor, and is itself dependent upon many influences which are to be termed accidental, such as for example timely obstetrical assistance. . . . If one were to allow for the importance of a constitutional factor, such as via the modification that it would depend much more upon how extensively the individual reacts to the variable severity of the birth trauma, one would deprive the theory of meaning and have reduced the new factor . . . to a subordinate role. That which determines whether or not neurosis is the outcome lies, then, in some other area, and once again in an unknown one. . . . For no trustworthy investigation has ever been carried out to determine whether difficult and protracted birth is correlated in indisputable fashion with the development of neurosis—indeed, whether children whose birth has been of this character manifest even the nervousness of earliest infancy for a longer period or more intensely than others. If the assertion is made that precipitate births . . . may possibly have for the child the significance of a severe trauma, then *a fortiori* it would certainly be necessary that births resulting in asphyxia should produce beyond any doubt the consequences alleged. . . . I think it cannot yet be decided how large a contribution to the solution of the problem [of the fundamental basis of neurosis] it [*i.e.*, difficult birth] actually makes' (pp. 124–126).

From his chapter on 'Analysis of Anxiety' in the same book, I quote the following:

'But what is a "danger"? In the act of birth there is an objective danger to the preservation of life. . . . But psychologically it has no meaning at all. The danger attending birth has still no psychic content. . . . The foetus can be aware of nothing beyond a gross disturbance in the economy of its narcissistic libido. Large amounts of excitation press upon it, giving rise to novel sensations of unpleasure, numerous organs enforce increased cathexis in their behalf, as it were a prelude to the object-cathexis soon to be initiated; what is there in all this that can be regarded as bearing the stamp of a "danger situation"? . . . It is not credible that the child has preserved any other than tactile and general sensations from the act of birth [in contrast to Rank's assumption of visual impressions]. . . . Intra-uterine life and early infancy form a continuum to a far greater extent than the striking caesura of the act of birth would lead us to believe' (pp. 96, 97, 102).

Here I realize we are symbolically and figuratively in deep water, but at the risk of finding myself in a sink-or-swim situation, I shall raise some questions now and repeatedly throughout the rest of the material of this chapter. It certainly seems clear that the birth trauma occupies no such exalted place in etiology or therapy as was once assigned to it by Rank; it seems indeed to have fallen quite into disrepute as an etiological factor in the neuroses. Yet we raise the question whether variations in the birth trauma are so insignificant in their effect on later anxiety—when birth is indeed the prototype of human anxiety —as we have been assuming. Is the birth trauma so opposed to the importance of constitutional factors as is implied in Freud's critique of Rank's position, as really 'to leave no room for the legitimate aetiological claim of constitutional factors,'[1] or may not the anxiety-increasing factors of a disturbed birth process combine with or reinforce the constitutional factors in the fashion of multiple determination of symptoms with which we are quite familiar? If the accumulated birth trauma of the past is so important as to leave an anxiety pattern in the inherited equipment of the race, is it then to be expected that the individual birth experience will have been nullified by this inherited stamp? If so, when does an anxiety reaction begin to appear—after birth, at birth, or is it potentially present in intrauterine life, to be released only after birth?

We are used to thinking of anxiety as having psychological content, but is there a preanxiety response which has very little

---

[1] I believe that elsewhere Freud himself has stated his attitude a little differently, and clearly does not in general consider the constitutional and the accidental as leaving no room for each other. He deals with this in a forthright fashion in his footnote to the first paragraph of his article on the 'Dynamics of Transference' (1912).

'We will here provide against misconceptions and reproaches to the effect that we have denied the importance of the inborn (constitutional) factor because we have emphasized the importance of infantile impressions. Such an accusation arises out of the narrowness with which mankind looks for causes inasmuch as one single causal factor satisfies him, in spite of the many commonly underlying the face of reality. Psychoanalysis has said much about the "accidental" component in aetiology and little about the constitutional, but only because it could throw new light upon the former, whereas of the latter it knows no more so far than is already known. We deprecate the assumption of an essential opposition between the two series of aetiological factors; we presume rather a perpetual interchange of both in producing the results observed. . . . The relative aetiological effectiveness of each is only to be measured individually and in single instances. In a series comprising varying degrees of both factors extreme cases will certainly also be found. . . . Further, we may venture to regard the constitution itself as a residue from the effects of accidental influences upon the endless procession of our forefathers." (Collected Papers, II, p. 312.)

psychological content? There are anxiety-like behaviour patterns in lower animals, even in those that are not viviparous. The human anxiety pattern varies greatly in its symptomatic form. Most commonly it contains cardiorespiratory symptoms which seem indeed to be the nucleus of the birth experience. But are there events besides birth itself, perhaps in the way of untoward events in intrauterine life or in the first few weeks following birth, which might constitute danger situations and be reacted to with something akin to anxiety in fetal life or in the first few weeks of postnatal life?

The fetus moves about, kicks, turns around, reacts to some external stimuli by increased motion. It swallows, and traces of its own hair are found in the meconium. It excretes urine and sometimes passes stool. It has been repeatedly shown that the fetal heartbeat increases in rate if a vibrating tuning fork is placed on the mother's abdomen. Similar increases in fetal heart rate have been recorded after sharp loud noises have occurred near the mother. This finding is reported by a number of investigators. Two of them, Sontag and Wallace (2), found marked increase in fetal movement in response to noise of a doorbell buzzer; this was especially strong and consistent when the buzzer was placed over the fetal head. Responsiveness to sound began at the thirty-first week of intrauterine life and increased as the fetus neared term (3). The fetus may suffer hiccoughs, even as early as the fifth month; and respiratory-like movements are noted in the last month. Sometimes the fetus sucks its own fingers, and cases have been recorded in which the infant was born with a swollen thumb (4);[1] and it is by no means rare for newborn babies to put their hands directly to their mouths. One questions what has been the role of sucking in these cases. Has a fortuitous meeting of hand and mouth served any function and been prolonged because of this? It would seem that the fetus is relatively helpless; and that while we cannot speak of any perception of danger, we still are faced with the quandary of what is the reaction to untoward conditions of intrauterine life, such as might in postnatal life produce pain and discomfort and be reacted to by crying. I raise the question whether the fetus which even cries *in utero* if air has been

[1] See footnote 1, p. 44.

accidentally admitted to the uterine cavity, reacts to 'discomfort' with an acceleration of the life movements at its disposal —sucking, swallowing, heartbeat, kicking. What is the relation of such accelerated behaviour to anxiety? This is not the more or less organized anxiety pattern which we are used to thinking of as the anxiety reaction, to be sure; but do not these responses indicate an earlier form of anxiety-like response of separate or loosely constellated reflexes? I realize here that I run the risk of encroaching on the domain of neurology and reflex reactions, and on the field of biology, which describes anxiety-like (frantic) behaviour in lower animals and even insects. So I must retreat again to an attitude of inquiry.[1]

## II

When we examine (vicariously) the behaviour of the newly born infant (according to Watson's studies (5) made in 1918–1919), we find three types of emotional reaction, described by Watson as 'fear,' 'rage' and 'love.' The behaviour which

---

[1] In the chapter on 'Analysis of Anxiety' (*The Problem of Anxiety*, pp. 105–107), Freud postulates a kind of anxiety signal which is different from the anxiety reaction itself, but sees the first as derived from the second, the latter being operative in the development of the actual neuroses, the former of the psychoneuroses. 'But when it is a matter of an "anxiety of the id," one does not have so much to contradict this as to emend an infelicitous expression. Anxiety is an affective state which can of course be experienced only by the ego. The id cannot be afraid, as the ego can; it is not an organization, and cannot estimate situations of danger. On the contrary, it is of extremely frequent occurrence that processes are initiated or executed in the id which give the ego occasion to develop anxiety; as a matter of fact, the repressions which are probably the earliest are motivated . . . by such fear on the part of the ego of this or that process in the id. We have good grounds here for once again distinguishing the two cases: that in which something happens in the id which activates one of the danger situations to which the ego is sensitive, causing the latter to give the anxiety signal for inhibition; and that in which there develops in the id a situation analogous to the birth trauma, which automatically brings about a reaction of anxiety. The two cases are brought into closer approximation to each other if it is emphasized that the second corresponds to the initial and original situation of danger, whereas the first corresponds to one of the anxiety- occasioning situations subsequently derived from it. Or, to relate the matter to actually existing disorders: the second case is that which is operative in the aetiology of the "actual" neuroses, the first is characteristic of the psychoneuroses.' What I am suggesting sounds as though it were comparable to this distinction, but it is really quite at variance with it.

Watson describes as a 'fear' response is 'a sudden catching of the breath, clutching randomly with the hands, sudden closing of the eyelids, puckering of the lips, then crying.' These responses are present at birth. Watson found no original 'fear' of the dark, and postulated correctly that later fear of the dark in older infants was due rather to the absence of familiar associated stimuli. The conditions which he found capable of producing a 'fear' response were: (1) sudden removal of all means of support, *i.e.*, dropping the child (or this same condition in a lesser degree—namely the pulling or jerking of the blanket or the sudden sharp pushing of the infant itself when the child is falling asleep or just awakening, and (2) loud sounds made near the child. Thus we see here a response (with the addition only of the cry) similar to the one which presumptively is called forth *in utero*, and provoked by the reversal of the most favourable mechanical features of intrauterine life, namely, the full support of the fetus, and the presence of a shock-absorbing fluid pad. The reaction to noise both in intrauterine life and immediately after birth raises the interesting problem as to whether this is real hearing or whether it is a tactile reaction to vibration. In favour of its being a reaction to actual hearing are the facts that embryological research has shown that the ear is functionally complete in anatomical structure and nerve supply long before birth (6), and that many clinical observations of prematurely born infants indicate that they are almost uniformly hypersensitive to sound; also that fetal reactions are greatest when the sound stimulus is applied over the fetal head. Of this reaction to sound I shall have more to say later. It seems possible, in fact, that the intrauterine situation in which the fetus is surrounded by water may furnish conditions in which sound is actually magnified: that is, the amniotic fluid may absorb mechanical shock but amplify sound.

The behaviour which Watson characterizes as 'rage' is indicated in the newborn infant by 'stiffening and fairly well-co-ordinated slashing or striking movements of the hands and arms. The feet and legs are drawn up and down; the breath is held until the child's face is flushed. These reactions continue until the irritating situation is relieved, and sometimes beyond. Almost any child from birth can be thrown into rage if its

movements are hampered; its arms held tightly to its side, or
sometimes even by holding the head between cotton pads.'
Here I would emphasize that this behaviour appears as an
aggressive reactive response to situations which are at least
faintly reminiscent of the recent birth experience, in which the
child was perforce helpless and the victim.[1]

Watson designates as 'love' the response characterized by
cessation of crying followed by smiling or gurgling, but does not
differentiate between a positive pleasure gained and relative
pleasure from relief of fear or discomfort. This pleasure response
he sees produced as the result of stroking, tickling, gentle rock-
ing, patting and turning upon the stomach across the nurse's
knee. These behaviour reactions of newborns described by
Watson would appear, then, as centrifugal and centripetal
responses possibly correlated with disturbances of intrauterine
life in the case of 'fear,' and with prolonged or difficult birth
processes in the case of 'rage.' This is too schematic, however,
and I shall presently be in danger of over-emphasizing a contrast beyond its value. Certainly in most instances they would
combine and reinforce each other. In brief, then, I would raise
the question of a preanxiety intrauterine response to (threatening) stimuli, consisting of reflex oral, muscular, cardiac and
possibly prerespiratory reactions. This precedes the anxiety
pattern established by the birth trauma, and probably aug-
ments it. It is inconceivable to me that there should be much
psychic content to this, and it may indeed be the stuff of
which blind, free-floating, unanalysable anxiety is constituted—

---

[1] Watson's division of the behaviour into 'fear' and 'rage' has been questioned by other writers. I am concerned here, however, with the actual observations, rather than with his theoretical designations. While there is a
considerable literature also on the related phenomena of the Morro reflex
and the startle pattern in infants and adults, I do not wish now to become involved unnecessarily in these questions. From going over a number of reports
in the literature it seems that reactions of newborns to loud sound and to loss
of support are generally observed, while the active reaction to confinement
of motion is less constant. (Some writers describe the slashing rage-like movements only in some babies, while other babies show a quieting of activity.)
This suggests to me that such behaviour of the newly born babies varies, perhaps according to the pressure and firmness with which the infant is held,
intense pressure producing the active 'rage-like' reaction; lighter holding
pressure, falling in the same category as patting, stroking, supporting stimuli
provokes the quieting response which Watson designated 'love.'

sometimes adding just that overload to the accumulation of postnatal anxiety which produces the *severe* neurotic.

There is one other phenomenon sometimes associated with birth: the frequent appearance in male babies of an erection immediately after birth. (In Part II of this chapter the corresponding reaction in the female is considered.) Although this phenomenon has been frequently observed clinically, I am under the impression that systematic studies of its occurrence are lacking. It has mostly been observed and then passed by. There is a possibility, however, that its occurrence immediately following birth is not merely coincidental but is the result of stimulation by the trauma of birth itself. In a verbal communication from one of the obstetricians on the New York Hospital staff, I learned that erections in male babies are not the rule but are by no means rare. The erection is usually present immediately after birth. As this man described it, 'I turn the baby over, and there it is. I have to be careful not to clamp the penis in with the cord.' It has never occurred to him to consider the cause of these very early erections and he had no idea whether they were in any degree correlated with birth traumata or prolonged births. Again I ask, is there any correlation of such birth erections with anomalies or disturbances of the birth process resulting in more than the ordinary—and presumably benign— sequela of tension?

That extreme emotional excitation may be accompanied by an orgasm even in adults has also been noted (7)[1] and is in line with Freud's early conception of the overflow of dammed-up libido. Cannon (8), approaching the same phenomenon from a physiological angle, says in discussing this, 'Certain frustrations which bring about strong emotional upheavals characteristically energize at least some parts of the parasympathetic division. . . . Great emotion, such as is accompanied by nervous discharge via the sympathetic division, may also be accompanied by discharges via the sacral fibres. . . . The orderliness of the central arrangements is upset and it is possible that under these conditions the opposed innervations discharge simultaneously rather than reciprocally.' Later he states that 'any

---

[1] Köhler, in his observations on chimpanzees, noted that any very strong emotion 'reacted on the genitals.'

high degree of excitement in the central nervous system—whether felt as anger, terror, pain, anxiety, joy, grief or deep disgust—is likely to break over the threshold of the sympathetic division, and disturb the functions of all organs which that division innervates.'

Mrs. Margaret Blanton (9), in some observations on the behaviour of the human infant during the first thirty days of life, published as far back as 1917, noted that erections occur immediately after birth, and mentioned specifically erections in four different babies whom she studied. Although this study meticulously and objectively recorded the infant behaviour, even measuring the angle of the erection, it is unfortunately of little value for our purpose as no systematic record of the behaviour in relation to the infant's biography to date is given; nor was the total number of infants observed specifically mentioned, leaving us thus in the dark as to the frequency of the observation. Mrs. Blanton made some other interesting and rather striking observations, however, which may possibly fit in with and certainly do not contradict the line of my questioning. She noted sneezing as occurring even before the birth cry. Strong rubbing (in contradistinction to patting or stroking—the rubbing, for instance, of the first real cleansing of the body) is accompanied, she says, by the most intense screaming and rage-like reaction that the infant showed at any time during this first month of life. The screaming is most intense of all when there is vigorous rubbing of the scalp and of the back. I would point out here that these are obviously the areas of body surface which have been most exposed to trauma during the birth process. She also remarks that the kinesthetic sense is probably the earliest developed of all the senses, appearing, as may reasonably be supposed, before kicking does in the fourth or fifth month. (What is the basis of this conclusion?) She quotes Miss Millicent Shinn (Notebook No. 2) as referring to the quieting influence of monotonous jarring as compared with smooth motion. Mrs. Blanton observed that walking with a baby quiets it even on the first day, and that in her experience, babies almost never cried when being carried through the hospital corridor. This too seems to support Ferenczi's and Freud's suggestion of the practical continuum of fetal and postnatal life; for the fetus has, in fact, been accustomed to being carried for nine months subject to the rhythmical motion of the mother's walking.

In regard to finger-sucking, Mrs. Blanton enumerates a number of instances occurring almost immediately at birth, the hand-to-mouth movement being so well established as to leave little doubt that it had already been established earlier. Here again we regret the lack of a systematic recording of the observations for each child. She indicates, however, that the finger-sucking was sometimes especially strong in otherwise weak or disturbed infants. 'One baby (a blue baby) two hours old, put fingers directly into the mouth. Another, a Caesarean delivery, very feeble, was seen sucking two fingers so vigorously, it required a decided effort to remove them. She [the infant] put them back at once without trouble. . . . Another, a malformed baby [type of malformation not specified], at ten days and in a dying condition, put finger in his mouth after four trials, and the sucking reflex was moderately good.' This is circumstantial evidence, to be sure, but it is especially interesting that these are the instances specifically noted.

I have recently come upon some further observations from a psychological laboratory which are somewhat supportive, though not conclusive, of the suggestions I have indicated. This is the experimental work of Dr. Henry M. Halverson of Yale (10). Dr. Halverson studied reactions of ten male infants, varying in age from one to forty-three weeks, who were subjected to various nursing situations. Here again the observations are mitigated for our purpose by the psychological interest in the experiment rather than the infant. Even so, Dr. Halverson's results are extremely interesting to us. He observed erections of the penis occurring quite frequently during some nursing situations; actually sixty times in two hundred and twelve different situations of eight different types.[1] It is first to be noted that the erections took place characteristically (with the exception of the first situation) in situations in which there was some frustration in the nursing—delay, difficult nipple, removal of breast

---

[1] The eight type situations were: (1) when the infant was being carried by the nurse, (2) two-minute delay in feeding, (3) breast removed, (4) easy nipple removed, (5) sucking at difficult nipple, (6) difficult nipple removed, (7) sucking at empty nipple, and (8) empty nipple removed.

or nipple. There were three situations in which there was an especially high frequency of erections in proportion to the frequency of the situation; (1) in sucking at a difficult nipple, where erections occurred twenty-four times in twenty-nine such situations; (2) on removal of the breast (prematurely), where erections occurred ten times in fifteen such situations; and (3) during sucking at an empty (air) nipple, where erections occurred thirteen times in thirty-nine such situations. On the other hand, an erection occurred in removing the difficult nipple only once out of twenty-nine such situations (Chart 1).

| FREQUENCY AND NUMBER OF ERECTIONS | Frequency of Situation | No. of Erections |
|---|---|---|
| 1. Infant carried or held by nurse .......... | 29 | 3 |
| 2. Two minute delay in feeding—gripping pressure only ........................ | 29 | 5 |
| 3. Breast removed ........................ | 15 | 10 |
| 4. Easy nipple removed .................... | 3 | 1 |
| 5. Sucking at difficult nipple .............. | 29 | 24 |
| 6. Difficult nipple removed ................ | 29 | 1 |
| 7. Sucking at empty nipple ................ | 39 | 13 |
| 8. Empty nipple removed ................. | 39 | 3 |
| TOTAL ............................ | 212 | 60 |

(CHART 1, from Halverson)

Halverson does not make clear whether this single instance was in an infant who had had no erection during the nursing on the difficult nipple but had developed one on its removal, or whether one of the twenty-four infants was doubly stimulated by frustration: first by the difficulty of the nipple, and then by the removal of even this modicum of sucking comfort. He also remarks that erections never occurred during sucking at the breast or at any easy nipple. The appearance of tumescence, according to Halverson, 'occurred decidedly most often associated with vigorous body movement, and fluctuating gripping pressure with the infant quiet or quieting.' In other words, the tumescence was associated with a general reaction to the frustration and did not appear as an isolated phenomenon.

Halverson also correlated the situations of the appearance of tumescence with those of detumescence (Chart 2). This brings out some striking findings: viz., that in ten instances where erections occurred in sucking at a difficult nipple, they disappeared when an easy nipple was given; and in nine cases where erections occurred when the breast was withheld, they disappeared when the breast was restored. These findings seem outstanding, as they indicate the importance of frustration excitement in the situation of tumescence. Halverson again

FEEDING
CONDITIONS UNDER WHICH ERECTIONS DISAPPEARED

| FEEDING CONDITIONS UNDER WHICH ERECTIONS OCCURRED | Sucking at easy nipple | Breast restored | Weak sucking and mouthing | Resting and mouthing | Sucking air | Resting | Sucking at own bottle | Nipple removed | Sucking at difficult nipple | Weak sucking | Infant removed |
|---|---|---|---|---|---|---|---|---|---|---|---|
| Sucking at difficult nipple | 10 | .. | 2 | 4 | 2 | 2 | 1 | 1 | 2 | .. | .. |
| Sucking air | 1 | .. | 3 | 1 | 1 | 2 | 1 | .. | 1 | 1 | 1 |
| Withholding breast | 1 | 9 | .. | .. | .. | .. | .. | .. | .. | .. | .. |
| Delayed feeding—gripping pressure only | 1 | .. | .. | .. | 1 | .. | 3 | .. | .. | .. | .. |
| Delayed feeding—held by nurse | .. | .. | .. | .. | .. | 1 | 1 | .. | .. | .. | .. |
| Sucking air—nipple removed | 1 | .. | .. | 1 | 1 | .. | .. | .. | .. | .. | .. |
| Easy nipple removed | 1 | .. | .. | .. | .. | .. | .. | .. | .. | .. | .. |
| Difficult nipple withheld | .. | .. | .. | .. | .. | .. | .. | .. | 1 | .. | .. |

(CHART 2, from Halverson)

summarized the behaviour as follows: 'Tumescence is accompanied by restlessness, frequent fretting or crying, marked alterations in muscular tension and vigorous body movements, most of which have no connection with sucking activity. Detumescence is accompanied by general quiescence, during which the muscles may be relaxed or *in a state of sustained tension*' (p. 412). (The italics are mine, as I would emphasize here that this might appear then as a residual tension or, paradoxically, comparative relaxation.) He believes that erections are probably quite common from birth, but are not observed because of the presence of clothing and the general taboo against noticing this phenomenon.

While these results of Dr. Halverson's experiments are harmonious with the assumption of anxiety even to the point of accumulation and a general overflow, any evidence of the association of any such susceptibility to discharge of anxiety or

the possible correlation of it with the disturbances of the prenatal, natal, or very early postnatal experiences is lacking, as
the experimenter made no effort to view his material from this
angle. Here, however, is a useful field for observation if the co-
operative interest of the obstetrician and the pediatrician can
be obtained; and while we still lack direct observations (which
Freud so earnestly wanted) as to the effects of difficult birth, this
nevertheless seems possible, and even a step nearer of attainment.

There are two other groups of observations in fields adjacent
to psychoanalysis that contain facts of some relevance to the
problems I have been discussing: (1) pathologicoanatomic
evidences of the degree of trauma resulting from birth or conditions associated with birth; (2) clinical observations on very
young, prematurely born children.

Concerning, first, the pathologicoanatomic evidences of
trauma occurring at birth, there are many facts available. The
mass of evidence is that *cerebral injury resulting from birth is very
much more common than one might suppose*. There is an excellent
review of this subject in a monograph by Ford published in
1926 (11), from which I shall select some findings pertinent to
our problems. While the study indicated that birth trauma did
*not* play the etiological role in the spastic paraplegias and
hydrocephalus that had been assigned to it,[1] the secondary
implications of the study are important. The pathologicoanatomic study was made, of course, on the dead victims of the
birth struggle; but the author notes, 'There is some evidence
that intracranial haemorrhage occurs in babies who survive
and may even show no clinical signs of (gross) birth injury. . . .
Old blood pigment is found in the meninges of babies up to the
ninth month even where there is no (clinical) evidence of injury
at birth.' Routine lumbar punctures done within a few days
after birth show modified blood in the cerebrospinal fluid in a
surprising number of instances without clinical indications of
trauma.[2] Please do not think that I am implying that anxiety

[1] It is of incidental interest that this was the conclusion of Freud also, in
a monograph published by him in 1897 on *Cerebral Birth Injuries*.

[2] F. R. Ford quotes a report of blood in 14 per cent. of the cerebrospinal
fluids obtained by routine lumbar puncture following birth in 423 coloured
babies. Only 6 per cent. of these babies had shown any clinical evidence of
cerebral lesion, and less than 3 per cent. died.

comes from blood in the meninges, I emphasize these facts simply because such a finding is a positive indication of one kind of trauma associated with birth and is in some measure an index of the degree of trauma occurring.

The same study also gives evidence that injury to the cerebrum, even to the extent of petechial haemorrhages in the white matter, results not so much from the trauma of the birth process as from asphyxia and strangulation which may occur with birth and may also occur in some degree through circulatory disturbances if the cord is caught around the fetal neck *in utero*.

Other pathologicoanatomic findings of note are evidences of disturbances of intrauterine life which leave gross effects on the fetus, without any clinically observable disturbances in the maternal health. Some fetal disturbances formerly thought to be due to defects in the germ plasm or to accidents at birth are evidently caused rather by local fetal illness. We are quite used to the idea that the fetus may suffer from systemic maternal disease; but it is pointed out (by Ford and Dandy) that in hydrocephalus, in which mechanical birth trauma was previously thought to play an important part, examination reveals adhesions and structural changes of meningitis resembling closely those found in meningococcus meningitis in adults, and that such occur without being associated with any history of maternal illness. There is further evidence of a very high incidence of intracerebral hemorrhage in prematurely born babies where the effect is not so much due to the pressure of labour as to the state of unpreparedness for extramural life of the tissues of the infant at the time of birth. Much greater sensitivity of the skin and fragility of the cutaneous and retinal vessels have been demonstrated in prematurely born babies than are found in the infants born at term.

It is well known that infants born without any cerebral hemispheres[1] may, nonetheless, carry out all the normal early activities, including sucking and crying. Evidently then, these

[1] Two such infants were born at the Johns Hopkins Hospital during the ten years I was associated with that hospital; numerous other instances have been reported elsewhere.

may exist at first entirely at a reflex level. Severe cerebral injury, however, seems to add signs of cortical irritation: localized twitchings and convulsions.

These findings seem to me important as indicating the frequency, the intensity and the far-reaching effects of birth trauma and of the variations in the birth process. They suggest the possible intensification of the organization of the anxiety pattern at birth at a reflex level and in the absence of psychic content. How this psychic content may later develop, partly out of dawning self-awareness during the first months of extra-uterine life, and partly elaborated through and coalescing with the infantile birth theories of the young child with contributions from the stories he hears regarding his own birth—this I hope to consider a little more definitely in a subsequent paper dealing with the clinical pictures in some cases of severe anxiety hysteria.

Surveying the clinical observations on young prematurely born children, we find interesting facts. There are two particularly important studies of behaviour, one by Shirley (12) at the Child Development Center in the Harvard School of Public Health, the other by Mohr and Bartelme (13) in Chicago. Neither of these gives us the very early day-by-day observations we desire, but they at least present some controlled observations. Shirley's report is the more valuable to us because it includes observations on sixty-five infants made periodically from three months to five years, while the other studies include fewer very young children. Shirley states that young prematurely born children (those up to the age of two and one-half years) were much more keenly aware of sounds and very early seemed more interested in their meaning than full-term babies of the same age. They were distracted by footfalls, voices, and incidental noises. Older prematures (those in the two-and-one-half to five-year-old group) often manifested the 'hark' response, stopping in their play and whispering in a startled voice, 'What's that?' at the hiss of a radiator, the chirp of a cricket, or the dropping of a paper. Premature babies were more fascinated by a yellow pencil used in the test than were full-term infants. Yellow objects were definitely preferred to red ones, and this preference for yellow seemed in many instances to persist through the early years. Premature babies seemed also to be more keenly aware of ephemeral visual phenomena like shadows, smoke plumes, dancing motes in a sunbeam, or reflections thrown by a mirror. The observer thought, however, that this visual-sensory sensitivity was less marked and less easily checked than the other characteristics she noted. Although premature babies seemed to respond as well as 'normal' babies in comprehension of speech and in making attempts to imitate words, they had more difficulty in achieving correct pronunciation, persisted longer in baby talk, and showed substitutions of letter sounds. (Mohr and Bartelme reported a higher percentage of stammerers in older prematures.) In general, prematures showed difficulty in manual and motor control. They had difficulty in pointing, showed tremors readily, spilled and scattered objects, and frequently went 'all to pieces' after making especially sustained efforts at manual manipulation. They were delayed in walking and tended to be clumsy. In activity, they went to extremes, tending to be soggy and inert or to be overactive and distractable, and had short spans of attention. In the older group (two and one-half to five years of age) these children might continue to work or play 'at a high level of interest and concentration until they collapsed in rage from fatigue and frustration.' The author also notes that premature children stood out above others in the desire to create artistically (especially through drawing and painting), although they were conspicuously less able, because of their poor motor coordination, to produce very effective results. The emotional responses of the prematures were noted generally to be volatile, with marked petulance, irritability, shyness, and a tendency to explode in a panic or a tantrum. There was a greater incidence of enuresis and day dribbling in the prematures than in others. The author submits no findings about thumb-sucking, but Mohr and Bartelme reported that more than 20 per cent. of their group showed thumb-sucking which persisted beyond twenty-eight months of age. In an attempt to make a quantitative study of these characteristics, Shirley made observations of premature infants comparing them with an equal number of observations of infants born at term. On the following page are three tables adapted from her report.

CHARACTERISTICS SHOWN IN TEST SITUATIONS

| Age group (6–24 months) | 50 Prematures | 50 Controls |
|---|---|---|
| Interest in yellow pencil | 16 | 0 |
| Distraction by sounds | 36 | 6 |
| Throwing toys around | 30 | 6 |
| Banging and slapping toys | 20 | 10 |
| Trembling and shuddering | 18 | 10 |
| Hesitate to touch toys | 10 | 12 |
| Comprehend but refuse to perform | 18 | 8 |
| Seek adult help | 22 | 6 |

(CHART 3, from Shirley)

CHARACTERISTICS SHOWN IN TEST SITUATIONS

| Age group (2½–5 years) | 22 Prematures | 22 Controls |
|---|---|---|
| Very distractable | 45 | 13 |
| Distracted by sounds | 18 | 4 |
| Short attention span | 13 | 9 |
| Trembling | 9 | 4 |
| Throwing toys around | 13 | 9 |

(CHART 4, from Shirley)

CHARACTERISTICS MANIFESTED DURING PLAY PERIOD

| Age group (2½–5 years only) | 30 Prematures | 30 Controls |
|---|---|---|
| Remarks about unusual sounds | 67 | 37 |
| Speech difficulties | 60 | 23 |
| Crying in play room | 80 | 57 |
| Rapid change from toy to toy | 43 | 23 |
| Jittery—nervous | 83 | 27 |
| Bowel movement during play | 40 | 30 |
| Five or more urinations | 27 | 12 |

(CHART 5, from Shirley)

Although these findings by Shirley, some but not all of which have been confirmed by other observers, deal predominantly with children already old enough to be surrounded by complicated life situations possibly outweighing the single factor of prematurity, the picture gives the impression of markedly increased infantile anxiety. How much this is due to the discrepancy between the earlier time development of sensory sensitivity and the later motor co-ordination, and how much it may be due to the traumatic factor, is not clear.

To summarize: (1) there is evidence of the possible existence of a preanxiety reaction occurring in fetal life, consisting objectively of a set of reflex reactions; (2) there seems to be an increase in the intensity of such responsiveness occasioned by the presence of untoward conditions of the prenatal, natal, or immediately postnatal period, such an increase presumably leaving a kind of deepening of the organic stamp in the pattern of response; (3) it seems evident that this preanxiety response is, in the fetal period, devoid of psychic content and probably is to be regarded as pure reflex whereas the birth experience, especially where there is severe trauma, would seem to organize the scattered responses of the fetal period with the addition of the birth cry and what it entails, into the anxiety reaction of which birth itself has been considered the prototype; (4) although the prenatal period is, as Ferenczi pointed out and Freud emphasized, practically a continuum with the postnatal life, the caesura of birth has not only the organizing effect of a single momentous event, but it also marks the threshold at which 'danger' (first probably in the sense of lack of familiarity) begins to be vaguely apprehended and it is therefore the first dawn of psychic content.

There are other problems which suggest themselves along these lines. There is first the question of whether an increased overload of preanxiety, something felt presumably as simple organic tension, is capable of producing a diffuse overflowing reaction including at one and the same time oral, sphincter, and genital stimulation at a reflex level. Further, is it possible that chance touching of the mouth by the hand may produce a premature oralization on the basis of the very earliest autoerotic response tending to promote relaxation of tension? Again, is similar specialized sensitization possible in the case of other zones, anal and genital? We ask, in other words, whether repeated accumulated simple organic tension of the fetus, diffusely discharged, might not deepen reflex response reactions in a way which would anticipate and tend to increase the various later polymorphous perverse stages; or whether some libidinal phase, probably most frequently the oral, might not be accentuated by being anticipated in fetal life, and a preliminary channelization for discharge established (14).[1]

## III

I am quite aware that these borrowed observations are by no means conclusive, and that it may justly be said that I am conjecturing. Having committed myself thus far, however, I shall go further and ask, 'What might be the effect of such early increase in the anxiety potential, provided this does occur, on infantile narcissism?'

Now narcissism is difficult to describe or define. It is, one might say, the great enigma of life, playing some part at one and the same time or in alternating phases in the drag of inertia and in the drive to the utmost ambition, and contributing its share to the regulating function of the conscience. Freud speaks of the 'narcissistic libido' of the fetus, in the passage already quoted, and suggests that its gross economy is disturbed by birth. We can hardly think of the fetal narcissistic libido being more than a degree of sensitivity and susceptibility to stimulus, bringing about the response which I have characterized as the reflex antecedent of the later anxiety response. Freud speaks elsewhere of narcissism as the 'libidinal complement to the egoism of the instinct of self-preservation, a measure of which may justifiably be attributed to every living creature.' (15) This is an extremely significant statement, for it implies that narcissism is coincident with life throughout and that narcissistic libido is, in fact, to be found wherever there is a spark of life. We can readily see, then, that there is a peculiar complexity to the conception of narcissism in the fetus which occupies a unique position between individuation and functioning as part

[1] Gesell and Ilg quote Minkowski as eliciting an oral reflex associated with movement of the leg when lips were stroked in a fetus at the beginning of the second lunar month of intrauterine life. Opening and closing of the mouth appeared as a discrete local reflex at about the eighteenth fetal week. They conclude that: 'it is safe to say that many of the elementary neural and muscular components of sucking and deglutition are prepared as early as the third or fourth month. . . . Even the hand to mouth reaction is anticipated in utero' (p. 15). Gesell notes (p. 123) 'that more boys than girls are thumb suckers; and also that thumb suckers are good sleepers, but otherwise are inclined to be more rather than less active and given to sudden fatigue.'

of a whole larger than itself. Practically, however, we would think that in the fetus the narcissism is reduced to its simplest terms, being almost or entirely devoid of psychic content. I can only think that the disturbance of the gross economy of fetal narcissistic libido which occurs at birth is just this: some transition from the almost complete dependence of intrauterine life to the very beginnings of individuation, at least to the quasi-dependence outside the mother's body instead of the complete dependence inside. That this transition is accomplished with a marked increase of tactile, kinesthetic, and light stimulation seems evident.

There are some attributes, derivatives or forms of postnatal narcissism with which we are familiar under whatever names: (1) the sense of omnipotence with its derivatives; (2) the over-valuation of the power of the wish and (3) the belief in the magic power of words; (4) the mirroring tendency, derived partly from primary narcissism and partly from an imperfectly developing sense of reality, the two in fact being hardly distinguishable. It seems to me quite evident that an increased early infantile anxiety can be expected to be associated with a complementary increase in the infantile narcissism (cf. Freud's statement quoted above); that, in fact, excess narcissism develops as part of the organism's overcoming of the excess anxiety before it can function even slightly as an independent unit in the environment. We might figuratively refer to the simplest primary narcissism in its relation to anxiety as surface tension which may be great or little according to the organism's needs. It is evident that in the birth experience the cry of the newly born infant is the main addition to the prenatal activity, and while it seems largely determined by reflex responses, it is quickly assimilated into behaviour both as a primitive emotional expression and a call for attention. That this latter function continues to be utilized in a way to materialize or substantiate omnipotence need hardly be remarked. The cry, in one sense, is the simplest forerunner of speech, though originally appearing as a simple discharge of nervous excitation.

Here I am not concerned with the vicissitudes of speech development other than to point out that the belief in the magic power of words is probably in line of descent from the utilization of the cry of rage at birth.

The 'mirroring' part of narcissism I believe has its simplest beginning in the incomplete psychic differentiation of the infant from its surroundings, which now include the mother—in the change in fetal narcissistic libido economy entailed in beginning individuation, in the pinching off of the amoebic pseudopod, to use a homely biologic metaphor. I am inclined to believe that this involves dim psychic content from the time of birth, content which is closely related to and dependent on vision, and which develops almost as early if not coincidentally with the cry as a means of communication. Mrs. Blanton noted that a large percentage of babies fixate on light at birth; other authors have noted that even within the first few weeks babies seem to have some recognition of a familiar face and cry when confronted with an unfamiliar one. I am inclined to believe that probably quite early this tendency to cry, *i.e.*, to show an anxiety response to the unfamiliar, becomes augmented by another factor, something which I would characterize as a kind of visual and kinesthetic introjection of those around the infant. The child reacts with a puckered, worried or tense expression when people around are cross or gloomy. This may come about through an association of mild discomfort (the restricting, frustrating sensations of being held or handled by a tense and jerky nurse or mother) with the gloomy expression which it sees; nevertheless the infant soon seems to make the connection directly, an anxious nurse being reflected in an anxious baby without the intermediate kinesthetic link. This is an observation of which sensitive nurses are quite aware. This is a kind of centripetal empathy; perhaps 'introjection' still remains the best word. At any rate I believe that babies vary greatly in this obligatory capacity to reflect those around them, and that it is the tense, potentially anxious infant that is the most sensitive reflector. This may, indeed, have something to do with the peculiar clairvoyant quality sometimes encountered in severe neurotics, and may be even more closely related to the marked facility of identification in severe hysterics who so readily assume the symptoms of those around them.

The infant's developing adaptation to the outer world soon

proceeds, however, beyond this introjective stage to a more definite sensing of the environment as separate from itself, involving in this, however, oscillations between introjection and projection. In Freud's article 'Negation' (16), he described the preliminary ignoring of reality as a transition stage in its acceptance, and stated that acceptance itself inplies a second stage of verification—the perception that the unpleasant experience is *really* true. Freud says in this paper, 'The first and most immediate aim of testing the reality of things is not to find in reality an object corresponding to the thing represented, but to *find it again*, to be convinced that it is still there.' This is certainly familiar enough in the experience of adult life when one sees some particularly shocking sight: there is an initial anxious tendency to block it out, and only by actually reviewing it or recalling it visually is it finally assimilated as a fact. This is, indeed, the familiar abreaction. All this is discussed in Ferenczi's paper 'On the Acceptance of Unpleasant Ideas' (17), as well as in his earlier one (1913), 'On Stages in the Development of a Sense of Reality,' in which he endeavoured to show also that the fixation point of the psychoses occurs at this stage. Now this touches what I have thought about the severe neuroses: that where infantile predisposition to anxiety is great due to an overload of potential in the prenatal, natal, or immediate postnatal experience or the combination of this with constitutional factors, new anxiety occurring at this period might pull down the whole load as it were, and by its peculiar paralysing effect on the organism, impair the sound synthesis of these two stages of reality. Such patients often have, in fact, an extraordinarily clear and vivid visual representation of reality, but one which is insecure and easily dislodged. This disturbed or fragile sense of reality is observed clinically in connection with the too easy identification of such patients with those around them. They are hunting eternally for satisfactory and secure models through which they may save themselves by a narcissistic identification (18).[1] On the surface it appears later as a scattered, superficial pseudo competitiveness.

While I have laid considerable emphasis on the possible exigencies of intrauterine life and the trip through the birth

[1] Do Wittel's 'Phantoms' have their inception here?

canal, I believe that severe traumata occurring during the first
weeks of postnatal life would have a comparable effect. I would
again emphasize that I see these factors as producing a *predisposition to anxiety* which combined with constitutional predilec-
tions might be an important determinant in producing the
severity of any neurosis; for such anxiety is a burden, ever-ready
to combine with new accesses of anxiety later on in childhood
and throughout life.

I know that I run some risk of being misunderstood. It is
possible that the same human tendency to which Freud refers
(in the footnote at the beginning of the article on the 'Dynamics
of Transference,' quoted here in footnote 1, page 28), the tendency to narrow the conception of causes to a single cause, or to
single out only one adversary to be attacked, may cause some
to conclude that I am just dusting off and reviving the birth
trauma theory with slight modifications and an intrauterine
embellishment, and that I am thereby avoiding dealing with
the events of the first few years of life. This is not my intention.
If I did so, I should be reducing treatment to a very fatalistic
management basis—little better and no deeper than therapy by
adroit management of the current situation of the patient
which, to be sure, is so often necessary in psychiatric practice. I
hope that by bringing this possible misconception to the fore in
advance, I may at least partially forestall it. In a later study I
shall present some clinical material with a statement of what I
have found useful in treatment of these especially severe neuroses. I shall indicate the ways in which I believe this excess
narcissism and anxiety may be managed during the course of
analysis—the ways which must be used, in fact, in order that
a 'regular' analysis dealing primarily with the disturbances of
libidinal development may proceed. Certainly the excess of narcissism in these cases is the presenting and terrifying problem
to the analyst. But I am inclined to think that the narcissism
can be educated sufficiently, if it is carefully done, to permit the
patient to stand the pain of the analysis, provided that due heed
is given at the same time to the blind anxiety which is the
cornerstone of this insecure character structure. Much can be
salvaged for such patients, many of whom are talented, intuitive
people.

SUMMARY

Freud considers that anxiety is the reaction to danger, and that birth is the prototype of the anxiety reaction. He sees this, however, as operating through the assimilation into the constitution (genetically) of the endless procession of the births of our forefathers. He doubts the importance of the individual birth experience in influencing the quantum of the anxiety response, largely because the birth experience is without *psychological* meaning; at the same time, nevertheless, he emphasizes the continuity of the intrauterine and the postnatal life.

From the various experimental and clinical observations cited, the question arises whether we may not look at this in a different way. The anxiety response which is genetically determined probably manifests itself first in an irritable responsiveness of the organism at a reflex level; this is apparent in intrauterine life in a set of separate or loosely constellated reflexes which may become organized at birth into the anxiety reaction. How much this total reaction is potentially present but not elicited before birth, and how much birth itself may, even in the individual life, play a reinforcing or an organizing role, is not clearly determinable at present. Certainly, however, 'danger' does not begin with birth but may be present earlier and provoke a fetal response which is inevitably limited in its manifestations and exists at an organic rather than a psychological level. Variations in the birth process may similarly increase the (organic) anxiety response and heighten the anxiety potential, causing a more severe reaction to later (psychological) dangers in life. Painful or uncomfortable situations of the earliest postnatal weeks, before the psychological content or the means of defence have been greatly elaborated, would similarly tend to increase the organic components of the anxiety reaction.

Observations on the special reactions of the fetus in intrauterine life and at birth give rise to new questions as to the effect of these on the later libido development. Further, where there is an increase in the early anxiety there is an increase in the narcissism. This situation favours an inadequate development of the sense of reality and furnishes additional predisposition to the development of especially severe neuroses or borderline states.

# PART II*

## PRACTICAL CONSIDERATIONS OF TREATMENT

IN Part I of this study, I advanced the tentative hypothesis that severe suffering and frustration occurring in the antenatal and early postnatal months, especially in the period preceding speech development, leave a heightened organic stamp on the make-up of the child. This is so assimilated into his organization as to be almost if not entirely indistinguishable from the inherited constitutional factors which themselves can never be entirely isolated and must rather be assumed from the difficult maze of observations of the genetic background of the given individual. I believe this organic stamp of suffering to consist of a genuine physiological sensitivity, a kind of increased indelibility of reaction to experience which heightens the anxiety potential and gives greater resonance to the anxieties of later life. The increase in early tension results in, or is concomitant with, first an increase in narcissism, and later an insecure and easily slipping sense of reality. I referred especially to the increase in the sense of omnipotence which may occur in a compensatory way to overcome or balance the preanxiety tension state of the organism, and to the increased mirroring tendency arising partly from the primary narcissism and partly from the imperfectly developing sense of reality. This increased mirroring tendency is the antecedent of the tendency towards overfacile identification of neurotic individuals, and in psychotics toward easy projection. The derivatives of omnipotence —the over-valuation of the power of the wish and belief in the magic of words—were also mentioned. With all these narcissistic weaknesses, the sense of reality is often poor and even when it seems quite good, it may be facile rather than strong and break

* Reprinted from *The Psychoanalytic Quarterly*, Vol. X, No. 4, October, 1941.

down readily under the fresh impact of anxiety-producing situations of later life. Further, owing to the pressure of early tension and anxiety, the ego development is exceedingly faulty; libidinal attachments are urgent but shallow and the ego drives not well directed toward satisfactory goals. The patient is not well individuated and often gives the impression of being in too great a state of flux, with many interests, many attachments, with the libido quickly and urgently invested and withdrawn.

The main general considerations of the treatment of the severe neurotic or borderline states depend upon the characteristics of development described in Part I. In order to organize my material, I shall discuss these problems of treatment from four main aspects: first, the handling of the overload of anxiety to produce an optimum state for the progress of the analysis; second, the education of the narcissism to better ego proportions; third, the analysis of the 'essential' neurosis; and fourth, the management of the residue of blind, unanalysable anxiety which is present throughout the analysis and which continues to operate in the life of the patient after analysis. I use the term 'essential' neurosis here to differentiate those neurotic elements arising after the development of speech from the predisposing constitutional ones present before this landmark.

I would for the time being divide the overload of anxiety of the severe neurotic into three subdivisions: first, *the basic,*[1] *blind or amorphous anxiety* which is always present in some degree and may in moderation furnish some of the drive of life, but which may be so heightened and combined with the anxiety of fresh dangers as to constitute a serious menace; second, the *anxiety arising in response to these fresh experiences of danger and frustration*; and third, *the secondary anxiety* arising out of the inadequacy of the neurotic defence and the additional dangers, real or illusory,

[1] I shall use the term 'basic anxiety' throughout the rest of Part II. In the first part I used the term 'preanxiety' to designate the condition of heightened irritability arising before the dawn of speech and contributing to the later conditions which I am describing in this present part. I feel justified in using the convenient term 'basic anxiety' as I am now dealing with the adult version of this earlier preanxiety—namely, the form in which it appears as anxiety, or at least amalgamated with anxiety from other sources. The question of the relationship of basic anxiety to the affect of anxiety is one which may well be considered, but cannot be dealt with in this chapter.

following the production of the symptoms themselves.[1] What we term secondary anxiety is familiar enough in the form in which it appears in the malignant compulsion neurosis, in which the compulsions or obsessions appearing as defences against the repressed erotic drives become themselves erotized and require a fresh line of defence to be erected in the form of new obsessional symptoms, until the patient is so involved in the complexity of his fortifications that the rest of life is virtually crowded out. At this stage a secondary atrophy of disuse (habit deterioration; functional dementia) finally occurs, and the end result may be not unlike the schizophrenic process. Although such a malignant development may occur in hysteria also, it is less frequent, less regular in its development and more dependent on the presence of a markedly increased predisposition to anxiety. This is to be expected on the theoretical grounds that the compulsion neurosis arises from trauma and fixation at an earlier level (and therefore closer to the factors producing basic anxiety) than is the case in the hysterical neurosis.

To illustrate the unhappy co-operation of the predisposition to anxiety with the anxiety of later life and finally with secondary anxiety, I shall describe a type of situation which I believe to be nuclear in the development of many severe neuroses.

If the traumata, distress or frustrations of the earliest months are particularly severe, the stimuli do not remain focused but overflow through the body and act upon various organs. We see direct evidence of this in the oral, excretory and genital responses at birth and under stress in earliest infancy. These responses may be activated simultaneously rather than in a relatively orderly progression. I shall illustrate the further succession of events by isolating the genital stimulation and response which arise so precociously as part of a widespread pain-helplessness situation. The response to this situational stimulus is automatic and spontaneous. It subsequently gains an additional pleasure value when the infant discovers the further

[1] A simple form of this is evident in the crying fit. 'It causes disagreeable visceral sensations, perhaps also pains, and it can end in exhaustion. Even if it does not last that long it can be traumatic for the infant. During the screaming fit the infant is not responsive to any attempts to quiet it.' (Benedek, Therese, 'Adaptation to Reality in Early Infancy,' *Psychoanalytic Quarterly*, VII, 1938, pp. 200–215.)

advantage accruing from body movements which also stimulate the genitals. The genital response next takes on a primitive masturbatory character, more obvious in girl babies than in boys. Although in the latter the appearance of an erection is the visible index of stimulation, the appearance of the.most primitive type of masturbation by thigh pressure may be the first evidence of genital stimulation in the girl. The occurrence of repeated and almost continuous stimulation of this sort may produce so prolonged a tonic state as to simulate Little's Disease, and to be capable of interruption only when mechanical obstacles or barriers stop the masturbatory activity.[1] At any rate, where a polymorphous discharge of tension has been carried on in the organism at a very early date, we may conceive of its leaving a heightened irritability for channels of discharge in later life, intensifying first the reaction to traumata of later infancy and early childhood which form the understructure of the essential neurosis, and then, at later periods in life heightening the anxiety of frustration and danger and aiding in turning the flow of activity backward along the old channels rather than continuously forward. If the anxiety is severe at these later periods in life (and it is likely to be severe because of the established predisposition) the overflow response of the earliest days or weeks of life may be repeated, and anxious erotic stimulation again occur. This is the setting of the frantic compulsive masturbation which so often precedes a psychosis. At these later periods in life, however, such masturbatory response is no longer the simple physiological response of the days after birth, but has accumulated the special wrappings of sado-masochistic fantasies (partly or wholly unconscious), guilt reactions, etc., which have invested its development in the intermediate stages. Thus the vicious whirl is set in motion.[2] The poorly developed sense of reality begins to go to pieces, bringing a threat of collapse to the ego; panic and sometimes

[1] I first became aware of the reappearance in a changed form of this initial genital stimulation in anxious states of later life through a series of clinical observations made during my preanalytic work. I have put these together in the section dealing with clinical case reports.

[2] Rado described the ego aspects of such a struggle in a vicious circle in 'Developments in the Psychoanalytic Conception and Treatment of the Neuroses,' *Psychoanalytic Quarterly*, VIII, 1939, p. 27.

dissociation ensue. This secondary anxiety may be further increased by inept and poorly directed treatment of the patient, and follows regularly in types of treatment which consistently undermine the patient's confidence in himself and limit his spontaneous activity, as in poorly advised and arranged hospitalization.

While I have singled out for description the course of the early genital response from physiological tension stimulus and response to masturbation, and have indicated its vicissitudes in later development, it is clear that a somewhat similar course may occur in the case of the nongenital areas (oral, anal, cutaneous) and that the selection of the one or of the other for first place is largely determined by the special traumata of later infancy (the roots of the essential neurosis).

Patients suffering from severe neurosis quite often come to analysis in a very acute state of anxiety or even panic. Subsequent panic states, however, seldom surpass those which brought the patients into treatment or those which were precipitated at the outset of treatment. If the experienced therapist watches the anxiety of his patient carefully and tempers the treatment accordingly, such panics will occur in the course of treatment only if some new danger appears. Even then the panic can generally be avoided. Obviously a patient who is frenzied or in a panic is in no state to be analysed. He is much too near to a state of psychic paralysis to lend himself to the analytic process. The first aim of treatment must then be to penetrate the panic and relieve some of the anxiety. In this the composed, firm, assured attitude of the analyst is of the greatest importance.[1] As is to be expected in such highly narcissistic patients, the tendency to exhibitionism is great and is unconsciously used by the patient, in reaction to the intense underlying fear, to excite the sympathy and counteranxiety of the analyst in a desperate effort to retain neurotic control of the situation. Such patients simulate the behaviour of psychotic patients and the inexperienced analyst may indeed be alarmed by them. It is extremely important in these early stages to have the understanding

---

[1] This need of the psychotic patient to be met with calm receptivity is emphasized by Dr. Dexter Bullard in his account of the organization of psychoanalytic procedure in the hospital. (*J. Nerv. & Ment. Dis.*, XCI, 6, 1940.)

co-operation of the people who are close to the patient during most of the other twenty-three hours of the day, whether this be in a hospital or at home; much of the gain of the therapeutic hour may be lost by hostile, solicitous, or too active friends or relatives. Naturally this means that the analyst has to be in contact, directly or indirectly, with some key person in the patient's milieu, and this may create problems later in the analysis. In my experience, this initial situation has been handled most readily when some other analyst has been in contact with the family of the patient as friend, relative, or professional interpreter.

A word about the role of reassurance: most patients seem to react badly to direct reassurance. A quiet attitude of knowing one's business usually suffices; on occasion one may remind the patient very simply that we are the doctor and he the patient. Such patients have often been treated previously with too much reassurance. They beg for and distrust it because they have in the past been overly placated, comforted and lulled with promises that could only come to naught. The same thing is true of advice. Although emergencies occur with appalling frequency at this stage, the analyst is in a better position if he does not permit himself to be drawn into the role of adviser. The patient is quick to seize upon any weakness, inconsistency, or falseness in the analyst's attitude, and if inadequate advice or superficial reassurance is given, it undermines rather than strengthens the patient's confidence. Calmness in the analyst induces calmness in the patient, and it is not generally necessary to be more 'active' with these patients at this stage than later, although it is very easy to be drawn into active participation. Because of the patient's insecure hold on reality, the analyst must maintain an attitude of clear, hard, unperturbed realism, and must refrain from giving verbal assurance.[1] Patients

---

[1] Years ago Dr. Brill emphasized the necessity for the therapist to reiterate consistently and firmly, a realistic negation of the schizophrenic's distortions. This was done patiently and without argument. But Brill was dealing with a group of patients who were more frankly psychotic than those I am reporting, and his therapy, although based on analytic insight and judgment, could not be considered psychoanalytic. (Brill, A. A., 'Schizophrenia and Psychotherapy,' Am. J. Psychiat., IX, 1929, p. 519.)

Dr. Zilboorg, reporting the treatment of a paranoid schizophrenic patient, also emphasized the preliminary state of reality testing before the analysis

respond well to a simple clear statement defining rather than
sympathizing with their disturbed state. It gives them relief and
a feeling of security to know that the analyst sees through their
surface situation and sees it as bad as it is, though not in the
exaggerated terms in which they have presented it. A negative
therapeutic attitude is encouraged if the analyst is too gently
sympathetic, shows solicitude or anxiety. Obviously this increases the secondary gain of the neurosis and draws it further
into the analytic situation.

Some patients will force an emergency or a crisis with a demand for a decision or for advice; and to ignore this is to push
the patient to an even higher pitch of frenzy and perhaps to
some disastrously convincing exhibitionistic act. Where I think
this may occur, I indicate a course of action to the patient,
usually with a succinct restatement of the possibilities which he
has already indicated to me. It is possible to put a little more
emphasis in one direction or another while being very careful
to leave the impression of autonomy with the patient (e.g., 'You
may find you wish this, or that; but the decision will naturally
be your own'). In this way the appearance of stubbornness or
evasiveness on the part of the analyst is avoided, the patient
gains in self-reliance, and the first step in the education of his
narcissism is begun.

There is one other tendency which appears throughout in
such severely ill patients and which must be 'managed' as well
as analysed. This is the habit which Stern[1] once graphically
and tersely characterized as 'scab-picking.' I had myself already
made use of the analogy of 'pulse feeling.' This can be so severe
as almost to crowd out other mental activities, and it must then
be dealt with before the initial stage can be passed and the
deeper work of analysis begun. It is usually adequate to call the
patient's attention to this process insistently and to interrupt

itself. His patient had been in a definite psychosis, and the subsequent recapitulation of the psychosis in an acting-out in the analytic situation was at
once more dramatic, and more massive than is the situation in the severely
neurotic patients of my own study. (Zilboorg, Gregory, 'Affective Reintegra-
tion in Schizophrenia,' Arch. Neurol. & Psychiat., XXIV, 1930, p. 234.)

[1] Stern, Adolph, 'Borderline Group of Neuroses,' Psychoanalytic Quarterly,
VII, 1938, p. 467. Dr. Stern's article touches on my own observations in
many respects, and mentions also the 'deep organic insecurity or anxiety,'
with which my study is largely concerned.

it repeatedly. This tendency is so clearly a kind of masochistic autoerotic gratification, analogous to compulsive masturbation and to some forms of brooding, that it must be repeatedly interrupted in order to turn the energy elsewhere even temporarily. The 'scab-picking' is itself partly a derivative of the active but poor co-operation of the strong superego and the weak ego; it frequently utilizes a highly developed scoptophilia turned back on itself. Late in the analysis, when the narcissism has been sufficiently educated to result in a strengthening of the ego, what remains of this self-watching tendency may be converted into a genuine capacity for self-criticism, indispensable for the management of the residual basic anxiety.

In general, then, the work of this part of the analysis is to increase the immediate reality hold of the patient, first through the attitude of the analyst, then through the relentless defining or clarifying of the immediate conscious attitudes and problems of the patient, and finally through the interruption of special self-perpetuating autoerotic tension states. While this must be done at the beginning of the analytic work, it is rarely accomplished adequately in the first stages of the treatment and usually has to be repeated in many different ways through the course of the treatment.

This stage of treatment differs from the beginning of any analysis only in its greater importance, not only early but often throughout almost the entire course of the analysis. Because of the patient's insecure sense of reality, the larger topographical outlines of the reality problems and the reflection of the unconscious factors on reality situations have sometimes to be gone over and over with almost monotonous repetitiousness. In this way there is an infiltration of this sort of insight into the microscopy of analytic work and there ensues a helpful organization of the latter in a manner which places it at the disposal of the patient. One must guard against making the analysis simply a tour of minute morphological inspection.

Analyses of these severe neurotic states are inevitably long. The sooner the patients and their relatives accept this and settle down to the analytic work, the better. The patient himself is usually under considerable urgency and scab-picks at the time element as well as at other aspects of the total situation, keeping himself in a state of pleasurable disappointment, attempting to extract promises and timetables from the analyst. To such patients and their relatives, I emphasize that analytic work involves genuine growth which cannot always be budgeted or scheduled.

Throughout the analysis there exists the need for a strengthening of the patient's ego through the education of his narcissism. As a part of this, a reduction of the tendency to easy and widespread identification should be accomplished.[1] This occurs partly spontaneously through the liberation accomplished by the analysis of the essential neurosis, but it has to be reinforced through a training in its actual recognition as a general tendency, and a self-critique must be established in regard to the tendency. By these means some of the otherwise dissipated energy may be reclaimed and brought back into the service of the ego. Many of these patients have a remarkable poverty of interests, i.e., very few external goals of ego achievement; or if they have any, they have too many and flit from one 'interest' to another, developing nothing satisfactorily. In the first instance, the analyst has to help the patient to find some satisfactory goal, and in the second, to select or organize those which he has already found. This cannot be done by prescription, suggestion, or even by direct encouragement, for the patient, reacting assertively to any positive direction (and rightly so since such direction would only increase the dependence with which he struggles), then lays the responsibility on the analyst and blames him for uncertainty or failure. Patients often demand such advice and would almost trap the analyst into giving it only to disregard or disprove it, and so prove their neurotic negative 'strength.' It is possible sometimes to accomplish the desired result by an adroit underlining of the patient's own inclinations, again emphasizing the patient's autonomy. 'You will find interests ready for you as you are ready to invest in them. It is unnecessary to force yourself (in one direction or the other), but only to take steps as you yourself feel at all ready for them.

[1] Schilder describes this florid tendency to multiple identification in the schizophrenic in his chapter on 'Identification in Schizophrenia' in his *Introduction to Psychoanalytic Psychiatry*. New York, Nervous & Mental Disease Monograph Series No. 50, 1928.

Even then you may be disappointed.' It is like helping a child with the first steps of walking.[1]

The analysis of the essential neurosis of such a patient is not fundamentally different from the analysis of any neurosis. The first stages of the analysis may have to be prolonged in order to strengthen the patient to bear the distress of the later analytic work. This has often been spoken of as the period of preparing a patient for analysis. In my experience, this work can hardly be confined to a preparatory time but has to be continuously reinforced throughout the analysis by constantly working through the material with reference to the current situation and the infantile roots of the behaviour and symptom patterns, never omitting the larger outlines of behaviour tendencies as a framework for the dissection of the finer details.

In the analysis of these severe neuroses, the risks involved in giving too early interpretations for which the patient is not ready are greater than ordinary. The temptation to do this may be great as the patients so often present rather florid material and have themselves some inkling of the symbolization involved, in this respect resembling the frankly schizophrenic individual. Patients meet premature interpretation by a marked increase in their defensive walling off or they seize upon the interpretations to construct an intellectualized formula which serves their narcissistic demand for magic and with which they may satisfy themselves temporarily and dazzle their intimates sufficiently to give the semblance of a cure. They improve temporarily because they have been given a magic initiation. This can be avoided by giving interpretations with special caution and always working back from the current situation to

[1] I combat the tendency to a negative therapeutic reaction here by being slightly negative myself: never praising, rarely permitting myself any enthusiasm, but definitely recognizing ability or achievement when it is shown, and always indicating to the patient that he may achieve further. I believe this attitude is more in keeping with the need of the patient for reality above all else; at the same time it diminishes overstimulation with subsequent disappointment, and avoids the pitfall of having the patient do things to please me. Others may find it possible to establish activity first on the basis of pleasing the analyst, and subsequently analyse this oversubmissiveness after the patient's activity has gained a certain momentum of its own. I presume these differences of procedure must depend in some measure on differences in the temperaments of the analysts.

the deeper roots, never allowing the analysis to become strangulated at one level or the other. Great analytic agility is sometimes required in order, on the one hand, not to allow the ever-ready deluge of anxiety to overwhelm the patient, and, on the other hand, not to permit the patient to rest on the relative comfort of somewhat reduced anxiety. To keep him at his analytic work, he should have enough anxiety to spur his effort, but not so much as to block it.

It is equally important, however, not to *overlook* the essential neurosis. The symptoms are often embedded in wider tendencies of behaviour, and the improvement from the concurrent education of the patient may be so striking that it may be easy to be fooled into dealing inadequately with the neurosis itself.

There are some peculiarities of the transference relationship to be considered. The transference at the beginning of the analysis is generally urgent but shallow, and characterized often by an ambivalent identification with the analyst. These patients ask everything and trust nothing (1). Later in the analysis it may develop into an intense obligatory erotic transference. Throughout it is a relationship of exquisite sensitivity.

These patients in the very nature of their organic sensitivity to experience have a remarkable faculty of observation, but not so good an ability to make use of it. The constant mirroring of life and the diffuse competitiveness resulting from this is evident throughout, especially in the dream material. The patients seem to hear and see everything about the analyst, his situation, his family, etc. They take in and register a mass of details without being aware of them. These reappear only slightly disguised in dreams which are full and remarkably elaborated. At the same time the patients are less able than are those suffering from milder neuroses to use the transference readily as a genuine medium of working out the reflected intricate patterns of their behaviour, and only seem to achieve this in the ordinary way toward the end of the analysis. While the mirroring tendency produces the semblance of the transference in most of the patient's dreams, the continued detailed analysis of its appearance tends either to confuse or merely to fascinate the patient. Consequently in the transference relationship too, one has to work early especially on the general larger patterns. Only after the patient's tendency toward identification has been somewhat reduced is it possible to do much detailed transference work with him.[1]

Because of the remarkable capacity for observation on the part of the patient, any changes at all in the analyst's arrangements are reproduced in the patient's dreams and attitudes. Sometimes these may by good chance bring out some special pocket of material from the patient. More often, however, they serve as artifacts and unnecessary complications in the analytic picture. For this group of patients it makes for a real economy of work to keep the immediate environment of the analytic work as constant as possible.

Later in the analysis the development of an erotic attachment to the analyst can readily cause the accumulation of transference anxiety. This is particularly intense in the patients under discussion, as there may be in them a considerable deepening of emotional experience and libidinal expansion occurring in the course of the analysis and not for the most part after it is over. In this sense the transference represents more than a 'transference,'[2] since there is an addition of new elements not previously experienced by the patient. Such a transference presents one of the greatest values and some of the severest problems of the analysis, as the dissolution of the transference demands the realignment of the deepest attachment the patient has yet felt. How much erotic tension piles up in the transference and how readily it is deflected onto and used in the reality of the patient's life clearly depends first on the specific life situation of the patient when he enters the analysis, and second, on how the analyst handles this emotional current. In these severe neurotics constant drainage of this is necessary, erotic tension never being allowed to accumulate and stagnate.

[1] In years past, in my psychiatric experience, I have seen patients quite often thrown into brief psychotic episodes by too assiduous and early work with the transference. I believe this still happens though not to the same degree, since the emphasis on continuous detailed interpretation is less. These episodes were not followed by any prolonged psychotic states. We used to refer to them as 'psychoanalytic deliria.'

[2] This was exemplified in an even more intense form in the affect hunger described by Dr. David Levy in 'Primary Affect Hunger,' *Am. J. Psychiat.*, XCIV, 3, 1937.

One should deal with it by always indicating directly or by implication the other love goals to which the current must return. The erotic tension thus escapes becoming fixed in a transference bondage or coming to an explosive rupturing.

The patient must become acquainted during the course of the analysis with the necessity of managing his own basic anxiety, which is not completely analysable and will always remain at least potentially with him. Neglect of this part of the treatment may cause the subsequent breakdown of much of the accomplishment of an otherwise effective piece of analytic work. The patient must acquire a considerable degree of self-critique and self-tolerance. In the course of the analysis, I gradually acquaint the patient with the fact that analysis will not be a complete revelation or a magic rebirth such as he demands; that he will in fact always have problems of tension and balance to deal with. This tempering of his expectations may be started very early in the treatment, with the same firm realistic attitude which is generally effective in combating his panic. If this is coupled with a clear statement of the fact that there are definite gains to be legitimately expected, it stimulates the patient to work rather than discourages him. Then as the work proceeds, he is gradually made familiar in a very simple way with the theory of basic anxiety. This is not given him as a packaged theory, but is interpreted to him as he refers to the material which, according to my mind, justifies such a theory. These patients always give some accounts of what they have heard regarding their own births, possible antenatal influences, and earliest postnatal experiences. These come to the surface often directly, sometimes combined with birth theories and fantasies of later childhood which again are revived in connection with current contacts with birth experiences. As patients speak of their own birth injuries, their earliest illnesses, accidents, the attitudes of their mothers toward and during pregnancy, I reconstruct for them the possible effects of such experiences on a young child, and indicate the inevitable contribution to the general tension and amorphous anxiety of the later adult. In this connection, it is interesting that one can in the course of such interpretation pretty well reconstruct what has been the specific experience of the given patient. He does not recover clear memories or confirmatory evidence which he can convert into words, but he reacts with wincing, increase of tension, or the appearance of confirmatory somatic symptoms when the old sensitive areas are touched, even when this has to do with events of the very earliest weeks and months of life.[1] It might be expected that this sort of interpretation would furnish the stuff for a negative therapeutic reaction and that the patient might fall back on the attitude, 'I was born that way; so what?' This has not been my experience. Perhaps it is counteracted by the special attention already paid to the education of the narcissism. These patients must learn to know and appreciate themselves as genuinely sensitive individuals, and come to utilize their sensitivity if possible. In this way may be built up a valuable self-critique which is then at the disposal of the patient rather than turned against him. Finally at the end of such an analysis there has generally occurred a reorganization of the individual. The level of the tension may still be somewhat elevated. But if the essential neurosis has been adequately dealt with, the organization is sounder, the behaviour more spontaneous, and the balance less easily tipped. Such treatment is, perhaps more than an analysis, an education; in procedure it necessarily lies somewhere between the classical psychoanalytic technique and the methods used with children.

CLINICAL STUDIES

In presenting the clinical material in connection with this part and the previous one, I give only one case history with any degree of fullness but shall first present briefly from a clinical experience extending throughout a number of years, the observations which formed the beginning of my queries about the effect of birth and other early traumata on the productions of a tendency to anxiety.

*A.* One of my patients, a competent and serious unmarried lady in her late thirties, suffered from hysterical symptoms. On the periphery of these was one which did not yield

[1] One sees here very clearly the significance of Freud's statement that the symptoms take part in the discussion. In this part of the analytic work, symptoms are the patient's main discussion.

readily to analysis. This consisted in certain irregular jerky movements with her feet. She complained that when she was driving her car, the free foot tapped rhythmically on the floor of the car. This was not a tic, nor yet a genuine compulsion, but an inconstant and semivoluntary act which she found herself repeating like a bad habit. She also noticed that when in company she was tense and felt people were looking at her, she was unable at times to keep from wriggling the toes sometimes of one foot and sometimes of the other. This embarrassed her, although it seemed to her that she did it only under scrutiny and to relieve embarrassment. It was obviously an autoerotic discharge in a state of mild anxiety, but like other neurotic symptoms, it turned back on its purpose and increased the state it seemed intended to relieve. The same patient gave a history of having rubbed her toes on the sheet in order to put herself to sleep in her childhood, a habit which was maintained until she was six or seven and which recurred subsequently especially during illnesses until puberty.

In the analysis of this patient's dreams, there were a number of associations which indicated the familiar foot-penis symbolism. This patient suffered from an unrecognized extreme envy of her brothers, among whom she was the only girl. I shall not attempt to go into the whole story of the neurosis, but I was puzzled by the route of selection of the foot in this particular case. I thought at first it was a simple displacement downward, occurring with partial or complete renunciation of infantile masturbation. It was evident that the foot and leg were equated with the penis (and also breast) not only in accordance with the familiar symbolism but also directly by association with her mother who had suffered a milk leg earlier, and then later became lame from other causes when the patient was at puberty. One could readily see that the foot-tapping was a combination of the illusory penis masturbation and an anxious exhibitionistic calling attention to her castrated plight. But the patient's original foot-rubbing to put herself to sleep was said to have occurred from 'earliest infancy.' Her mother had told her that she had been a quiet baby and had slept well, except for the foot-rubbing and some thumb-sucking. It seems clear that the foot erotism had preceded the problem of castration anxiety and penis envy and had certainly antedated the mother's lameness and knowledge of the milk leg story.

B. In seeking the possible derivation of this patient's symptoms I recalled another patient who some years ago had told me that at the height of an orgasm she would have peculiar tingling sensations in the toes of both feet. There were certain similarities in the developmental histories of the two patients. Neither remembered childhood masturbation but had come upon masturbation in adult years when it occurred 'spontaneously' as part of a diffusely felt sexual arousal with sensa-. tions emanating from the genital areas and spreading throughout the body. In the patient under discussion this had occurred in the setting of a quasi intellectual erotic stimulation (reading and looking), and seemed to her a short-circuited response. In both patients the masturbatory habit was a recurrence of the most primitive thigh-pressure type. In neither case was there any clitoris masturbation. In the second patient, the masturbation was accompanied by fantasies of intercourse which, in the patient's imagination, consisted simply of holding the penis within her vagina, i.e., clearly a possession of the penis in this way. It seems probable that the masturbation which had been initiated so late was only a recrudescence of what had occurred and had been renounced very early in life.

This type of genital sensation without awareness of any preliminary stirring or fantasying but consisting rather of sensations suffusing suddenly upward from the genital region and extending throughout the body, reminds one of the distribution of dissociated and disclaimed erotic sensations described by schizophrenic patients as due to electrical or hypnotic influences.

There is one other fragment of a case history, which I recall from my early clinical experience, of a young woman who was at first considered to be a very severe case of hysteria. This young woman had an autoerotic orgastic tic with a sucking muscular movement culminating in a snapping noise sufficiently loud to startle bystanders. I have recently been able to learn the bare details of the later history.

C. This young woman first came to the hospital at twenty-three because of especially violent quarrels with her father in which she threatened to kill him and also threatened suicide. The family was one in which talent and instability intermingled and fused. The father was a brilliantly able man, who sank later into a cranky senile state. I saw this patient first twenty-one years ago. She was the third among five children. One had died of meningitis, and one had had a manic attack precipitated by the torpedoing of his transport during the first World War. In the years since, a younger sibling, too, developed a psychosis, so that four of the five children developed severe psychic disturbances. Genetically determined constitution may be considered to have had a possible influence here; however, the early individual history is also of note. The patient was a seven-month baby, cyanosed and weighing four pounds at birth. Because of a neglected *ophthalmia neonatorum*, her vision was permanently impaired and a constant lateral nystagmus developed. There were many fainting attacks in childhood. She was never able to study adequately, both because of the reduced vision and because of inability to concentrate. She had a particularly severe temper with sudden exceedingly violent outbreaks occasioning chagrin and a religio-moral struggle for control. She became a religious fanatic and wished to be a Deaconess. Masturbation occurred throughout the entire childhood, and she could recall no period in which it was even temporarily in abeyance. The childhood history was so full of sexual traumata, explorations and experiments with other children and with a variety of animals, as to give the impression that this frustrated child was in a state of continual autoerotic overflow in which her impulsive discharges set up new excitations until she was involved in a frenzy of polymorphous perverse excitement with almost no relief. In this patient, too, masturbation by thigh pressure was the earliest and still predominant form of masturbation, although to it had been added a great variety of autoerotic practices.

In the hospital she was at first extremely scattered, distractable and restless; she then developed the tic, which was clearly an effort at relief. 'If it does not occur my eyes get misty and roll up into my head, and my brain gets confused.' She described it as 'a contraction and expansion of one of my organs.' It occurred, however, without her volition and became a thoroughly automatized tic. She complained also of pain and a feeling of paralysis in both legs and sensations in them 'like mercury in a thermomter.' Withal she moved about freely.[1]

Obviously this case presents a mesh of complications. But I quote it here because of certain similarities in symptom constellations with other cases. Having recently obtained an abstract of the history of the younger sister of this patient who suffered a psychosis some seventeen years later, I have learned that all of the children in the family were born by extremely difficult labours. It thus appears that this part of the family situation, dependent on the pelvis of the mother, and an accident as far as the children were concerned, may have combined with and reinforced the later results of the pathetic neglect which the patient suffered as a child.

In thinking over the possible relations of this pressure masturbation to the toe, foot and leg symptoms in these cases, I believe that I may have come upon a somatic rather than a purely symbolic link in the possibility that in severe pressure masturbation of this type, where the body is held in a state of prolonged, frenzied, autoerotic tension and the legs crossed in scissor fashion, there may actually be referred sensations of tingling in the legs and feet. This seemed to me the more probable when I recalled having seen several times in my student days on a pediatric ward, cases of very young female infants in exactly such states of unrelieved tension, with the body in a condition of rigid tonicity and legs crossed scissorwise. I recall that one of these little patients was at first thought to be suffering from Little's Disease because of the history of birth trauma and the superficial resemblance of the posture to spastic paraplegia. Separation of the infant's legs with soft

[1] I wish to thank Dr. Adolf Meyer for permission to use these and other clinical observations from the period of my work at the Phipps Clinic.

cotton pads was followed by the cessation of this masturbatory tension and a relative degree of general relaxation. The recollection of these instances of very early masturbation in girl babies then related itself to the observations of erections following delivery of boy babies, and the line of query which was developed in Part I began to take form (2).

Anyone who has attempted to give a fairly full account of the analysis of a single case knows how difficult this is. The mosaic of the analysis is inevitably complicated and delicate and while a few relatively simple patterns stand out boldly in almost all cases, what pattern unit stands out most sharply depends on the angle from which the whole is viewed. Thus, what looks like a diamond to one person may look like a cross to another. It is often important to establish *some* pattern unit, at any rate, and go along from there. In dealing with the following case history, I have found it impossible to present all my data and have consequently organized it for purposes of presentation along the lines already indicated. It was the tendency of this material to organize itself along these very lines, however, which stimulated my attempts to bring together my observations and to formulate ideas about treatment of this group of severe neuroses.

*D.* This patient came to me at the age of twenty-eight, a trim young woman of small stature, probably not more than five feet or five feet one inch tall. Her figure inclined to boyishness, especially in the straight slimness of the hips, but this was by no means conspicuous. The upper part of the torso was feminine and the breasts well developed, but with inverted nipples. There was a slight excess of hair on the forearms and a little heaviness of the hair of the upper lip. She walked in an overly energetic tense fashion, with her head thrust forward, her arms swinging freely. Her speech resembled her gait in being hurried, urgent, inaccurate, and often ahead of itself. She was accompanied by a nurse companion, as she was afraid to go any place alone.

At the time I first saw the patient I had already been given the general facts of the formal history, and all arrangements had been made in advance for her treatment. Another analyst was in touch with the family and had done the not inconsiderable job of explanation and interpretation of treatment to them. The patient came with the anticipation of being analysed, but she accepted analysis as a last and probably futile resort and was not kindly disposed to it.

The presenting symptoms were those of a severe anxiety hysteria, with phobias, a tendency to doubt and some compulsive activity. She was afraid to be alone, afraid of high places, and especially of windows above a ground level. In attacks of panic she was afraid of losing consciousness. At other times she described herself as dazed and without positive feelings, 'as though I were looking inward instead of outward,' and again, as though she 'just stared out.' Sometimes she felt as though she were not herself, and her face felt stiff. She felt like an infant and was afraid of drowning in her tub. Again, she felt very tiny, like 'just a tiny atom lost in space.' Sometimes she insisted she was feeble-minded. Going to high places, having to eat alone, going to the hairdresser, or being in any situation in which she sat directly facing another person, were all situations in which she was likely to have anxious feelings mounting almost to panic. At this particular time she could not bear to look in a mirror, which was as bad as having anyone else look at her. She was tense almost to the point of frenzy, but there nevertheless appeared an element of play acting in her manner.

She had really been sick most of her life, and while one could recognize stages of change in her symptoms, there had been only a few relatively short periods when she had seemed reasonably well and active. She had never finished school or held any position. (Tests, however, had indicated her to be well above average intelligence.) She was married and had a daughter of four, and kept up an intermittently active participation in the social affairs of her friends. She had been more or less in contact with psychiatrists and psychoanalysts since the age of seventeen. At that time her parents consulted an analyst who advised that they take her to Vienna to Freud. A neurologist thought a European pleasure trip would be better. Later she was successively in the hands of a psychiatrist, a child guidance specialist, and what appears to have been an 'analyst' without training. She spent two years with this man and become quite familiar with the general symbols and some of the concepts of analysis. Next an analyst advised against analysis and the patient then entered a psychiatric hospital. There she remained for about seven months, showing marked improvement at first and then getting rapidly worse, with the appearance of more marked frenzy and desperation than at any time previously. She was now so bad that it seemed impossible for her to live outside of a hospital and in order to start the analysis it was arranged that she remain hospitalized but commute daily accompanied by a companion. All arrangements were made with the help of another analyst who was a friend of the family and proved an invaluable aid during the first months of the treatment, acting as an interpreter and shock absorber in the situation.

I shall not attempt to describe the minutiae of the therapy. It proceeded essentially along the lines I have already described. At first the patient behaved in a crazily frenzied fashion reminiscent of the 'antics' of patients in a psychiatric hospital. She would refuse to lie on the couch though she knew from her previous experiences that this was expected. Sometimes she paced about threatening to throw herself on the floor, or walked up and down wringing her hands. She went through the motions of choking herself and threatened to jump in front of a train on the way to the office or to jump from a window. She would sometimes ask me how I dared to let her go around outside of the hospital. She attempted to entice me into some commitment about the outcome of the analysis, the length of time, my expectations, etc., and she tried a number of bullying methods. She told dreams and quickly gave crude symbolic interpretations, sometimes saying, 'I suppose *you* would think that means thus and so.' She now repeated in order to discard them the many symbols learned in her previous 'analytic' experience. She was mildly obsessed with a great variety of sexual thoughts—a kind of pansexualization of thought content which may have been partly induced by the previous rather blunt therapeutic efforts. It was usually futile for me to say more than a sentence or two, as she would turn her head away and say, 'I am not listening to you. I don't hear anything you say'; or 'I can't hear you, because I can't concentrate.' A little later she was able to hear more of what I said, but often attempted to convert the session into an argument, amply demonstrating the basis for her having been affectionately dubbed 'a last word artist' by her parents when she was a child. When she asked me if I were a good enough analyst to treat her, she was surprised when I simply said, 'Yes.' (This served to check temporarily the potential sado-masochistic argument with which the patient was used to drowning out all therapeutic contacts. Somewhat later I was able to help her first to see that she blocked her own progress in this way, and later to begin to analyse these tendencies in herself.) She was an inveterate scab-picker, sometimes drawing her husband and her mother into the process by scaring them with her behaviour and inducing them to call me up, then demanding verbatim accounts of what our talk had been.

During the first two or three months there was a gradual simmering down. Her failure to arouse counteranxiety in me was probably the most effectively 'reassuring' factor. Gradually I began the most elementary explanations. Ignoring the symbols which she displayed so generously, I began with simple suggestions that her feeling like a little atom was a kind of picure of her feeling lost in the world, that she didn't really feel grown up and able to take care of herself, and that being unable to be alone was like being a child again. Even this was too much for her at first, and when she once grasped the idea that she was reacting to a feeling of insecurity in many ways, she was relieved that at last she had understood something. This is just an indication of the extreme simplicity with which we began. The gradual deepening of her understanding, the emphasis on her appreciating herself as an individual, her increasing ability to assimilate more and more interpretation and the extreme caution with which progress could be made, can be imagined from the content of the patient's history. These first weeks were essentially a stripping off of the secondary adornments of pseudo-psychotic behaviour which she had picked up in a psychiatric hospital together with much of their complement of secondary anxiety. She began to feel that she had rights and independent functioning. The use of the simplest sort of explanations permitted her to abandon the analytic vocabulary which she had previously acquired and which served only as a meaningless burden to her, having already lost even the quality of being magic words.

This girl was the first child and second pregnancy of a young mother. An earlier tubal pregnancy resulted in operative interference and a stillborn fetus. The maternal grandmother died suddenly ten minutes after the patient's birth. The mother then went to her father's home to live and to take her mother's place with the grandfather. The family remained there until a second child was born twenty-seven months later. (This story was part of the family saga and the patient could not remember when she first heard it.) The patient was delivered by Caesarean section because of the mother's contracted pelvis. She was a fretful baby in spite of the fact that she sucked her fingers from earliest infancy, presumably beginning the first week of life. At a very early age she began sucking her blanket. She recalls that later she sucked the blanket and then smelled it before falling asleep. In summer she had to have a piece of flannel to suck and smell. Intermittent finger-sucking occurred until the patient was fourteen or fifteen. It then was gradually replaced by smoking which is still a deeply fixed habit and is largely an oral pleasure; she inhales little and is as well satisfied with an unlit cigarette in her mouth. Another childhood habit was rubbing her foot on the blanket in order to put herself to sleep. In adolescence she twisted her hair with her fingers continually. She was nursed until she was a year old and was then weaned on principle rather than exigency. She wet the bed throughout her entire childhood up to the age of seventeen, when there was a further extension of neurotic symptoms. She was constipated intermittently in childhood and was given enemas frequently. One of her early recollections was of being held struggling and fighting on the bathroom floor while the mother inserted the enema nozzle. She masturbated throughout childhood. This was a rather ineffective clitoris masturbation described by the patient as 'touching myself but not working at it.' The details of the beginning of her speech are not known to the patient, but she recalls having had a mild speech defect, something of a lisp which gradually disappeared at eight or nine. Later in life she complained a good deal about getting mixed up in her speech: under any excitement she used words which had the approximate sound of those she wanted—a mild degree of malapropism under stress. There were no serious illnesses except mastoiditis in the patient's infancy. She had had occasional spurts of fever, however, often accompanied by brief delirium, and on one occasion a series of convulsions.

When she was twenty-seven months old, a younger sister was born. The mother was permitted to go into labour, which proceeded unsuccessfully for some time; then forceps were applied and the child was severely injured. From the first it was feared that the baby would not develop normally, and by the time the baby was two or three years old it was evident that she was both deaf and an imbecile. At the time of the birth the mother had gone to another city for delivery, taking the older child with her. On the train returning home, my patient, then twenty-seven months old, developed acute mastoiditis necessitating a mastoidectomy. She remained in the hospital nine weeks and later had to have very frequent dressings. She fought so against these that an anesthetic was given, and she is supposed to have had chloroform almost daily for some time. (This is the mother's account. The patient herself has always thought it would be impossible to have been anesthetized as often as the mother reports to have been the fact.) The patient's earliest conscious recollections is of being held by her nurse, looking out of a window in the hospital and watching some negroes on a near-by roof. The mother devoted herself to caring for the patient but was under great stress in her position as successor to her own mother and in concern over the next pregnancy. (A certain oedipal ambidexterity was patently needed.) After the sister's birth, first the patient and then both the children were in charge of a *Fräulein* who was very strict and methodical and punished them severely for spilling anything. The two children were brought up together until the sister was about six, when the latter was sent away to a special school.

The patient's neurosis developed in successive stages and with increasing intensity: (a) at seventeen, when she first went away from home, (b) during her engagement, and (c) after the birth of her child. It just happened that the birth of this child came in a period when there were many deaths in the family, so that again birth and death were juxtaposed even as they had been at the time of her own birth when her grandmother died ten minutes after she was born. At the time the patient entered analysis, she stated that her sexual response was good, *i.e.*, that she usually had an orgasm in intercourse. It developed, however, that she was averse to intercourse and had an inadequate orgasm overly readily.

In considering the etiological factors in this young woman's illness, I shall confine myself to the simplest statements in regard to the two groups; the very early, *predisposing* ones, and those producing the *essential* neurosis. In regard to their effects, it is not possible to make a clear-cut distinction between those predisposing causes resulting from the genetically determined constitution and those arising predominantly from the very early distresses which I have conceived of as leaving an organic (constitutionally assimilated) imprint in their wake. I believe that these two groups of factors are inevitably together and sometimes fused.

In this case, we have a history of competence and some brilliance on both sides of the family, but with an incidence of neurosis which seems very high. In addition the mother was tense and apprehensive during her pregnancy with the patient, as her previous pregnancy had ended in a defeat and suffering for her. She was, incidentally, a rather undaunted sporting type of woman, with considerable bravado as a cover for her disturbance. Although there were no particular data regarding the patient's nutritional state at birth, my surmise from the contents of her symptoms and dreams would be that she had not been a markedly undernourished baby. She was born by Caesarean section. It is interesting here that the patient does not describe any sensation of a band or localized 'brain stiffness' or head pressure feelings which are so commonly described by schizophrenic patients and by some neurotics, but rather feelings of light-headedness in her panic states, as though her head would 'fly to pieces,' and a feeling of stiffness in the face. The last was definitely a reproduction of the chloroform mask and disappeared readily on analysis. That she was an uneasy infant from the very first was attested by the crying, excessive sucking, twitching and rubbing which began in the very first weeks, and the convulsions and easy deliria within the first two years. The mother's constant watchfulness and tension almost certainly was reflected in her face[1] and in her handling of the young baby. The mother prided herself on taking care of the little one alone, in spite of her own emotional burdens and practical responsibilities at the time. The mother described the first few years of her children's lives as 'a hell of worries' to her. It does not seem to me too far fetched to consider that the patient's truly extraordinary sensitivity to facial expression, strikingly apparent in the first few months of her analysis, had its roots in this early period, although it may have been augmented in infancy by the birth of the somewhat mutilated sister and by her own abundant experience with anesthesia. Subsequently it was sustained by a severe father who exerted much control through frowns and scowls.

Similarly the direct effects of the Caesarean birth became amalgamated later with the images called up by the verbal accounts of it which she heard, and gave substantiating form to some of her later birth theories. We see further in this girl's birth a situation which favoured a sense of abnormality and, with the death of the grandmother following so closely, gave rise to questions of her own identity, expanded her omnipotence even to the point of killing, and intensified her guilt feelings, etc.

For the *essential* neurosis two events were especially important: the birth of the younger sister, a mutilated half-dead baby, when the patient was twenty-seven months old, and a rape by a grown man occurring when the patient was five years old. The patient's own mastoid infection and operation, following so closely on the sister's birth, had psychologically the importance of birth to her, and the repeated experience with

[1] Therese Benedek quotes C. Bühler as observing that the infant recognizes the face of the mother or nurse at an earlier age than it recognizes the bottle. She draws the very pertinent conclusion that the confidence inspired by this recognition is a stage of object relationship preceding positive object love. This regularly occurs by the third month. 'Adaptation to Reality in Early Infancy,' *Psychoanalytic Quarterly*, VII, 1938, p. 203.

anesthesia merged with her death and rebirth fantasies. It is interesting too, that there was a recurrence of the mastoid following the mother's miscarriage when the patient was about seven. The time of the birth of the sister was remembered quite readily by the patient, but its emotional significance was completely annulled in consciousness and had to be unfolded to her in analysis against the customarily stern defences of the obsessional neurotic. For the rape, however, occurring as it did at the beginning of the latency period, she had a deep hysterical amnesia.

SUMMARY

In presenting this clinical data I have had to condense and simplify the material very greatly and have attempted only to sketch it in such a way as to indicate the fundamental outlines of the work. In the last case cited, the work began with the problem of management of the anxiety-laden behaviour and the establishment of a better grasp of immediate reality. The education away from narcissism extended throughout the entire analysis, permitting the patient an increasingly useful self-critique. The interpretation was gradually deepened until the essential neurosis could be reached. I believe that these general principles are applicable wherever there have been many severe and early traumata, whether or not there is any possibility of antenatal and natal contributing factors in the underlying anxiety.

This is a group of patients who are coming to analysts with increasing frequency, asking and needing help. It is clear that the consideration of these cases takes us back to the need for more observation with infants, work which appears to me the source of the richest material for psychoanalysis.

I want to give due appreciation to the work already published by others dealing with many aspects of these problems. I think of the publications of Brill, Zilboorg, Sullivan (6), Schilder and others of about a decade or more ago; more recently there have appeared the publications of Hill, of Tidd (8) at the Menninger Clinic, of Fromm-Reichmann and

Bullard (3) at Rockville; and in the New York Psychoanalytic Society the papers of Stern, Franz Cohn (4), Lorand (5), and Thompson (7). By and large these have dealt, however, with conditions as encountered in the franker psychotic states, or with relatively circumscribed problems of interpretation or of method. My own study may perhaps serve to bring these observations and considerations together in a general form, and especially to demonstrate them in the severe neuroses or borderline states which so often occupy a sort of no man's land between the hospital and the analyst's office.

## CHAPTER III

# INFANT REACTIONS TO RESTRAINT: PROBLEMS IN THE FATE OF INFANTILE AGGRESSION*

CLINICAL discussions concerning an intellectually retarded boy of four, who had been severely and frequently tied up by his mother were the stimulating source for this study. Questions were raised concerning the relation between the severe prolonged restraint and the intellectual impairment, and whether therapeutic unshackling of the child might also initiate a comparable intellectual freeing. Such cases are not uncommon in outpatient clinics, and the more dramatic ones find their way into press reports. Clinical reports are in general singularly naive and overoptimistic. It is probable that in many such cases the restraint was actually enforced partly because of the child's original impairment rather than the opposite, and that subsequently the two factors of original intellectual deficit plus severe restraint act together to the child's further detriment.

The term *restraint* is a broad one. But in all forms of restraint there is the common situation that the free response (usually partly motor) of which the subject is capable is not permitted. Restraint may be applied through physical means as in binding the child's body or shutting him up, or through psychic channels by the use of threats, warnings, and prohibitions.

It is further apparent that the problem of the effects of restraint on a young infant is indeed complex, involving at least the questions of whether the restraint approximates a passive limitation of motion, whether it involves pain and sets up marked counterreactions, the time at which it occurs in the infant's life with reference to the special developmental stages of spontaneous growth, and finally, whether it is restraint of a single part of the body or involves most of the body. With these questions in mind, some review of the observations available was

* Reprinted from *The American Journal of Orthopsychiatry*, Vol. XIV, No. 2, April, 1944.

attempted from three angles: (a) clinical observations of psychiatric patients, both adults and children, (b) experimental work, chiefly in the field of psychology, (c) observations regarding customs of restraint in certain folk groups, mainly the custom of swaddling infants as found in widely diverse areas in the world.

## CLINICAL MATERIAL

Restraint for infants varies from the extremely common tying up a child's hands to stop thumb-sucking or masturbation, to a rare case where the child may be kept in a near-embalmment state. Such cases in a clinic are generally not well studied, nor is careful study often feasible. The mother who restrains a child in this fashion is apt to be stupid, hostile to the child, and guilty. Consequently she rarely tolerates treatment of the child for a long period. The clinician must depend too much on clinical impressions gleaned over a period of years and covering a number of cases. Occasionally in psychoanalytic work with adults one glimpses through the dreams or symptoms of the patient many of the infantile situations, including those of restraint, which are seen firsthand but too briefly in the children's clinic.

The problem of reaction to restraint and forcible limitation of motion was thus presented in a very complex and late form in a twenty-year-old girl who was brought to my office as a last resort several years ago, with hope of a cure.

The presenting symptom was that she had failed in her first year in college. The mother stated that the girl was bright but extraordinarily slow throughout her entire life. The mother dated the slowness in fact from the time when, soon after returning home from the hospital where the child was born, she had laboured for an hour and a half to get the infant to take the breast. She explained that the nurses must somehow have known how to manage the baby, for she had been all right in the hospital. Mother had been depressed during pregnancy and later, and felt the physician should not have permitted her to nurse the baby. Instead he had only cut down the number of feedings. There had seemed to be plenty of milk, but the mother spent most of her time trying to induce the baby to nurse. The baby cried a great deal and the mother was frantic. This went on for five or six months. In telling the story the mother remarked with grim facetiousness, 'First babies should be prohibited by law!' She had prided herself on keeping her temper all through the years, and now was a quivering mass of self-restraint.

The patient had been somewhat slow in learning to walk, but the facts of the situation were not entirely clear. From eighteen months to two years of age she wore braces on her legs. The mother's reason was that she thought the child's legs a little bowed and not properly developed. The physician had been averse to using braces but she had been insistent. At the same period the baby was wearing aluminium mitts. It is not clear eighteen or nineteen years later whether this had been as protection against thumb-sucking or masturbation. Mother gave no history of either. She recalled that the baby had liked the mitts and called them 'toys,' but she hated the braces and would bang them against her crib. The child had a nurse until she was ten or eleven. Wet the bed until about this time, but got over it the following year. She was ushered into puberty by being given a book on what girls should know.

Throughout, the child was 'unbelievably stubborn.' At nine or ten she would stand on the street corner looking skyward for a time before crossing the street. The mother interpreted this, probably correctly, as a negativistic response to her own anxious admonitions to look in both directions before crossing. Once when the mother purchased some blooming geraniums and set them out in a pretty border, the child broke the stems of all the plants. Again, the mother bought a lovely antique sideboard which had sixteen panes of very old glass in it. The child broke five panes in a single effort.

The mother stated spontaneously that she had wanted a boy for her first child, and then hastily explained that this was because she herself had no brothers and thought it would be easier in any family if the first child were a boy. She said she was all mixed up about sex and in a terrible state during the pregnancy. She wanted the child to be a boy for the child's own sake. In adolescence, the young girl was unattractive; had a 'large abdomen, pipe stem legs, and looked funny.' She cared nothing for clothes. Her posture was bad in spite of postural exercises and dancing classes, where she was awkward and taller than even the boys. In adolescence 'she had all the ills possible. If you can think of any more, she had them too.' She wore special corsets to support her back which had a slight curvature. She was repeatedly treated by an orthodontist, but would not wear the dental braces consistently. In high school she was bright but seemed slow of tempo. With some tutoring she did well in examinations, even winning a special prize, and was able to enter one of the leading colleges.

The mother seemed to be in a chronic psychosis, which she covered up rather than compensated, driven by terror of husband's abandonment of her. She described her husband as 'so well balanced that he has no understanding of anything else.' He had been 'wonderful' to her, though completely non-understanding. He was a gentleman of one of the more orderly professions, and I could vouch from my contact with him for the nonunderstanding his wife described. He told of his wife's nervous illness before the birth of the baby, but stated that he 'did not intend to have *that* go on' and that he had cured her himself, though he could not remember exactly how. He was an ambitious, successful, ruthless, sentimental man.

The daughter's condition was really unique, best described as an angry ambulant catatonia. Treating her soon became a hopeless task. The same sort of restrictive measures, but with incredible ramifications, were applied to the girl's visiting the psychiatrist. Because of the parents' sense of disgrace, the girl was not permitted to live outside the family lest someone discover she was seeing a psychiatrist. She was instructed in minute detail how to avoid or evade detection should she meet anyone in or near my office. She would ring twice before entering as a signal that it was she and that the way should be cleared. She must walk upstairs rather than ride in the elevator in order to avoid the elevator operator. The psychiatrist must never telephone her for fear the identity might be revealed to the servants. If she telephoned the psychiatrist, she must never leave her name with the secretary. She must pay the fee in cash so the psychiatrist's name would not appear on cheques seen by the bank; and probably also to impress on her the amount she was taxing her parents.

This account gives a circumstantially comprehensive picture of the strait-jacket in which the girl lived, at first an almost complete physical one consisting of a series of metal braces, and then an expanding psychic strait-jacket supplemented by forced propulsion along certain demanded lines. By the time she came to the psychiatrist she was practically a synthetic person, a kind of living marionette in which there were not only the external strings of control but the opposing forces from within. It seem clear that the girl was hostilely appersonated by the mother, and the major part of her energy was used in a series of blind attempts to separate herself. While there are many clinical descriptions of children and young people subjected to long periods of restraint, I know of no case where the restraint was so complete, so varied, and so subtle as this one.

### EXPERIMENTAL WORK

The experimental work to be considered may be divided into two subdivisions—one having to do with positive restraint of motion of infants, and the other dealing with a more negative restriction, viz., the elimination of ordinary stimuli in the infant's life which would promote activity or provide situations for practice.

While there were earlier observations along these lines, Watson's work was so publicized that it influenced the experiments on infants for a decade or so afterwards. About 1917, he published his observations of three types of emotional behaviour responses in newborn babies which he thought corresponded to the later emotions felt as rage, love, and fear. From 1917 to 1930, he developed, restated, and popularized his ideas until they became well known in this country. The psychological literature of the 'twenties contains many more references to Watson's work and accounts of experiments substantiating or controverting it than has been true in the decade since. In this review we are concerned only with the responses which Watson characterized as *rage* and which he describes as follows :

'Observation seemed to show that *hampering of the infant's movements* is the factor which apart from all training brings out the movements characterized as rage. If the face or head is held, crying results, quickly followed by screaming. The body stiffens and fairly well co-ordinated slashing or striking movements of the hands and arms result; the feet and arms are drawn up and down; the breath is held until the child's face is flushed. In older children the slashing movements of the arms and legs are better co-ordinated and appear as kicking, slapping, pushing, etc. Almost any child from birth can be thrown into a rage if its arms are held tightly to its sides; sometimes even if the elbow joint is clasped tightly between the fingers, the response appears; at times just the placing of the head between cotton pads will produce it' (1).

In this passage and in some others, Watson stated quite definitely that he considered the restriction or hampering of motion as producing the reaction; and the reaction which he described was certainly a vigorous one. He both stated and implied that the reaction occurred when the hampering was by slight constraint. He did not, except by implication, recognize any possible difference in reaction of the infant according to the intensity of the holding exertion, *i.e.*, the difference between light contact and deep intense pressure. Neither did he clearly meet the question whether the infant's response is influenced by jerkiness or sudden change in the experimenter's pressure in holding. Workers who followed Watson gave various reports. The Shermans (2), in 1925, described diffuse defence reactions of the hands in a newborn baby if pressure was exerted on the chin while the head was held steadily in an assistant experimenter's hands. The 'defence movements were not at all as violent or as extensive' as Watson described as rage, however. Taylor (3), at Ohio State, who somewhat attempted to follow Watson's method of arm and nose restraint, could evoke no constant patterned responses and concluded that he merely evoked a generalized activity. Other workers there (4) had earlier attempted a more quantitative method of recording observations of infant reactions, including those to holding the nose and the arms. They concluded that the reaction was general rather than specific, that the reactive activity was greatest in those bodily segments which are nearest to the region stimulated, and that a decrease in the magnitude and frequency of the activity roughly corresponds to the distance from the zone stimulated. This seems to me the nearest, in the experimental work, to any consideration of the possibly varying effects on the infant's reaction according to where the restriction of movement is applied. It would seem that there might be some difference in infantile reaction when, for example, the whole trunk was held gently and firmly from that when the hand or wrist was held and the infant was otherwise free to try, as it were, to get away from its limited captivity. The latter situation might favour strain and frustration, while the former would tend more to produce a struggleless submission. It seems possible, from the report of Pratt, Nelson, and Sun, that they may sometimes have had such a 'quiet' response from the babies, but their whole report is in terms of how many movements of each type occurred, and one can scarcely keep sight of the reacting infant (5). It appears further that they obtained results similar to but less intense than Watson's, and that they utilized less intense stimuli.

At the University of Virginia, Wayne Dennis with the aid of his wife (6) conducted experiments on a pair of twins, which are more extensively reviewed later. He found that at two months the twins reacted with Watsonian rage in variable degrees and to a variety of stimulations, including holding the head between the experimenter's hands so that it could not be moved, and pressing the subject's nose with the experimenter's forefinger, as well as by using strong taste stimuli— saturated salt solution, a very bitter quinine solution, and dilute citric acid. In these latter experiments it is evident that the discomfort of too intense or unpleasant taste stimulation is added to the question of restraint. The Dennises state, however, that it was necessary to use very vigorous restraint to provoke the so-called rage response. They concluded that it was the intensity and persistence of the stimulation rather than merely the limitation of movement which was the especially provocative factor. Dennis objects to the characterization as rage; he prefers the simple descriptive terms 'struggling, thrashing, and crying' or, when the reaction is present in a lesser degree, simply 'restlessness and crying.' It seems to me that these early reactions may be interpreted as very simple aggressive defence, whether or not we call them rage or the precursors of rage.

The Dennises found that when in the tenth month their twin subjects were held with pressure on the nose or with their bodies or heads immobilized, far from showing a disturbed reaction, the babies responded with a smile which sometimes lasted as long as five minutes before fussing began. They recognized that this smiling was due partly to the peculiar attachment of the subjects to the experimenters on whom they were so emotionally dependent that they tolerated and 'liked' any attention given them so long as it was not severe or acutely painful. Dennis concluded rightly, I believe, that it is probably futile to attempt to test for 'instincts' or native emotional reactions after the very early weeks of life, as every stimulus which is presented, even if it has never before been employed, bears some relationship to the (individual) experience of the child. In other words, there can be no isolated stimulus. He states quite definitely that restraint of movement achieved without the use of intense stimulation does not cause negative, i.e., rage-like reactions in the newborn, but that intense and enduring stimulation, of which rough restraint in the sense of interference with customary behaviour sequences is an example, gives rise to negative reactions of frustration.

The recognition that stimulation is very soon incorporated into the fabric of experience and does not remain unrelated to other experience leads to another comment or question. In most clinical situations which come to us as psychiatrists, the restraint which has been applied early has not been in an impersonal or even unemotional setting. The type of restraint most frequently encountered clinically is punishment restraint of some sort in which the affect of anger or disapproval of the person who applies it has also to be reckoned with in the total situation. The nearest we can come to impersonally applied or at least unemotionally enforced restraint would be in studying the forms of aggression shown in a group of babies who were early subjected to plaster cast treatment as in the case of clubfeet treated by nonoperative methods. Here, of course, there would be still other factors to be considered, but such a comparative study might be worth while.

Considering further the factor of the emotional attitude of the restrainer, the question arises of the tendency of even a relatively young infant to reflect in some degree the attitude of the person who holds it (7, 8).[1] My belief is that such an induction or increase of emotional pitch by empathic reflection is appreciable, and that it may indeed occur at an earlier age than would at first be thought possible. The literature on this subject is not very extensive, and the problem is not readily subjected to experimental methods. But there is some evidence of a basis for its occurring in infancy in the observations of C. Bühler (9), the Dennises,[2] and Gesell (10), all of whom remark on the early focusing of the infant's gaze on the face of the mother or nurse.

Other factors entering into the restraint situation are discussed by Dr. Wayne Dennis in an article in which he summarizes his critique of Watson's rage theory (5). Dennis here brought out the question of the contrast between the quiet reaction of the infant to general, slight, or moderate restraint of motion and the thrashing, active, aggressive reaction to severe or sudden restraint of motion. He thought this contrast might be due to a similarity of the first condition to the intrauterine state of the infant, while the latter condition caused definite thwarting and, if the restraint was sufficiently intense, there might be pain. Independently I made a similar suggestion in Chapter II, Part I. This has also been remarked by various other writers, discussing swaddling and other restraint customs which will be later reviewed.

While there is an extensive literature on the effect of practice on learning, that on the effect of deprivation of practice situations is not as well rounded. The idea of determining

---

[1] This question is one I discussed in Chapter II, Part I, the 'Predisposition to Anxiety,' or in *Psychoanalytic Quarterly*, X, 1, 1941, pp. 66–94. One sees this emphatic reflection of the person watched in the eager, stimulated aggressive expressions, and clenched fists of the members of a prize-fight audience. I believe this 'absorption of emotion by reflection' may be one of the most potent factors in the heightening of emotional reactions in a crowd resulting in mob force.

[2] Mentioned later in this article in the résumé of the Dennis monograph.

what infants would do if not subjected to ordinary stimulations from other human beings seem to have stirred the imaginations of philosophers and psychologists for ages. This may be an academic form of the narcissistic question of the independence and self-sufficiency of man so well romanticized in *Robinson Crusoe*. Herodotus is said to have reported the case of two children reared without contact with speaking adults to determine if these children would develop speech (quoted by Dennis).

The most comprehensive report that I have located is contained in the monograph of Wayne Dennis (6). This offers some interesting material which has both direct and tangential bearing on this discussion.

Dr. and Mrs. Dennis took a pair of twin girls five weeks old and attempted to rear them with a minimum amount of stimulation and minimal practice situations. They kept the babies through the fourteenth month. Although there are striking defects in their observations and interpretations from a medical angle, the experimenters have brought out a valuable human document. In a résumé of their work, two groups of responses may be emphasized here: the emotional responses of the babies, and the developmental locomotor behaviour, *i.e.*, sitting up, reaching, standing, walking.

For the first six months the experimenters were able to maintain quite rigid conditions. The twins were not permitted to see each other. They were handled with as complete unemotionality as the Dennises were capable of. They were taken from their cribs only for feeding and bathing or for specific experiments. If either child cried at other than feeding time, one experimenter entered and investigated, and usually changed a diaper. There was no response if the infant cried when the experimenter left. They did not speak before entering the room, did not speak to the twins, and did not speak to each other while feeding or caring for the twins. There was no demonstration of affection, petting, fondling, cuddling, or smiling. There were no rewards or punishments, and a definite effort was made in the direction of 'indifference' while handling the babies. Acts which would provide examples for imitation were avoided.

The result of this emotionally sterilized environment is a

little surprising in that it was the experimenters rather than the babies who broke down and could not maintain this unnatural status. By and large, one might summarize the developing situation as follows. Since the babies had no one else to become attached to, their emotional responses became focused on the experimenter to a provocative extent. At seven weeks the babies were observed to follow the experimenters with their eyes, and to smile occasionally when they appeared. 'From the time that the infants first showed visual regard for adults, they were most attentive to *faces* rather than to other parts of the person at whom they were looking.' At eight weeks their hunger-crying would stop when an adult appeared. Between nine and twelve weeks they began to laugh and coo; but also to show something resembling impatience about feeding. Their hunger-crying stopped on the entrance of an adult but promptly began again if the feeding was not immediate. Between thirteen and sixteen weeks, they began to show behaviour suggestive of the beginning of disappointment reactions: they cried when the adult turned from the crib, and if they were picked up as though for feeding and then put down again, they cried more lustily.

During the fifth and sixth months the twins showed especially strong fright-like reactions to certain noises. But they smiled and laughed persistently when approached unless they were hungry. Also, in the sixth month they developed 'a response which for some time seemed to serve as an expression of interest, of wideawakeness, of excitement, and of well being.' This was called by the experimenters *extension of the extremities*. In this response the arms or the legs or both would be rigidly extended and perhaps moved slightly. This often occurred when the experimenters bent over the crib, but might also occur when they were not near. It was often accompanied by smiling and 'loud vocalization.' From this time on the twins laughed more. One of them would laugh almost any time she was touched. When in their eighth month one of them seized the experimenter's hair and face as he bent over the crib, it seemed they had finally more or less captivated the experimenters and begun to set themselves free from the tepidness of their handling. For the experimenters began gradually to break down and talk and play with the twins a little every day. The babies were then allowed to associate more with each other, and the negative morale of the experiment dissolved considerably.

It is unnecessary in this résumé to recount full details of the locomotor development. Neither twin learned by herself to sit up alone by a year. An effort was then made to test them for their ability to support their weight on their legs, and neither baby gave any indication of doing so, giving only a few momentary kicks. After many repetitions on that day, both were supporting their weight for a few seconds, and after four days of such practice were able to support their weight for several minutes when thus balanced by the experimenters.

While the Dennises were chiefly interested in what they called the *autogenous behaviour* of the infants, of equal interest to the psychiatrist is the degree of deferment of certain behaviour responses under conditions of prolonged deprivation of stimulus. Of additional interest is the fact that the Dennises indicate that such delayed behaviour could be brought out readily as soon as stimuli and practice situations were amply provided.

There is a sort of sly humour of nature in the experiment, which was designed if not to frustrate, at least to deprive the babies. But in the emotional interreaction of the twins and the experimenters, it was the latter who in a way found themselves thwarted by the conditions of the experiment. So great was the twins' positive reaction to them that they found it almost impossible to get moving pictures of their 'negative' reactions. As soon as they approached or even moved in arranging the camera, any crying or fussing would stop and smiles would supplant the negative attitude. This is certainly reassuring!

To summarize, it appears that it is not simple hampering of motion that provokes aggressive rage-like behaviour in the young infant. Indeed, consistent, moderate and general restriction of motion may first quiet the infant, and intense and sudden restriction of motion with deep constriction, binding or jerking, seems to provoke negative responses. It seems possible that within the first year, though not immediately after birth, the infantile reaction may be increased by the angry or tense attitude of the person applying the restraint, and this may be of considerable clinical importance. The indication is that special types of restraint, plus an angry or tense restrainer, may provoke a strong emotional response leading to a reciprocal fear and then to anxiety. Depending on the duration and special degree of interference with expected activities, it further acts by direct limitation of practice. There is, however, no evidence that a permanent impairment of intellectual function itself is produced.

### FOLK CUSTOMS

The folk customs which suggest themselves for study in connection with these problems of restraint are chiefly the various forms of swaddling. This practice occurs in different forms and degrees, especially according to whether part or all of the body is swaddled, as well as the time in the development of the child at which such restraint is applied. Dennis (5) has reviewed much of the literature on the subject, and the accounts here studied are taken largely from articles mentioned in his bibliography. The interest in this report, however, has a different point than that on which Dennis focused.

The practice of swaddling the infant from birth until six months or a year old has been common throughout the centuries and in widely different localities—the papoose of the American Indian, the bambino of the Italian, and Baby Bunting of our own folklore, being widely separated examples. Then there are the customs of binding parts of the body, notably the head and the feet, although there is no part, it seems, that entirely escapes this attention in some folk custom. Our interest is directed, however, only to those restraints which are applied soon after birth and continued for some time. In reviewing the literature certain general impressions stand out, viz., that the swaddling of infants has some practical utilitarian value; has commonly been used by the *hoi polloi* in various groups; and that it is in its own way the antecedent to the cradle, or the play pen of today. In most instances the swaddling is not extremely tight, painful, or continuous. The infant is released from its confinement for several hours during the day. The swaddling, whether with or without a cradle board, serves as a kind of portable cradle in groups that do not move on wheels. In contrast to this, the head-binding and foot-binding, which are painful and deforming and the utilitarian value of which is not readily discernible, are generally marks of aristocratic distinction. Head-deforming was and still is carried on in many parts of the world, being commonest among the Indians of the northwest part of North America, especially the Columbia River region, and least common in Australia. It is said to have been practised recently by the Haida and Chinook Indians in America, by certain tribes in Peru and on the Amazon, by the Kurds of Armenia, by certain Malay peoples in the Solomon Islands and the New Hebrides. The deformation was always done in infancy and often in both sexes. In some places it was reserved for boys and sometimes, as in Tahiti, it was reserved for a single caste (11, 12, 13, 14). The binding of aristocratic Chinese girls' feet continued until 1910. In this review, special attention is paid only to those reports which include some description of the infant's reaction to the swaddling or deformative binding.

Winifred de Kok (15) describes the swaddling of Italian children as an entirely happy proceeding, and concludes that the swaddling offers a comfortable support and protection to the newborn which, far from irritating, serves as a happy bridge across the abrupt birth passage and vaguely approximates the intrauterine conditions until the baby is a little more prepared for the world. She speaks further of the ease with which the bundled baby may be handled, and of the complacency of the Italian baby in its modified strait-jacket. The papoose of the American Indian was generally 'comfortably swaddled' on a cradle board with a round protruding protection for the head, for all the world like the hood on a baby carriage. The restraining jacket was laced over the baby and was comfortably padded within.[1] This same form of body swaddling was used by the Chinooks and other Columbia River tribes, but the special head deforming pressure was added.

A study of the swaddled infants of Albania offers a peculiarly interesting comparison with the Dennis experiment on the twins. In 1934 two Viennese psychology students, Lotte Danziger and

[1] This seems undoubtedly to have a function similar to that of the restraining pack—whether wet or dry, often useful in quieting disturbed patients, as any hospital psychiatrist will recognize.

Liselotte Frankl, published a report (16) of their painstaking study of Albanian infants in and near the little city of Kavaja.[1] From their report it seems that they approached their study with some of the same interests of the Dennises in setting up their experiment. Only the Viennese students wished to study the babies in their own special environment which included peculiar conditions of the infants being removed from most but not all stimulations. The Albanian children are swaddled from birth, and it is no halfway swaddling that is described either. The swaddled bands are applied tightly and the whole swaddled bundle further bound into a crude cradle. It is said that the infant generally screams when the swaddling is applied, but that the mother continually rocks the cradle until the crying gradually dies down.

The swaddling restraint is kept on almost continuously during the first year. Although the Mohammedan law prescribed that the baby should be bathed daily during the first year, the investigators did not seem to see many mothers bathing their infants. Feeding is often carried on without removing the child from its trappings. It is subjected to a further form of passive restraint in that whenever the mother is out, the cradle is put in one of the sleeping rooms which is commonly windowless, the only light coming through cracks in the roof. As soon as the mother comes home, however, she is wont to take the cradled baby out into the lighted living room where other adults and older children may be present. The investigators were not able to reach accurate conclusions as to whether the amount of time spent in the cradle varies at all with the age of the baby. Their description indicates, however, that the night and certainly the greater part of the day is spent in the dim back room. The baby is rarely taken out of doors during its first year. The babies are not played with or dandled. On the other hand, there is no absence of expressions of affection, parents and grandparents lean over the cradle, talk and smile to the baby. In this respect, the Albanian infants have the edge on the Dennis twins. It is noteworthy and unfortunate that neither the Dennises nor

[1] This study attempts to apply quantitative and semi-statistical methods in so small a number of cases that it hardly seems warranted. Its general observations are extremely interesting, however.

Danziger and Frankl say anything about the management of urination or defecation during these early months. To the psychiatrist and psychoanalyst, aware of how much these functions participate in the expression of both anxiety and aggression, and which may be affected by restraint, this is a rather glaring omission.

Danziger and Frankl compared their observations on the behaviour of ten Albanian babies with similar observations on Vienna children. Their general conclusions resemble those of the Dennis experiment. All but one of their ten infants showed a distinct retardation in general development when compared with the Vienna group, but the difference was not so striking as might have been expected, especially when the amount of individual variation is taken into account. The babies showed distinctly less good motor activity, co-ordination, and general body mastery than the Vienna group. At six to ten months the babies sat up but did not crawl. When they reached for objects, the reaching was only approximate and not well directed. Even when not tightly swaddled, they showed little spontaneous movement during this first year, and then it was superficial 'surface movement' which died out readily unless stimulation was continued. Three of the ten infants showed enough spontaneous movement to be worth calling it that, but at best it was weak and poorly directed. When at seven to eight months the child was offered some object, it would make movements indicating some general motion of grasping, but head movements would then occur. It would appear that the child felt drawn toward the object, but moved only diffusely and uncertainly toward it. It was noteworthy, however, that one of the babies, who at ten months showed a marked retardation in motor ability and made no attempt to slap two objects together or play with hollow blocks, seemed suddenly to 'catch on' and in two hours of freedom seemed to have made up for about four months of retardation. It appeared that the latent development was there, but simply had not previously been called into definite form.

In social responsiveness and control, however, the Albanian children were better developed than the Vienna children of the same age group. Unfortunately the authors do not describe very

TGP-D*

clearly just what they mean under this heading. I presume it means indicating by facial expression or behaviour the awareness of and obedience to other human beings. The authors attribute this difference to the fact that, although the babies spent so much time in the dark, when they were brought out, social-emotional contact was the one realm permitted to them. Curiously, the authors have very little to say specifically about sounds or speech. Perhaps this too is included in their social development. It may be that because they are deprived so much and so generally, the babies grow especially in the dimension in which they are permitted freedom, just as a tree seeks the sunlight. The situation again somewhat resembles the Dennis experiment, in which the concentrated spontaneous emotion of the developing babies finally dissolved the self-imposed masks of the experimenters.

Regarding the next three to four years of life of the Albanian infants, Danziger and Frankl state that the young children play little and have no toys, but are wont to stand around watching and listening to the activities of the grown-ups and are quickly drawn into participation in the work of the family. From the account of the investigators, there is no evidence whatsoever of any lasting intellectual impairment.

The head-moulding carried on by the Columbia River Indians, especially the Chinooks, is also a restraint process starting at birth. Here the restraint is applied with such force as actually to deform the shape of the head. Swan (12) gives a detailed account of the process. The baby at birth is placed in a cradle made of a piece of cedar log, hollowed out and lined with softest cedar bark, then covered with soft skin and cloth. A pad is put at the baby's neck and a soft little pillow of wool and feathers on the forehead, enclosing a flat stone The body is laced into the soft wooden cradle with protective thongs, but the pad on the forehead is laced on very tightly and with increasing pressure, so that the head is unbelievably flattened by the end of the first year. Both Cox (17), a trader with the Indians along the Columbia River in 1814, and Paul Kane (18), an artist writing in 1925, gave graphic accounts of the infant's appearance during the course of this flattening process. Kane says, 'the eyes seem to start out of their sockets with the pressure,' and

Cox—'The appearance of the infant while in this state of compression is frightful, and its little black eyes, forced out by the tightness of the bandages, resemble those of a mouse choked in a trap.' Observers all agree that the flat-headed Indians, whose heads as a result of this treatment sometimes do not exceed an inch in thickness at the top, suffer no intellectual impairment and are no duller than those who keep their round heads. Incidentally, the latter are contemptuously called 'rock-heads' (instead of blockheads), and the flat-heads are the more aristocratic.

Kane remarks that the infants seem quiet and placid when the head pressure is on, but if for any reason it is removed, they cry loudly until the wrappings are replaced. Cox also mentions the placidity-under-pressure of the infants, but says nothing of any outcry. Kane offered the explanation that the pressure deadened the sensitivity of the child and only when it was removed did the child become aware of pain. This may be true. It may also be true that since the pressure is gradually applied, the child gradually becomes accustomed to the discomfort, and in a sense misses it when the pressure is suddenly released. I am reminded of an account given by a guide in Guatemala a few years ago that some of the runners who carried heavy loads to the market place, filled their emptied baskets with stones to about the weight of the original load because they felt more comfortable running with a load than without one!

Cox, who was more scandalized than sympathetic toward these Indians, describes them as follows: 'Their good qualities are few and their vices are many. Industry, patience, sobriety, and ingenuity comprises the former. Otherwise they are thieving, lying, incontinent, gambling, and cruel. . . . Each tribe accuses the other of envy, hatred, malice, and all uncharitableness. They are continually back-biting. Their bravery is doubtful, but their effrontery is great. When one of them was stopped for stealing an ax, he denied it completely. When it was pulled out from under his robe, he laughed and said it was a joke. One of the men gave the culprit a few kicks. He took them with *sang-froid*. When he rejoined his companions, they bantered him on the failure of his attempt.' Another man was seen eating the insects which infested his body, and explained when asked, that he ate them out of revenge because they bit him.

From a cursory review of the literature, it appears that swaddling and head binding are practised immediately after birth, and that binding of the feet, amputation of the hands or fingers or other parts of the body seem to be done later than infancy. In one group the grandmother gives up one digit for the birth of each grandson.

While the folk custom material is colourful, it might be considered too anecdotal for much specific interpretation. Still these practices, especially swaddling, have occurred seemingly independently in so many different parts of the world, that the question arises whether there are common factors in their production throughout. The impression emerges that swaddling and head binding actually do have some psychological relation to birth, as well as does the time relation—swaddling being some sort of reinstatement of intrauterine conditions, and head binding a kind of prolonged caricature of the head moulding which may occur spontaneously in a particularly difficult birth.

In the later mutilations (hand or foot binding, or amputation) a relation to castration for punishment or purification is suggested, while in the grandmother situation the mutilation would seem a combination of castration and rebirth. Throughout there is the dubious distinction of the economy of masochism which justifies itself only through the trait of endurance. However, it would take more anthropological background than is here available to understand these customs adequately. It is especially difficult to determine the exact heightening of the sado-masochistic elements of the character which would seem to be the inevitable result. One approaches the circular problem of the underlying sadistic aggression from which such frightful practices of restraint originate and then in turn contribute to the character of the new individual.

### SUMMARY

It is apparent that the problem of the reaction to restraint in infancy is a difficult and complicated one. What the analyst sees in any stage after infancy is not only the original reaction, but

the fusion of this with later experiences; quite often the interpretations belonging to these later periods reprojected back
onto the early periods. Analytically, one must do a careful job
indeed to dissect out what rightfully belongs to the various
stages. Occasionally one has a chance to check this against the
accounts of parents, early baby diaries, or hospital records, and
to compare them with the direct observations on infants.

It must be recognized that *restraint* is not a simple term: that
there is the positive restraint of binding and holding so as
actually to limit motion; that there may be a negative sort of
restraint through deprivation of situations for activity. Then
there are the factors of the intensity (tight or loose swaddling,
the suddenness or unevenness with which positive restraint is
applied; whether it involves the whole or part of the body, and
if it therefore promotes resignation or escape reactions. There
is further the question of the relation of the type of restraint to
the special era in the development of the child, *e.g.*, the almost
certain difference in reaction dependent on whether a baby's
legs were tied down immediately after birth or at the time of the
sixth month, when Dennis notes the pleasurable activity of
extension of the extremities which seems to correspond with a
stage in development when the baby would under normal conditions begin preliminary standing-up exercises by pushing against
the mother's lap or against the floor if held in a near-standing
position. Finally there is the important question not only of the
infant's primary reaction to restraint, but of the augmentation
of the emotional reaction by the reflection of the anxious or
angry attitude of the restrainer, which must indeed be fairly
frequent in the cases which find their way into our clinics.

It seems, however, from the material reviewed as well as from
a number of years of clinical experience that even the reaction
to severe prolonged and painful restraint does not produce any
general intellectual impairment. It may temporarily retard
development through limiting stimulus and practice situations
as in the case of the Dennis' twins. More important is the indication that prolonged restraint, with its accompanying frustration
or submission, may be a factor in producing retardation of
another kind, namely, a slowing of tempo. This in itself produces some impairment of efficiency of intellectual functioning,

without destroying the intellect *per se*. Such slowing of tempo
may also be a factor in chronic negativism, stubbornness, blocking, or lack of good and sustained concentration. In extremely
severe cases it may produce a condition somewhat resembling
the functional deterioration of chronic psychotic states. The
relation of such retardation to the generation of anxiety is a
problem beyond the scope of this chapter. The slowing may
itself be the result of the chronic anxiety associated with very
strong aggressive urges, held in check and shown chiefly in the
extreme ambivalence exhibited by such patients. The tendency
for such early restraint to increase the sado-masochistic elements of the character is clear, but the exact pattern cannot well
be established or even indicated from this material. In any
event such a heightening of the sado-masochism would appear
later combined with and canalized by subsequent life experiences. From a few observations on patients in the course of
a psychoanalytic treatment, I have thought that prolonged
early restraint, producing a condition in which stimulations to
the body far exceeded possible motor discharges, also resulted
in an increasing general body erotization and was a factor aug-
menting the problems generally associated with this condition.

## CHAPTER IV

# URINATION AND WEEPING*

DURING the course of the treatment of some neurotic conditions, certain interrelations between urination and
weeping were noted. In general these may be grouped into: (a)
Relatively normal mechanisms in which weeping and urination
both serve as tension-discharging functions and may come into
play alternately or simultaneously. Both weeping and urination may be increased in states of chronic tension or anxiety.
(b) Specific types of neurotic weeping which are determined by
a displacement of urination urges on to weeping. A similar displacement but in the opposite direction, i.e., the diminution of
the urge to weep resulting in an increase in urination urges,
may also occur. The clinical observations which stimulated this
study, however, have been chiefly along the lines of displacement of urination urges on to weeping with resultant peculiar
types of neurotic weeping. My own cases have been women
patients.

It is a matter of general observation, so common as to need
little substantiation, that both urination and weeping are normal tension-discharging activities. The enormous increase in
enuresis in the 'evacuated' children in England (1)[1] and the
frequency of enuresis in army camps (probably considerably
above its incidence in civilian life) are rough indications that
urination is one of the readiest outlets of anxious tension. It may
in addition be the result of complicated neurotic patterns of
either primary or secondary significance.

A group of neurotic patients encountered in civilian practice
(2) referred to as constitutional neurotics, commonly show until
adolescence a multiplicity of neurotic tension-discharging symptoms: they may have temper tantrums, be thumb-suckers, develop transitory tics and tremors, have nightmares, and many
other symptoms. Chronic or intermittent enuresis is very frequent

* Reprinted from the *American Journal of Orthopsychiatry*, Vol. XV, No. 1,
January, 1945.
[1] Similar observations are reported by numerous other writers.

until puberty or after.[1] Quite frequently it may be noted that if the tension-discharging symptom is dammed up by habit training or even by the social pressure of the obligatory effort toward maturity in adolescence, the enuresis may stop but there is an outcropping of a latent neurosis or psychosis which has previously smouldered.[2] Some of these constitutional neurotics do not break down if they are fortunate in their early emotional life and, also, if they possess inherent talent or abilities which have been developed in childhood and which give them a hold on reality and a justifiable self-confidence. But even such positive developments cannot always save such fragile personalities. If they do remain reasonably compensated, these patients develop into high-strung, competent, often successful individuals of great drive and great sensitivity. Careful scrutiny, obligatory in psychoanalytic treatment, always reveals the residues of the complicated and intense early struggles by which the compensation was established.

Among other neurotic patients there are some who do not have this 'constitutional' multiplicity of neurotic discharges, but who develop special forms of weeping accompanying neuroses. My own observations include two forms of neurotic feminine weeping: one, *shower weeping* (or flooding), and the other, *stream weeping* (crocodile or movie tears).[3] The first type usually weeps inordinately without much sobbing or crying and with very little provocation. As soon as she becomes at all emotional she overflows into floods of tears. The second type of weeper does not show much obvious emotion, being in fact singularly well-controlled in her behaviour. When certain sensitive subjects are touched upon, however, a stream of tears trickles quietly down her cheek. While there is a strong element

---

[1] Huschka reviews many of the factors which contribute to enuresis in children who have other disturbances of behaviour and quotes Michaels' conclusion that enuresis in this character is 'a prototype of psychopathic personality' (Michaels, J. J., 'Parallels between Persistent Enuresis and Delinquency in the Psychopathic Personality,' *Am. J. Orthopsychiatry*, 11: 260—1941).

[2] This was very striking in the cases reported in Chapter II, Part II, 'The Predisposition to Anxiety,' especially in the case cited on p. 73. (Also in *Psychoanalytic Quarterly*, X, No. 4, October, 1941.)

[3] The term *weeping* especially emphasizes the tearfulness, *crying* stresses the sounds, and *sobbing* the muscular movements of mouth and chest.

of exhibitionism in both types of weeping, these types can be readily differentiated from the ordinary hysterical sobbing of the tantrum type so often shown by temperamental women.

In my experience both types of neurotic feminine weeping are derived from an emotional conflict and struggle about urination in the infantile period of life. In both there has been a strong penis envy or fascination focused on the urinary function. In the first type of patient, there is a greater acceptance of the feminine functioning, albeit a quasi-hopeless attitude. One might say that she has wept in early childhood because she has no penis with which to urinate and she continues to weep excessively throughout her adult life. In the second type, the neurotic weeping is actually a substitute for the male urination which has been observed in childhood. The penis envy of these women has been transformed into periodic aggressive demands for the male organ running parallel with illusional ideas of its possession. Two such patients complained repeatedly of sensations of dryness of the genitals during intercourse, and showed a stream of quiet tears as they talked of this sensation. One of these patients showed further a body-phallus identification which was striking. The psychoanalytic interpretation of these cases will be presented in Chapter V.

The main considerations of this chapter, however, deal with the normal or ordinary relations between weeping, vision, and urination in the successive stages of the child's early development. While it may be a little arbitrary to separate these three functions from others such as sweating, defecation, and even salivation—all of which also are obvious biological discharge mechanisms—such a separation seems warranted in this study for the sake of limiting it to a practical clinical usefulness, rather than making an extensive psychobiological theory. The development of the child in regard to these three functions is, for the sake of clarity, considered with reference to cross sections in the child's life at specific ages.[1]

All babies cry at or soon after birth. Crying involves certain

[1] In the selection of the specific ages for cross section, I have followed very much the presentation of Gesell, A., Ilg, F., Learned, J., and Ames, L., *Infant and Child in the Culture of Today*. New York, Harper & Bros., 1943. I found this book most useful and quote liberally and gratefully from it. While not all observers would substantiate the precision of Gesell's

general muscular responses and seems to be provoked by pain (or its precursor) or soon by the discomfort of physiological frustration. I do not find any record of differences observed in the amounts of crying at birth in boy and girl infants. Urination occurs soon after birth and there is evidence of its having occurred *in utero* also. Its subsequent periodicity depends upon a complicated neuromuscular growth involving both sphincter and bladder wall structure and innervation, and can never be separated either from its relation to the total structure or from the working of the infant as a whole. It is very clear that later in life both crying and urination are much influenced by psychic states as well as by physical frustrations. It is thought that there is some capacity for visual localization or at least some reaction to light and dark in the infant at birth (3). The eye, too, is an enormously complicated developing structure whose functioning at once becomes integrated in a complicated fashion into the total development of the baby. Tears or weeping do not generally appear at birth.[1]

Tears first appear at about *one month*, which is also the time of observable focusing of the eye of the infant, which by six weeks can follow in response to a moving object or light.[2] During this first period of life urination occurs readily and very frequently, and crying occurs sometimes if the baby is allowed to remain in a wet diaper. A little later the baby will cry in its sleep on the occurrence of urination (4), either, as Gesell thinks, because the uncomfortable sensation of wetness penetrates the sleep or, as it would seem to me, because there may be the beginning awareness of muscle tension just preceding and almost simultaneous with urination. Crying and urination may both be discharges for the discomfort of the bladder tension.

By the *third month* the urination appears with a more definite

developmental stages, many of the observations coincide approximately with those of other experimenters. I know of no other study as systematic and detailed.

[1] It is interesting that psychical (emotional) weeping is peculiar to the human species and to some species of bears. Walls, G. L., *The Vertebrate Eye and its Adaptive Radiation.* Bull. No. 19, August, 1942. Bloomfield Hills, Mich., Cranbrook Institute of Science.

[2] M. Blanton, C. Bühler (in *The First Year of Life*, New York, John Day, 1930, pp. 27 and 40), A. Gesell (3), and others are in practical agreement about these observations.

periodicity and with larger volumes on a single urination (4, p. 328). At the same time there has developed a true ocular fixation which, accompanied by directed arm movements, begins to influence the posture (3). Perhaps the vision is now the leading acquisitive function. Weeping, which first served largely to wet, nourish and clean the cornea, and wash away physical irritations, is now definitely associated with crying and is in the service of the emotions as well.

About the *sixth to seventh month*, the first sex differences in urination appear, in that girls may develop a longer interval (up to two hours) between urinations and may begin to respond to the pot. This seems to be correlated in time to certain other muscular development, in that the baby now will reach for objects, change them from one hand to the other or even pick them up if dropped, and it is also the time when back musculature is strong enough and sufficiently well controlled so that the child has begun to sit up.[1] There is in this stage a combination of factors tending to produce a lesser degree of spontaneous urinary control in the boy than in the girl.[2] The male genital which is by its exposure always subject to more ready stimulation than is true in the case of the girl, is now brought into the view of its possessor by the sitting posture; while the coincident development of the eye-hand manipulatory ability permits and stimulates the male child to touch or handle his organ very much more than is possible for the girl.[3] Such stimulation also causes a stimulation to urination.

By *ten to twelve months*, the development brings about further combinations of influences. Children of both sexes are sitting up well and strongly; most can creep, a few are beginning to walk. The dry periods are longer and assiduous training may have seemed to take hold and establish habits of urination which are, however, fragile and break down again. The eye-hand movement is developed further, and the child now points

---

[1] Cf. footnote 1, p. 101.

[2] It is a general folk observation that boys are harder to train than girl babies.

[3] Dr. David M. Levy has told me of a 7-year-old girl who attributed her cross-eyed condition to her persistent examination of her own genitalia! Whether or not the girl was correct in her explanation, the strain of such a self-examination is clearly very much greater in the girl than in the boy.

and probes at his excreta as well as other objects. A new difference between the sexes appears, in that *girls frequently laugh as they urinate*. Gesell (4, pp. 328–329) who notes this offers no explanation. It seems to me, however, that this may be due to two facts: (a) that there may actually be a tickling sensation from the rush of urine in the girl which is absent in the projected stream of the boy; (b) the boy is more interested in and observant of his own urination, as he can see it and begin to direct the stream in a way which is not possible for the girl. Certainly the factor of visual attention plays a greater role in the boy than in the girl. His fun comes later when he has confident control of his urination in a way that the little girl so often envies. It may be, too, that there are different visceral sensations on urination in the two sexes, due to the difference in the length of the urethral canal in the two sexes and a difference in the sense of pressure.[1]

At *fifteen months*, the strains of standing and walking are less, the span of time between urinations is increased, but the reaction to the stimulus of the toilet is uncertain, sometimes resulting in withholding of the urine.[2] There is similar behaviour in the bowel situations, and to some extent in manual control of grasping and release, so that the child often lets go of an object with an exaggerated release. He is also beginning to talk at this age.

From *eighteen months* on, social influences begin to be more important, chiefly through toilet training, but also through the increasing capacity of the child to reach and explore his surroundings. Gesell (p. 148) makes certain observations at this age, which if consistently verified and not artefacts due to unrecorded training, are exceedingly important in our understanding of further developments. He states that at this age, children fall into two groups in regard to their bowel movements. One type has its bowel movement in close association with the meal; the other defecates less regularly and between meals. He also thinks that the first type often has a high

---

[1] It is my impression that, later, girls urinate from the pressure of laughing more readily than boys do.
[2] This is interpreted by Gesell as due to the child being in a transitional stage in which contraction of the sphincter eclipses relaxation (4, p. 329).

language ability and will refer to the bowel movement and the toilet by name, but the same words are generally used for urination and defecation, indicating that there is as yet no clear differentiation between the two functions. I would suspect that this type of child might later readily become preoccupied with fantasies regarding the primary gastrointestinal economy and with alimentary birth theories, but I have not verified this clinically to my own satisfaction. An infant of the second type, with irregular time of bowel functioning, more often has his movement alone, in the midmorning while standing in the crib or play pen. There is resistance to the toilet, and stool smearing episodes are more frequent.

Gesell also states that although infants at this period use a common word for urination and defecation, the urination does not follow clearly the two types of defecation procedure. My own impression is that in the first type of infant, with bowel movements following regularly on meals, urination often follows defecation, although it also occurs at intervals between defecations.[1] This age of a year and a half is also the time when susceptibility to shaming is seen, a clear indication of the strength of social pressure.

It is reported (4, p. 148) that at about *twenty-one months* a further difference between boys and girls is noted in that some children, chiefly boys, are unable to have their bowel movements unless they are completely undressed. This has been attributed to the general tendency of the child at this age to undress and run around naked. I would make further suggestions, viz., that it may depend upon a lingering confusion of urination and defecation complicated by the fact that boys may now have begun to stand up to urinate, and there is further a slight confusion between the penis and the formed stool.[2] It is certainly a matter of general observation that children at this

---

[1] In slightly older children, these postdefecation urinations may be regarded as cleansing urinations. This is perhaps more frequent in girls than in boys, probably due to the difference in anatomical structuré actually permitting the urination to wash the girl's genitals more than is possible in the boy.

[2] I have known little girls, only a little older, to make this substitution of stool for penis quite clearly and to say, 'I have mine behind,' referring to the stool and accounting for the apparent lack of a penis in front.

age are aware of and concerned with their excretory products as well as with the process of production. At this time also, there is a dawning sense of possession and differentiation of mine and thine. The way in which this revolves around the problem of the differences in anatomical structure between the two sexes is repeatedly evident in any nursery in which children of different sexes undress and bathe in each other's presence. It is obvious that vision is all important in the acquisition of this knowledge, and that visual stimulations and shocks may leave a definite imprint. At this time, however, girls are achieving nocturnal dryness considerably ahead of boys.

During the next period, up to around two and one half or three years, there is a definite increase in sophistication and pride in the toilet habits and their products.[1] Children learn now to interrupt and resume urination. A sense of control and a pride of mastery is apparent. This is a considerable contribution to the sense of self. The child is now interested in the toilet habits of others, including adults and animals.[1] The sounds of urination also becomes important.

The age at which the little boy has assumed the standing position in urinating varies greatly according to the ambitions and zealous training of the parents as well as being influenced by the opportunities of copying older children and adults. Little boys may be taught to urinate from a standing position as early as twelve or fourteen months—as early in fact as they have learned to stand firmly in an upright position. At this early stage, however, the enforced training in standing urination may be too great a strain on the child and actually result in an insecurity and anxiety about the performance. By about two and a half, most boys are standing urinators. It is natural that the boy takes additional pride in this just as children of both sexes have developed pride in the control of the time and place of

[1] One of my adult patients remembered some interesting childhood observations and fantasies about animals. To her a cow was always feminine, but a horse was masculine when it defecated and feminine when it urinated. She explained that the poor cow splashed both on urinating and defecating and might soil itself badly with its own feces; the horse, on the other hand, defecated proudly—with its tail up it expelled its neat, well-formed fecal balls without even having to stop to do so. Only when it urinated was it reduced to a somewhat feminine role as it must stop to function and usually splashed as well!

urination. But the access of pride in the boy may be enhanced by the fact that in his last weeks as a sitting urinator his stream urination has actually made it difficult for him to urinate tidily in the toilet. What has been in danger of being a liability becomes now, by the change of posture, a definite asset as he gains prowess and precision in directing the stream of his urination from a standing position. Urination soon develops game and contest possibilities and it is his turn to laugh.

By three years the control of urination is reasonably well established. (Gesell remarks that it is now 'in focus,' the very phrase indicating the participation of vision in the procedure.) At four and five there is increasing poise and margin of safety in management. Little boys throughout are more subject to nocturnal accidents than are little girls. This may be due not only to the exposure and consequent chance stimulation of his genital and to his touching and handling it with greater ease than does the little girl, but it may further be due to the relation of urination to weeping, and to the role of each as an aggressive outlet.

Lachrymation, which begins at four weeks, primarily to moisten and nourish the cornea, soon had become associated with crying in children of both sexes, and developed into weeping, serving as well to wash away or relieve psychic or emotional irritations and give discharge to tension and frustration.

The social attitude towards weeping is certainly different for the two sexes. The woman may weep, but the man may not. It seems probable that this difference in social custom came originally out of the fact that the male child's urination early assumes the significance of achievement of an aggressive activity to an extent much greater than that of the female child ever can. In consequence, it is a greater outlet for his tension and a projectile weapon as well. How much this is true is strikingly apparent in the fact that the little boy may put out a fire with his urination, but the little girl can never do this without the greatest risk and almost certainty of being burned. But even though the taboo on male weeping may have come primarily from its being less needed, the pressure of training and shame about weeping is often put very early on the little boy. He must 'be a little man' and not weep if he is hurt or disappointed, although he may sometimes be permitted to cry or yell with a minimum of tears in anger or in rage. This restriction on weeping is borne down upon him often just at the time or before he has achieved urinary control and before he has real confidence in himself in this respect. It is on this basis as well as from greater stimulation of the genital, I believe, that we see greater susceptibility to early enuresis in the boy than in the girl.[1]

With the little girl, however, we have another story. When the little boy rises from the sitting position to the standing one in which he learns to direct his own stream neatly ('to make a river'), this is an impressive sight to his sister. She is often then seen to attempt to imitate him, only to return abashed to the sitting posture. Infantile feminine envy of this masculine urination is recognized as a very common component of penis envy, and is probably dependent only on the incidence of the actual visual observation of the boy by the girl. My experience with adult patients has led me to believe that when this observation of male urination occurs in the setting of general or severe frustrations from other sources, the little girl may show an increase

---

[1] The recent plight of the 3½-year-old daughter of some friends has illustrated rather clearly the interrelations between vision, urination, and weeping. This child, the youngest and only girl in a family of three siblings, had a moderate congenital bilateral ptosis of both eyelids. She seemed otherwise a well-developed, bright child and got along quite well, viewing the world through narrowed eye slits, although one may guess that this was a natural peeping situation. When recently she was operated on for a correction of the ptosis, the ophthalmologic surgeon requested the parents not to visit her while she was in the hospital as he did not wish her to get upset and cry until she was well over the operation. This may have been because he thought crying would strain the surgical site. During the few days in the hospital, the child accepted the bandaging of her eyes submissively, became extremely bossy otherwise, called repeatedly for water, urinated freely, and began biting her toys fiercely. When the bandages were removed, she made no attempt to open her eyes until the day that the parents came to visit and take her home. At home she developed a marked stuttering, relapsed into both day and night enuresis, and bit other children viciously. These reactions lasted for a full month after the operation. Ferenczi, as well as others, has well pointed out the relation of the flow of speech to the urinary flow. In this case, it seems, the child needed some aggressive outlets for the anxiety, distress, and visual (and emotional) isolation of the operation. On her return home a further conflict was set up about this with increased anxiety at the resentment toward the parents for having deserted her. Her aggressive demands increased and her conflict expressed itself largely in the speech, as well as in enuresis. She had been a 'good soldier' about not crying, but at what a price! In this instance, the little girl had been coerced about weeping in a way that is more frequent with boys.

in her weeping. This gives an outlet for her tension and becomes particularly marked when her envy turns to a kind of hopeless acceptance of her inability to urinate as a boy does. (There may, of course, be other items of envy and discouragement displaced on this as well.) The weeping itself is of a feminine type, of the *shower* variety and very copious.

On the other hand, some girls never accept their inability to achieve the masculine type of urination. They weep not hopelessly but with a quiet resentful approximation of the *stream* which now comes from above rather than below. These girls take pride in the fact that they show little emotion. But in their neuroses their stream-like, quiet exhibitionistic weeping appears whenever the sensitive subject of penis envy arises almost to consciousness. While the detailed psychoanalytic case material will be presented in the next chapter, the broad outlines of these underlying mechanisms may be seen as intensifications of situations observed in the normal development of children.

### SUMMARY

In this chapter[1] I undertook to scrutinize the relations between weeping, vision and urination as they appear in the normal development of infants. The significant facts were as follows: tears appear at about four to six weeks of age, at about the time of the first focusing of the eye and probably the first awareness of muscle tension preceding urination. As early as six to seven months a sex difference in urination is noted, in that girls tend to develop longer intervals between urinations and are more readily trained to the pot than are boys. This corresponds in time to the development of directed eye-hand movements and to the beginning of the sitting-up period. It seems probable that the greater frequency of male urination at this time is due to the greater exposure—and consequent chance stimulation—of the male genital, especially in its being touched or handled more frequently by the male infant himself as it is brought into visual range by the sitting posture. From then on it seems that urination

[1] The interpretations were based on observations reported elsewhere, especially by Gesell and his co-workers in *Infant and Child in the Culture of Today*. New York and London, Harper, 1943. Specific references are given in this chapter.

is a more complex, sensitive function in the male than in the female child, eliciting in the male more visual attention and accessory muscle co-ordination, and ultimately leading to a greater sense of mastery and power in its management and control.

This is especially evident when the male child, generally between the ages of one and two years, is further confronted with the obligation of learning to urinate in a standing position. As mentioned earlier in this chapter, at ten to twelve months little girl babies often laugh as they urinate while boys seldom do. Urination is a more serious business for them. They are also more subject to urinary accidents than are girls, a susceptibility (reported by Gesell and Ilg as being apparent up to four or five years of age) which may be further increased when there is a special prohibition against weeping before a confident mastery of urination has been gained. Later, the very fact that male urination expresses greater power, and is an aggressive weapon as well, renders it a better outlet for tension, and may be one reason why weeping is less necessary to the male than to the female. It is a general observation that in many situations of 'nervousness' in which women weep, men show an urgency or frequency of micturition. That the little girl between two and six usually envies the boy his urinary prowess, attempts to copy him and shows an increase in her excited curiosity about her own urination, is an everyday observation of nursery-school teachers and others who have young children of both sexes together.

It appears then that there is at first some degree of correlation between the physiological stages of development of control of visual focusing, general muscle co-ordination and bladder-sphincter control, and that there is a natural reciprocity between urination and crying as tension discharging mechanisms. In the boy these three functions converge earlier and to a greater extent. Urinary control is at first less certain and then becomes a more effective expression of aggression than in the girl in whom urination is a simpler tension-relieving mechanism. Later the girl is naturally more susceptible to any reinforcement of visual erotization because of the fascination of male urination which may then take over much of the castration problem. This is a brief indication of the high lights of differences in the development of urinary control in the two sexes.

## CHAPTER V

# PATHOLOGICAL WEEPING*

IT is not my intention to deal with all the aspects of pathological weeping, but to limit myself to clinical observations on
certain forms in which the weeping was apparently related to
underlying childhood disturbances of urination. . . .

From an accumulation of clinical impressions, I had long
noted that psychotic patients who wept freely rarely had coincidental urinary symptoms or disturbances of bladder control.
Subsequent analytic experience permitted a clearer and more
detailed examination of this relationship.

Two types of neurotic weeping met in the analysis of several
women patients are presented here. The form and character of
both types of weeping were found to be determined by a displacement on to weeping of the urge to urinate. The weeping
then appeared as a secondary coincidental symptom. In no instance was the weeping a presenting symptom or even spontaneously complained of by the patient.

The observed neurotic weeping was *shower* weeping or *stream*
weeping. In the shower type there are copious tears with very
little provocation and without much sobbing or crying. Sometimes these floods of tears appear indiscriminately with any
emotion. In the stream type, little obvious emotion is evident
but a stream or trickle of tears rolls down the cheek when
certain sensitive, deeply repressed subjects are touched in the
analytic work. In both types the weeping, *i.e.*, lachrymation, is
the main evidence of the disturbance and is singularly free from
associated muscular reactions. In both, a strong element of exhibitionism is present together with marked penis envy and some
visual fascination focused on urination. Shower weeping indicates some acceptance of the feminine role but a rather
discouraged attitude about it. This type weeps in anger and
in partial resignation because she cannot approximate male

* Reprinted from *The Psychoanalytic Quarterly*, Vol. XIV, No. 1, January,
1945.

urination. Stream weeping is a substitute for male urination, the penis envy appearing in periodic aggressive demands for the male organ accompanied by fantasies of its possession. In one case, described later, the patient seemed to be continually reassuring herself about the possession of a penis and weeping partly to demonstrate her possession and partly from relief. An extreme body-phallus identification was present and may always be prominent in stream weepers.

Two cases illustrate the two types of weeping. The shower type is illustrated by the first patient who had been analysed twelve years before I first saw her. Her analyst had subsequently died. During my work with her she wept a great deal although she did not seem greatly depressed. Although it did not seem that she wept when she was alone, during almost every analytic hour floods of tears would come up as she talked. She had a curious, slightly imperious way of asking me for Kleenex with which to wipe her eyes—rather than using her own handkerchief—as though to call sharply to my attention her need to clean and dry her eyes. The exhibitionist demand for a tender ministering was obvious.

This patient brought me several dreams which were variations on the same theme. One of them, the middle section of a triptych of dreams appearing the same night was as follows:

I was standing outside a bathroom—of which the door was wide open—waiting for a large coloured woman to finish cleaning. I was conscious of wearing a sweater which was front side back, buttoned up so that it was awkward to wear. Next I was waiting in a hallway like the the top floor of one of the old brownstone houses. A stairway from the floor below had a slight curve before it reached the top floor and there was a railing along one side of the hall guarding the well of the stairway. If you went up the stair, the bathroom which was bright and sunny (*i.e.*, in a way open rather than dark) would have been at your immediate right. On the top step of this stairway was a little girl child, almost a baby. Before the woman had left the bathroom the child had gone into it (although I had not seen her go) and had fallen, so that she was stretched out on the bathroom floor on her back. I went in and looked at her. I realized that she had fallen with great force but she was not crying, she was lying motionless. Then I noticed that the upper part of the head was abnormally large. 'She is not crying because she is becoming an imbecile,' I thought. Later after I awoke, my thought was that she had water on the brain. I seemed to know somehow in the dream that the child was a girl.'

It is impossible to go into all the association to this dream; only the more important items referring to the urination-weeping problems will be mentioned. The patient's family name was derived from a word which means 'brown' and they often jokingly referred to themselves as 'the brownies' or 'the coloured people.' The patient was the oldest child of a large family. Two brothers came after her. In her earliest childhood two boy cousins, one of whom was a little older than the patient and the other about her age, repeatedly visited the family. In her infancy she had been a fretful first baby, nursed solicitously but not very successfully by the mother.

The dream house shows the obvious common reference to the body structure. This appeared very clearly in the patient's associations. The coloured woman, like the brown stone character of the house, referred to the brown mother, as well as specifically to a brownstone house in which the family had lived when the patient was a child. In addition it had the meaning of brown stool or feces. Urination and defecation were evidently confused and an effort was made to clarify what comes from in front and what from behind. (This was the main motif of the first dream of the trio, of which this was the second.) The *sweater which was front side back* referred not only to this question of front function (urination) or rear function (defecation) but also to the infantile observation that she had to unbutton her drawers behind whereas her older boy cousin and later her brothers more handily unbuttoned in front to urinate. She had indeed to act the same in order to urinate and to defecate, while the boy could unbutton in front to urinate. The *openness* of the bathroom which is emphasized both by the open door and also by the open sunny character of the room, referred to the openness of the mother's genital space which was unencumbered by a stool-penis, and further to the openness of her own genital area which was innocent of dark pubic hair. This was, indeed, an attempt at reconciliation to the lack of a penis like the cousin's.

It became quite clear in other work with the patient that the setting of the birth of the younger brother had been an

extremely disturbing event. Its effect had been not only to wrench
the child prematurely from the mother's care but since it came
at a period when the differentiation between urinating and
defecating was not very secure and when there was a beginning
sense of possession—of what was hers and what was his—it had
reinforced the no-penis problem. At this stage the penis of the
cousins and of the brother was still confused with the stool which
was dirty. But the penis had also assumed positive value as a
possession and its absence was beginning to be felt as a lack, the
result of discrimination against her.

The *little girl child, almost a baby,* who falls limp to the bathroom floor is the patient herself who received so bewildering and
shocking a blow when she wanted to be cared for by the mother
(cleaned by the negro woman) and was devastated by finding
herself displaced by the birth of the brother. The displacement
from below upward is thrice emphasized in the dream: first, by
the location of the bathroom on the top floor of the house whereas the patient's recollection was that the bathroom was on the
second floor, halfway up the house; second, by the idea that the
fallen child has *water on the brain*; and third, by the representation of her drawers as a sweater that buttons behind. The limp-
ness, the imbecility of the child—so great that she does not cry
but develops water on the brain—refers to the sense of helpless-
ness of the little girl, the beginning of a clear penis envy, the
prodrome of floods of tears throughout her life.

This patient's neurosis was primarily a hysterical one. She
was pushed by the rapid birth of two younger brothers into a
premature turning from her mother to her father but maintained a deep underlying yearning for the mother. Her oedipus
period was characterized first by a special intensity and then by
a trauma which further focused her castration fears. There was
an overt hysterical breakdown at adolescence which she tried to
resolve by turning from sexuality and partially identifying herself with her father, whose profession she subsequently followed.
It is obvious that she had strong homosexual tendencies, yet she
made a predominantly feminine identification, though a discouraged one in which she never did justice to her own feminine
attractiveness. While she had never married, she had no overt
homosexual relationships. There was one prolonged hetero-

sexual affair which embodied some genuine love. She was past thirty-five when she underwent her first analysis and approaching fifty when she consulted me. Perhaps more could have been done for her if she had come to analysis earlier. As it is, she is an able, warm-hearted, attractive woman who feels that she has missed much in life and still weeps somewhat too readily.

The current situation in which the trio of dreams appeared is interesting. Her mother had died two years before the dream. She had accepted this and the recent breaking up of the old home in which she had not lived for many years, with apparent relief and great calmness. She then began to show an undue worry about her old father and his retirement to a farm he had in the country. The third section of the triptych showed this conflict quite clearly: a fusion of an oedipal conflict with the deeper preoedipal one when she was wrenched prematurely from her mother and forced to seek her father's solace and care.

The stream type of neurotic weeping is illustrated by excerpts from the second case. This patient was a married woman of thirty-five. The presenting symptoms were those of an anxiety hysteria of two years' duration marked by an exacerbation of a severe claustrophobia which had been present to a lesser degree throughout her life. There was also a fear of fainting and a fear of becoming addicted to drugs. The overt form of the neurosis began when the patient fell ill from an acute infection. Her feverish state seemed to revive disturbances of early childhood based essentially on an insecure sense of reality.

On superficial examination she presented the appearance of a marked hysterical blandness; deeper examination indicated that the disorder was very severe and might be considered of a 'borderline' nature. Very striking was a peculiar scheming attitude toward life: an outspoken, appallingly frank graspingness coupled with a neurotic generosity. Her love relationships were poor, a fact which she herself recognized and stated with startling candour. At twenty-one she had married a partially impotent older man intending to divorce him as soon as she had found someone more suitable. Once married, she never found the suitable partner, but became fretful, sleepless, increasingly good and generous, but obviously unhappy. She attributed this to her husband's inadequate sexual performance. A physician suggested that she would be better if she had a child. Although she had till then thought little of this deprivation, she seized the suggestion with a peculiar intensity and embarked on a long struggle to get a child willy-nilly. This was complicated by the husband's poor status and by the fact that she herself had had pelvic inflammation which made conception improbable. Before she discovered the latter, she had gone to extraordinary lengths to procure a child first from her husband, and failing that, from other men—both by the natural method and by artificial insemination. At the time she began treatment, she was living with a man for whom she had but slight affection. She demanded intercourse with nymphomaniacal frequency. Her plan was to get the child and then abandon the lover. She stated this with a forthright, unabashed simplicity, and seemingly with no regard either for the lover or the hypothetical child. It is clear enough that the patient suffered from an overwhelming penis envy.

The patient's appearance and behaviour presented peculiarities. She was a slender, very trim young woman, more than ordinarily neat. She wore the same hat day after day, a close fitting turban with a stiff round platelike part above the snood. The whole effect, both in hat and posture, was of stiff uprightness. She would not take off the hat even when she lay on the couch, except in the heat of summer. She rationalized this by saying that she did not wish to muss her hair and that the hat was so small that it did not get in the way. Her blandness was apparent in her face which was unusually smooth. Her nose was smooth, firm and not remarkably large or small. She stated that in childhood her brothers and sisters had been wont to call her 'Long Nose' because her nose was longer than theirs. She also referred to herself as 'nosey' because she seemed to pick up so much information about people around her that she suspected she must be unconsciously prying. Her mouth was small and feminine. Her eyes, however, were her most striking feature: they were large, usually wide open, moist and luminous.

Connected with this feature were three outstanding symptoms: her peculiar bland emotionlessness, her urinary frequency and her really extraordinary weeping. At first, while she would say, 'I am so angry,' it was said with a placid mildness and no flicker of a muscle. As the analysis progressed and I began to break down this glossy shell, the frequency of urination and the weeping appeared, generally alternately. She complained of feelings of dryness around the urethra and the mouth of the vagina during intercourse. In the analytic hour she would get up and glide from the room to the bathroom to urinate. Once during a period of anxiety she developed a bladder tension, never feeling satisfied with urinating but returning again and again to attempt it, until she set up a real urethral irritation. At other times when subjects arousing jealousy or envy were touched, leading back to the fundamental problem of penis envy, a trickle of tears flowed quietly down her cheek. It first appeared in the patient's dreams and later became a verifiable fact, that she wept only from the eye that I could see, although at other times she might have tears from both eyes.

From the dream material it appeared that the vagina, which was confused with the urethra, was her most important mouth, and that she was continually in search of the missing breast (penis). From her life story (before her marriage she was trained as a dancer), from her unique headdress and posture, as well as from the content of many dreams, it was evident that there was a very strong body-phallus identification, a fact which was to be expected from the dramatically clear baby-phallus concept.

It is impossible to give much of the developmental background. The following facts are noted for comparison and contrast with the first case. This patient was also one of a large family, the third child with two older brothers and a sister only fifteen months younger, as well as other children several years younger. Thus she was preceded, rather than followed, by two boys. Her father was much depreciated by the mother who boasted of her ability to get along without a man and the fact that she only permitted him access to her when she was willing to have a child, while at the same time she looked to her sons for everything—they were more hers than was her husband. Thus the family stage was set for the turning of the little girl's envy toward her brothers. This is in contrast to the first case in which the girl's awareness of a contemporary penis was not as acute because her brothers were younger. She envied them more their babyhood and their possession of the mother and was prematurely pushed into pride in being older. The penis envy generated toward the cousin and later reinforced toward her brothers was relatively weaker.

In the second case there were many other determinants including repeated primal scene experiences which occurred so early that there was no adequate differentiation between the sexes in the eyes of the little onlooker. However, an experience when the patient was about six appeared important in the determination of the pseudostoical calmness and the repression of any emotional display followed by its reappearance in the exhibitionistic stream weeping. She remembered at this time playing with a group of children—mostly boys in which the two little girls were merely tolerated—engaged in competitive jumping games during which she had been pushed by her younger sister from a ledge several feet high, injuring her shoulder in the fall. Fused with this memory, and partially hidden by it, were ones of similarly competitive urination games in which she could only be an onlooker. At the time of the accident the frightened brother and sister begged her not to cry and not to tell, as both feared they would be blamed by the frantic mother. The matter could naturally not be long concealed and the patient was taken to a hospital for treatment. Here the forceful superstitious mother battled the doctors and refused an operation, with the result that the little girl went two or three times a week for a while to have the shoulder treated. She recalled the pain of these proceedings and the determination to show no feeling in order to avoid the mother's frenzy, to win praise for her stoicism from the doctors and to gain a superiority over the other children. That in this way she was retaining her penis equivalent and avoiding the imminent castration is amply suggested by the patient's dreams. One recurrent dream, presented in many versions, boiled down to the fantasy that the younger sister was trying to take the patient's man away from her. The patient awoke with anxiety lest this happen.

During this period at six, when she was stoically undergoing treatment of the shoulder and not permitting herself to weep, she seems to have been able to retain bladder control. A little later, however, she developed fainting spells whenever injury to anyone else was threatened. Even before the shoulder injury, the patient's castration anxiety had been gravely aroused by the birth of her second sister to whom she later became greatly attached. This child was born at home. The patient heard about, fantasied, and possibly witnessed some of this birth. As soon as she had returned to school after her own injury, she made unusual progress in her work and caught up with her brother with whom she spent much spare time reading. She officially forgave the younger sister but thereafter refused to play with her and even during her analysis condemned her for her roughness and vulgarity. Her compensation by means of an intellectual superiority worked reasonably well until puberty.

In this second case, there was a special visual erotization arising from the repeated early primal scene experiences, the witnessing of urinary games and the probable witnessing of the birth of the sister. The castration fear which was aroused by seeing the urination soon afterward became intensified by the fear of operation and was mainly met by an attempted denial and displacement. A superiority and an equivocal illusion of the possession of the penis was maintained through the repression of crying. It seems probable that the peculiar type of tearfulness dates from this time—a kind of defiant compromise. It may be significant that the patient not only did not complain of the tearfulness, but never spoke of it as 'weeping' but as 'tear-ing,' which also is one of the slang terms for male urination.

The infantile situations of the first case are in some respects less clear. The penis envy was in itself less focused on the function of urination, but there was a greater struggle with toilet habits *per se*, due to a rather severe toilet training. The envy was more directed toward being cared for as a baby like the younger brother and the penis envy itself seemed associated with the permission to be dirty.

The presentation of the material of these two cases in general outline serves to bring out the salient differences in the pathological weeping of these two types. These observations are probably relatively common in analytic practice, and it is a little surprising that they have not been dealt with more specifically in the literature. Abraham, in his article 'The Development of the Libido' (1), refers to a patient who, '. . . during menstruation which used to excite her castration complex in a typical way . . . scarcely ever stopped crying,' and adds in a footnote, 'It may be mentioned in passing that the copious flow of tears represented her unconscious wish to urinate like a man.' Lewin's article (2), 'The Body as Phallus,' which presents much that is pertinent to the second case with her obvious body-phallus identification and the onset of her overt neurotic illness during a fever (which promoted the body-phallus fantasy as well as disturbing the sense of reality), contains a reference in its summary to tears and saliva being equated to semen and urine. Zilboorg (3), in an article on the transformation of instincts, cites a rather comparable case. About a woman who always cried after intercourse, he says, '. . . . let me state simply that her spells of crying frequently, if not always, seemed to take the place of neurotic, symbolic, substitutive, masculine orgasm. . . . Feelings of hate, frequently coupled with a sense of tearfulness, mounted as soon as the penis began its withdrawal and were experienced regardless whether an orgasm was attained by the woman or not.' Ferenczi (4) mentioned the sudden relief (relative pleasure) from urination in a frightened child and that it stops the child's crying, but he did not develop the theme further.

Winnicott (5) also cites a case of a girl who became enuretic after the death of her brother, in whom the enuresis disappeared promptly when weeping was induced. In van der Heide's case of pollakiuria nervosa (6), a twenty-three-year-old girl had a phobia of urinating in public and showed many of the same components as in my cases: urinary envy of the brothers, peeping and exhibitionism, hostility toward men and the desire for the oral incorporation of the father's penis. In his report there is no special mention of weeping except that the patient cried much during the first interview. It would seem that this patient frequently vomited rather than wept.

While in this paper I have attempted little more than a presentation of clinical material in a kind of vignette form, some aspects of the problem of pathological weeping may have broad psychosomatic implications. In their studies of asthma, French and Alexander (7) have presented their interpretation of the asthmatic attack as a repressed cry of a very early and predominantly vocal sort. More specifically, Saul (8) raised the issue of the relation of urticaria to weeping and demonstrated that in some situations the urticaria would disappear when weeping was induced. He did not make quite clear why there had been a suppression or repression of weeping or why the skin was selected as the site of the displaced weeping.[1]

In general one wonders whether the extravasation of water from the body is not basically an expression of aggressive defence, whether it appears as the result of a channelled excretory process (as in lachrymation, sweating, urination, etc.) or as local or general transudative edemas resulting from severe or prolonged non-specific traumata (as in the wheal formation of the skin (9) or the pleural and peritoneal edemas of the acute 'alarm reaction' of animals (10)).

[1] A clinical observation of alternating attacks of asthma and weeping similar to Saul's report of the relation between urticaria and weeping has been made in the Menninger Clinic. (Lane, Selma, 'Psychological Factors in Asthma,' *Bull. of Menninger Clinic*, VIII, No. 3, 1944, p. 76.)

## CHAPTER VI

# VISION, HEADACHE, AND THE HALO*

## REACTIONS TO STRESS IN THE COURSE
## OF SUPEREGO FORMATION

O N several occasions patients have brought material which showed quite clearly some connections between visual shock, headache, and the development of a halo. Schematically the sequence is as follows. The child receives a stunning psychic blow, usually an overwhelming visual experience which has the effect of dazing and bewildering it. There is generally the sensation of lights, flashes of lightning, bright colours or of some sort of aurora. This may seem to invest the object, or objects seen, or it may be felt as occurring in the subject's own head experienced literally as seeing lights or seeing red. This is depicted in comic strips as seeing stars. The initial experience always produces the most intense emotions, whether of awe, fear, rage or horror. Extremely severe lancinating pain may be part of the disturbing experience.

The emotion is felt with great force, as if an explosion or a stab had occurred within the head. There is usually at first a feeling of unreality, or of confusion. The shocking stimulus arouses an erotized aggression which demands subsequent mastery. Sometimes the little voyeur feels impelled to repeat the experience as though to test its reality. Peeping or fantasies of peeping are accompanied by sensations of tension and strain in the eyes or across the frontal region. Headaches occur later when new situations reactivate the original trauma. Mastery is attempted by successive repetition in fantasy (reality testing), partial repression, or by the development of severely binding superego reaction-formations of goodness which are supplemented by or converted into lofty ideals. As the tense goodness relaxes a little, the headache improves and the ideals are loftier but less exigent.

* Reprinted from *The Psychoanalytic Quarterly*, Vol. XVI, No. 2, April, 1947.

Figuratively, the child develops a halo to which, if it remains too burdensome, he reacts either by throwing it defiantly away —conspicuously in some psychopathic and psychotic states—or by endowing someone else with it. Such children and adults seem to overvalue enormously those whom they love, projecting onto them the extreme ideals and demands they first required of themselves. Quite often the loved one is seen as a saint on a pedestal, worshipped rather than loved, and kept almost inviolate in an overestimation which is in actuality a devaluation.

The infantile origins of this state, especially with reference to the superego, will be traced in two patients who have been psychoanalysed. The symptomatology is fairly common, and may be recognized in varying degrees of intensity in different neuroses. It often appears strikingly clear in schizophrenic patients. It is my clinical impression that it is commonest with definite obsessional and compulsive trends, even when these are not the main symptoms of the disorder. Only those parts of the case histories and of the dreams which have a direct bearing on these aspects of the superego will be given.

### CASE HISTORY I

This patient sought psychoanalysis because of overconscientiousness, lack of adequate forcefulness for effective functioning, fear of active aggression in others, and some symptoms indicating a repressed scoptophilia.

At the beginning of analysis the patient remembered almost nothing of her childhood before her seventh or eighth year, although she had been told certain facts by her parents and her sisters. She learned from her mother that she had been a frail overly sensitive baby, definitely smaller at birth than had been her older sisters. She was a nervous, wakeful baby, too readily startled by sound, very easily aroused from sleep; hence, a habit of afternoon naps was continued until about the age of nine. She was permitted to attend only the morning session of school and had to rest during the afternoon that she should not become unduly excited.

From a rather long analysis, the impression was gained that she had been one of those quivering, eager, easily stimulated children who sometimes hide behind a mask of vagueness. Intellectually she was somewhat precocious, but passive and too easily hurt. She elicited a good deal of protection from those around her. When she was sixteen the parents inconsistently sent her away to college, hoping to counteract her shyness and dependency. She was the most timid of three sisters, none of whom was particularly forceful.

It is noteworthy that a rather marked degree of myopia was first discovered when the patient entered school at about six, after which she wore glasses. She recalled a sudden increase in clarity of vision which the glasses gave, and the contrast of the external world in focus with her previous blurred peering.

She recalled no early sexual curiosity or experiences. She had been carefully informed by her mother about the birds and the flowers, and believed she had first masturbated in her twenties.

The patient had been nursed at the breast at least during the first year, weaning having been postponed for convenience while the family was cruising on a yacht. Perhaps during that year, and certainly during the second and third years, the patient had resorted to holding her breath—practically her only expression of anger—for which and for an infantile spasm she had been immersed in cold water. During this first year, too, she had slept in her parents' bedroom, or in the close quarters of their cabin aboard the yacht. Later she had a room of her own, but sometimes slept with her two sisters in a screened porch which after her sixth year she often shared with her brother, born when she was five.

Her third year was especially eventful. She had a tonsillectomy under a general anesthetic; afterward she was given the excised tonsils in a bottle of preservative to cherish as a memento of the occasion. That same year all three sisters had scarlet fever, for which they were quarantined separately as they did not fall sick simultaneously. The patient got it after the other two, while visiting a relative to whom she had been sent to protect her from becoming infected by contact with her sisters. During the illness she developed a mild nephritis in the course of which she was catheterized. Soon after this illness, her mother fell in attempting to get on a streetcar, and miscarried a stillborn boy, which

especially grieved the parents as they had long wanted a son.
Two years later, when the patient was five, a healthy boy was
born. This whole matter of the miscarriage had been completely
repressed by the patient, but presented itself so insistently during
the analysis that the patient finally asked her mother about it
and received a verification.

The infantile sexual experiences in the development of this
patient were approximately as follows. During the first two
years there were primal scenes which were not clearly visualized
by the child, perhaps because they often occurred in the dark,
perhaps also because of her markedly defective vision. She
picked up the sounds, however, got the sense of turbulent motion, registered and reflected the heavy breathing and returned
the aggression in her own attacks of holding her breath.[1] These
attacks were then checked by immersing the child in cold water.
The patient had been in an adjoining room when her mother
miscarried, had gone into the mother's bathroom and discovered
something in a pail as well as bloody linen. This made a profound impression and had the effect of an overwhelming visual
trauma, but was dealt with by fairly quick repression, being
fused with the memory of the tonsils in the bottle. Between three
and five there was an increasing awareness of male genitalia.
She had had, even earlier, some blurred impression of her
father's genitals and attributed similar equipment to the
mother. Before she was five she was visited by two male
cousins, both several years older. One was a rather dull, enuretic
boy, and in becoming aware of this boy's genital she did not
elevate it to any particular position of grandeur, although
certainly there had been this general feeling about her father's
(and mother's) penis in the earlier primal scenes. With the other
cousin, a mischievous headstrong boy, there was some sort of
mutual sexual investigation which appeared in the analysis as
a cover memory of having been terrified several years later when
this boy tried to push her down a hole. In this sexual experience
too, she had seen and been tempted to touch, or had actually

---

[1] Dr. N. C. LaMar has told me of a case of his in which a child of three
and a half years was known to have walked into the parents' bedroom while
the parents were having intercourse, to have been obviously 'shaken' by the
scene, and to have had her first attack of asthma the following night.

touched the boy's genital. In this same age period between four and five, there was a memory of coasting with her father on the sled behind her, and of being so aware of his genitals that she thought she could feel them. She felt a frightened exhilaration with a fear that the situation might get out of control. This memory recurred several times in association to 'out of control' dreams, which also evoked association to the story of Ethan Frome. In other words, the child was in an early oedipus period of considerable intensity.

The patient's brother was born, presumably, at midnight. The patient saw nothing, and how much she heard or reconstructed in fantasy from what she soon overheard is not quite clear. The event had for her the accoutrements of the birth—and the death—of a hero, bringing associations of the *Erlkönig*, and fantasies of a doctor racing at midnight through a colossal storm of water and wind. It seemed pretty definite that this event was not nearly as overwhelming to the patient as the mother's miscarriage had been.

Between the patient's third and sixth years there was some mutual masturbation among the three girls on the sleeping porch, for which the oldest sister, about twelve, was blamed by the mother. My patient had two types of masturbatory fantasies: one of being blindly smothered by a large overwhelming pressure which descended especially upon her head; the second, sadistic fantasies of hurting others, sometimes by magic, sometimes by direct torture. In the first, she was passively succumbing; in the second, actively attacking. The fantasies of smothering, on analysis, proved to be a fusion of rather forceful and prolonged breast feeding, identification with her mother in the primal scene, of having been anesthetized, and birth fantasies. The sadistic fantasy became detached from masturbation and appeared at the age of about eight as symptomatic play when, at a seaside resort, she caught little fish left in shallow pools by the receding tide, and in solitary secrecy burned the tiny creatures alive. She was always startled that she, so mild a child, could have done so cruel a thing.

The birth of the brother was a severe disappointment to the patient in typical oedipal fashion, except that she seemed to renounce all hopes of ever having a child, probably on the basis of guilt (masturbation) and fantasies that she had been responsible for her mother's miscarriage. Early in treatment there was an extreme resistance to analysing the hopelessness of her pregnancy wishes. She would simply sigh and say in a bored fasion, 'Why bring that up? Haven't I enough problems without that?'

The birth of the brother focused the child's penis envy. She regarded his genitals as 'a cute little flower' (the mother's term for all her children) and had impulses to touch them. Her awareness of his circumcision increased the notion of her own castration, also her ambivalence toward him to which she reacted by extra devotion to the brother which extended to small animals and toy animals. In relinquishing the idea of having a baby herself, she denied herself dolls but accepted in their place small stuffed animals. The burning of the fishes was a return of the repressed hostility clearly expressed in play. This displacement from penis to fish found symptomatic expression in a mild phobia of seeing, eating or touching any fish. The reaction to large fish was additionally determined when, at six years of age, she saw her grandfather urinating into the water as he stood fishing from the shore. With her new glasses she could see quite plainly, and the sight awed and aroused in her a latent excitement connected with memories of past experiences and fantasies of birth, castration, death, dismemberment, fused together. The induced erotized excitement and aggression were quickly repressed, reappearing in dreams first of weeping and finally of rage. She became increasingly good, still more passively compliant than formerly, and withdrew into fantasy. Sexual interests were repressed and did not reappear with anything approaching normal intensity until analysis. She was fearful and ill at ease with boys, could not fall in love with any man although she made a conventional marriage at the proper age and was the formally adored wife of a quite unindividuated husband in a kind of make-believe marriage. She had only the highest ideals, found it difficult to bring any definite accomplishment to completion. She was whimsical, gentle, wrote delicate poetry and stories in which the theme of flames and burning reappeared frequently. She complained of vague feelings of unreality, sensations of heaviness, and occasional headaches which were not severe, consisting of aching superimposed on a general feeling of cloudiness and ineffectuality. In the early part of the analysis, she repeatedly asked with a childish naïveté, 'Could I possibly have felt that way?' or, 'Is it possible for a child to have such feelings?' as if requiring an authority she did not possess to permit her to claim her own feelings.

The patient's dreams clearly revealed the infantile sequence of events reconstructed, and demonstrated strikingly the light and colour effects, which reached a climax with clear visualization of the adult male genital. This order was influenced by myopic vision. In other cases the intensity of the visual element appears earlier. It depends seemingly on the visual acuity and the intensity of the emotion aroused.

Early in the analysis the patient told a dream of a large puffing locomotive coming toward her, in danger of getting out of control. She first related this to outbursts of temper of her father toward whom her feelings were partly fear and partly disapproval because of them. This theme of an engine with a large headlight had been in college the inspiration of a poem in which it was a dragon breathing fire, beautiful, awe-inspiring, and frightening. At times it was associated with the trolley car whose lurching caused her mother's miscarriage. However, I shall present dreams from only a few days in which the patient was working over, as she did again and again, the sequence of events which I have indicated.

After a period of marked scoptophilic fantasy, especially in the transference, she awoke one morning with the opening words of 'The Star Spangled Banner' obsessively in her mind. Subsequently she dreamed '. . . About nuts and bolts, as though they might fall apart some way,' with associations of having investigated contents of drawers, of male genitalia, and of her enuretic cousin whose name reminded her of a comic strip robot who had buttons all up his front; if the wrong one was pushed, the machinery would jam, and the robot get out of control. There was a cover memory of children at Hallowe'en peeping in the window, and of her father squirting soda water at them in fun, at once associated with the possibility of having seen her father's or some other man's genital urinating.

In the next hour she related the dream:

My brother had died, but he seemed to be confused with my father; yet I was wondering how I could break the news to my father. I was utterly overwhelmed and wept so hard that I awoke.

During the dream she felt a tenseness across the eyes, almost from cheek to cheek. Later in the dream:

It seemed that brother was really my child, and I felt vaguely guilty toward my mother; but I was responsible for something happening to my brother and was distressed that I would have to tell father.

This dream had been stimulated by learning that her brother's wife's father had died, and realizing that she felt hostility toward her sister-in-law at a time when she wanted to feel only sympathy. In addition to the obvious oedipus, there was the trend of guilt, envy, and hostility toward the male with weeping substituted for urination.

During the next hour, as she heard the radiator make a rhythmic racket, she turned and said jokingly but sarcastically, 'If *you* just speak to it, it will be quiet.' In the transference, I represented the mother and the grandmother who ruled their respective husbands with a calm piety that suppressed both sex and aggression. She then told a dream in which she had felt enraged.

This rage was so great it was like a fit. It was directed against an elderly white-haired man, a grandfather. He was not giving me the recognition I should have had and I was screaming at him. I had a pillow that I was trying to use as a club, but it would not do. Then a great big policeman came in, a kindly person with his shirt open at the neck like a woman's. He was going to put me away, but he was good and kindly and represented good law and order. Father came in and I thought the policeman and father confronting each other was going to be tough. It felt almost as though my rage would make me cross-eyed.

The patient associated me with both figures, the grandfatherly man who looked like a psychiatrist of her acquaintance and did not give her the recognition which was her due, and the orderly policeman who took kindly protective custody of her and did not condemn her. Her anger at having soft parts instead of a firm penis, the conception of the woman as having a male genital, some excited expectation of a primal scene, and the reference to strain on her eyes in looking, are all clearly represented in the dream.

The following day she dreamed:

I was writing a legal brief in self-defence. It was being written on *yellow* foolscap paper. Before writing on the foolscap I had been writing in a stiff-backed notebook with *green* covers.

This brought memories of having worn a dunce cap at a children's party and of having wept because she felt neglected; then of feeling that her mother was remote and too good. The patient had such a shorthand notebook on which was printed the amusingly suggestive description, 'Tumbler, lies flat, stands upright, turns quickly. Eye-ease paper.' She recalled that her pious grandmother had influenced her at puberty, against her inclination, to attend Sunday school. The unconscious question seemed to be whether grandmother too, like mother, had a penis.

In the next hour the patient reported that she had had a headache following the previous hour, and had awakened in the night with a feeling of confusion as though she might have hurt someone. Falling asleep, she had a terrifying dream which had the quality of a memory.

Someone was standing on a rock fishing. The rod was given to me, or else I wanted it, but I did not know how to use it. Then I was to be shown those bright-coloured things, spoons, that are used in trolling.

The memory of grandfather urinating into the water while fishing and other associations lead to the castration problem. The bright-coloured spoons were glittering and artificial like Christmas-tree ornaments. The patient had seen the grandfather's penis as an illuminated, highly coloured object, partly as a means of denying its existence as if to say, 'It can't be real. It is brightly coloured artificial bait.' She asked in a puzzled way, 'What colour is the penis? . . . Isn't it just skin-coloured?' The theme of colours continued during the next few days, with black, blue and scarlet predominating, in fantasies of sexuality as excitingly damaging and bloody.

A horse stood outside a fence looking at the mangled body of a small dog which had been killed by a larger dog. Someone put a great big brightly coloured tam-o'-shanter over the horse's head so that it would not see the body of the dog.

In this dream the dreamer is still trying to resolve and relieve the guilt of forbidden seeing (dog fight = primal scene), for the horse represented her father, whose affectionate nickname was Tam, and the protective blinding brightness covers his head, as a few days before it had the grandfather's penis. Incidentally, the mechanism of pseudoimbecility and the magic cap of invisibility (1) is here nicely dramatized.

In my clinical experience the two events of childhood which are most likely to produce visual overstimulation are, first, the sight of the genitalia of an adult of the opposite sex; second, any glimpse of the process of birth. My fairly definite clinical impressions include too few cases to warrant assured generalizations. Either of these 'visions' is most stimulating in the pre-oedipal period, and definitely less so in the latency period.

The sight of female genitals has never, in my case material, been directly invested with a shining light, but is represented as something dark, gloomy or forbidding, but behind which some glorious adventure or secret hall may lurk. 'The blue embracing caverns of the night' (2), was quoted by two patients in an almost identical symbolization of intrauterine fantasies. Redness sometimes represents an illusory feminine penis, sometimes a bleeding castrated one. The halo of the vision is either given an intrauterine extension of this kind and appears as the mysterious luminous blue; or, it is a white or red shining light displaced to the head, as the figure of the Madonna, or of the red-headed woman (frequently a phallic prostitute) in dreams and fantasies. The memory of the adult male genital, however, is often represented as glowing white, blue, or even a red-white-and-blue (probably a fusion of experiences and fantasies) as in the case of the patient who awoke obsessed with the words of 'The Star Spangled Banner,' but could never consciously recall whether the erect penis of the man possessed any colour. She recalled, however, having seen the erect penis of a dog and of a horse, in each instance being impressed with the bright colour of the organ.

I am inclined to the opinion that the pedestal which is so

often spoken of as the site of elevation of the opposite sex is determined in part by the observation of the erect genital of the father, seen by the girl as a luminous object and by the boy as a monumental column beside which his own organ is very diminutive. The original visual stimulation is but one component in determining this isolation mechanism, which is further determined by all other experiences which increase the fear and hostility between the sexes and promote unconscious homosexuality.

### CASE HISTORY II

This patient came to analysis in an acute homosexual panic, fearful of killing his wife and children, and most intensely jealous of his brother to whom he had previously been attached, but whom he had recently thrown into the closest relationship with his wife and then become frantic lest a sexual relationship might have developed.

Prematurely born, his anal and urinary aggressions were quite repressed in infancy from excessively severe, too early toilet training. This repression caused inner sensations of bursting for which urination gave the readiest relief, and formed a prototype for the discharge of erotized aggression. The patient was an eminently successful man of really enormous energy, drive, and ambition. It was conspicuously apparent to his friends that he idealized and kept women on 'pedestals.' He was jocularly companionable with women but totally inhibited sexually with all but his wife, and with her only under certain conditions. He lived in the country so that he could escape from her to play golf at any moment. He could not tolerate to be confined with her in close quarters; yet so far as he knew he was passionately devoted to her, and unaware of any hostility until it erupted symptomatically in phobias.

In the rather long intervals between coitus with his wife, this man masturbated with fantasies of intercourse with his wife or with a red-headed waitress whose name was Joy. He dreamed:

I was looking for my wife and found her standing inside a door crying. We had been to a party which was not a success and which had ended in my getting angry and throwing the food, two buns

with fish in them, at a man who had served them to me while I
stood in front of a counter. Even though I threw the stuff right
at his head this man ignored me. When I found my wife, she was
weeping because the party had ended so badly. She had on a plaid
wool dress. Our three-year-old son was beside her. She said something about a headache and the fifteenth of the month. I thought
it referred to something about the baby. Then I realized she meant
it was a good time to have intercourse. I kissed her and, by God,
I would have had intercourse only just then the alarm went off.

This dream represented the patient's current difficulty in having
intercourse with his wife after a jealous quarrel because of feeling exploited by her and their nineteen-year-old daughter. It
states clearly his ambivalence about intercourse and fear of
making his wife pregnant('fifteenth of the month'). The dreamer
is identified in some measure with every character in the dream,
and its infantile content is being in bed with his parents, jealous
of his father and wanting the breast of his mother by whom he
felt rejected. Everybody's head is injured except the dreamer's
and the baby's. His wife complains of headache and he throws
buns at a man's head. He associated this with his mother's
frequent complaint of headache, and remembered in childhood
hitting his sister in the face, causing her to have a nosebleed,
because she had stolen some cherries from his hat. Awakening
from this dream, he had headache around his eyes which he
attributed to a sinusitis.

Another dream:

My wife's brother, Ray, was getting ready to dance with a twelve-
year-old girl who wore the epaulettes of a commander with grooves
between the stripes. Then somebody was talking about the *New
York Sun*. I said, 'That is a good newspaper; if you want any
qualifying statement, it is a God-damn good newspaper and you
can quote me as saying so.'

To this dream the patient commented that *Sun* was generally
the name of a morning rather than an evening newspaper.
From his early morning wakefulness and urinary tension, he
was led to recall that when he was about eleven years old he
rubbed his penis with his brother's, who was about six, and felt
intensely guilty. In the dream verbal profanity takes the place

of sexual aggression, and reflects the conflict about how much aggression may be considered as legitimate and conservative. The grooved epaulettes are a bisexual symbol associated with a time when he had been frightened by seeing his sister nude. Here too the dreamer is identified with everyone in the dream, with the aim of establishing his superiority. Ray especially was a highly esteemed man—too polite and downtrodden by his wife—but otherwise practically an ideal to the patient,—'The pride of the navy, and a shining example to others.' This, indeed, is an approximate description of the patient during his adolescence when he was secretly seducing his brother.

In so far as these patients may be representative of my general experience, I would say that such strong visual stimulation adds very much to the stress of the superego formation at whatever time it occurs. It seems especially to combine with the problems of the formation of the superego between the years of two and three when toilet training is being established; also, naturally, it combines with the oedipus when ego ideals are in their incipiency. It is very much less disturbing for the child to have such experiences during the latency period when social outlets for the discharge of aggression are so enormously greater. While both of these patients border on that group of patients predisposed to exaggerated somatic reactions to trauma, the typical halo reaction-formation occurs also in patients whose birth and early development have been without known trauma.

The question is raised whether directly investing the adult penis with a halo (in contrast to its displacement in the case of the adult female genitals) is not due in part to the fact that there is a greater degree of focusing required, and that consequently defects in the vision of the voyeur, such as myopia or muscle strains, play a greater role in producing a central image with a peripheral luminous blur. For the male child observing the adult penis the intensity of his focusing may be modified somewhat by his knowledge—visual and tactile—of his own organ. The shock is then greater in not seeing the penis.

In the psychoanalytic literature there are several references to the phenomena which I have described, although I know of none in which it has been related to the development of the superego. Schreber (3) boasted that he could look at the sun without being punished or dazzled. During the period when he believed that his organs were being destroyed, he thought they might be restored by divine miracle, or 'rays.' At a later time in his illness, he believed that he was to be emasculated so that he might be impregnated by the rays of God. In interpeting this, Freud remarked that the 'sun is nothing but another sublimated symbol for the father,' and that Schreber had discovered again this mythological method of expressing his devotion to his father. Indeed, the Earth mother and Sun father are common symbols of mythology. Abraham in his paper, 'Transformations of Scoptophilia' (4), referred to the Schreber case, giving confirmatory reports from folklore and clinical cases among which one of his patients had two dreams resembling those of the patients here reported.

1. He was in school and the headmaster came into the room and spoke to him. At first the patient defiantly opposed his orders, but later had to obey them, while there appeared over the master's head a blinding light, at the sight of which he fainted.
2. The father appeared to him as a ghost of a dazzling white form, rather than the faint pale white generally worn by ghosts.

Abraham made no special comment about conscience here although it is obvious in the manifest content of the first dream. The second dream is a fragment. One wonders whether the returning ghost was a punitive authority, as the headmaster in the first dream so clearly was. In a footnote Abraham stated, 'I might briefly mention that in many neurotics the father is not represented by the sun but by lightning, i.e., by another phenomenon of light in the sky. Lightning here more especially represents the punishing (killing) power of the father.' It seems that in Abraham's case the fainting in the dream may have been the expression of the stunning blow which, if lesser, might have been a headache. Dr. Edith Jacobson has called my attention to an article by Marie Bonaparte (5) which presents much material suggestive of the observations I have outlined. Her case focuses on certain stresses of the oedipal period, with the identification of a little girl with a glorified mother who had died at the child's birth. This child who at the age of four suffered a pulmonary hemoptysis (the memory of which was subsequently repressed), had a hallucination of a brilliantly coloured bird, possessing all the colours of the rainbow, resting on her lower abdomen. In analysis she associated the rainbow, which penetrates the earth, with the opal which was her father's gift to her mother, a stone of rainbow colours bringing bad luck. This was further associated with the father's penis which was responsible for the mother's pregnancy and death. The patient remembered vividly the red trousers her father had worn, about this same time or earlier, as an army officer. The girl had later in life identified her father with an exalted ambition to conquer the world with the force of her brain. In another article (6) Bonaparte states that at the same age the child had witnessed in broad daylight repeated sexual intercourse and fellatio between her nurse and the coachman (actually the father's illegitimate half-brother). This primal scene was first reconstructed by the author from dreams and screen memories but was later verified in conversations with the coachman-uncle, much as my patient verified the facts of the miscarriage. The data presented by Bonaparte in these two articles do not particularly emphasize the superego which is represented chiefly with reference to the oedipus.

I have found only one other extensive reference to this subject by Stragnell in 'The Golden Phallus' (7). Investigating dreams in which yellow or gold appeared, Stragnell came to the conclusion that gold was always associated with the father, 'a tabooed love object . . . a person of authority from whom emancipation cannot be obtained.'

In the cases here presented, the symptomatology is not as important as the character structure. The possibility is suggested that the phenomena described may have some relation to the scintillating scotoma and headache of migraine, which occur conspicuously in compulsive characters in whom individual attacks can sometimes be traced quite precisely to situations in which large quantities of aggression have been aroused without the possibility of adequate discharge.

Two psychophysiological problems suggest themselves: first, what are the pressure systems in homeostatic balance in the infant, and what homeostatic interrelation exists between the bladder or lower bowel and the intracranial space; second, what part does vision play? May visual sensations constitute some sort of intrapsychic shock which may later be neurotically reactivated; or is there a secondary stimulus centrally aroused by any shock, resulting then in an intensification of visual stimulation, as it were, because the eye is more closely part of the brain than is any other organ of special sense (8)? Dr. Ernst Kris has offered the valuable suggestion that the halo and colour effects which I have described may be related to the peculiar characteristic of peripheral luminosity, or sharpness of edge, which commonly invests cover memories. It may be that this latter is due to the intensity of the emotional shock of the initial experience, no matter what its content, and that the sensation of light is then displaced to the cover memory. It also seems possible that these phenomena may have some relation to the 'colour shock' findings of the Rorschach test.

## CHAPTER VII

# ANATOMICAL STRUCTURE AND SUPEREGO DEVELOPMENT*

AN attempt is made here to trace some of the influences of the gross differences in anatomical structure in the two sexes on character and superego development. Is there validity in the suggested correlation between these structural dissimilarities and certain differences in the character of the ego development, in itself fusing with and affecting the organization of the superego? No absolute proofs are available. It seems, however, that if a causal dynamic relationship appears on examination to be a probability, this weighs on the side of the correlation being more than a chance one.

It should be clear that the anatomical factors dealt with here are not considered to be the only or generally important ones in character and superego formation, except that they are primary nuclear ones in determining early divergence in such development. Even in questions of sexual differences, cultural patterns are undoubtedly strong reinforcing or neutralizing forces, but in so far as the body is the greatest part of its own first environment, it seems justified to stress the influence of the reactions within and to it of the developing ego. It is difficult to separate from the supergo certain general character or personality traits which contribute to and amalgamate with the ideals to determine individual standards of behaviour and value. For example, frankness and honesty may be partly derived from ideals, and partly from more primitive sectors of the character.

The development of the superego may be described in four stages: (a) Primitive roots exist in the early introjective-projective stage of development of the first months of life, roughly the first eighteen months to two years. (b) Further impetus to character formation occurs in the habit-training years when the

* Reprinted from *The American Journal of Orthopsychiatry*, Vol. XVIII, No. 4, October, 1948.

morality of the nursery—the being good or bad—is so much dependent on the child's struggle to master body urges, especially eating and toilet functions, and to accommodate the body rhythms to comply with adult demands. (c) The struggle of renunciation at about the age of five (the oedipus period) is probably the most important era in the growth of the superego, which may in fact exist only in the definite self-criticizing form from this time on. This renunciation is furthered by a degree of physical and intellectual maturing in the child, forcing a marked extension of his world and experiences beyond his own body. It is also advanced by the intense emotional relationships and infantile sexual urges toward members of his own family, especially toward the parent of the opposite sex. This renunciation, *i.e.*, the successful overcoming or loosening of the oedipal attachment, is aided by the child's increasing identification with the parent of the same sex (the desire to be *like* rather than actually *to be*), and by a deferment of sexual demands. It is a time in which growth and development have increased the child's concept of time and the idea of growing up becomes a possibility. This may even depend somewhat on the child's ability now to perceive size and space relationships more precisely, and consequently to realize himself as smaller than adults. This ability the child of eighteen months to two years certainly does not possess in a comparable degree. It is therefore a period in which renunciation can be tempered by deferment and a generally expanding environment dilutes the genital urgency. Interest is more directed into learning and exploring in the outer world. (All this will be discussed in more detail later.) It is, then, the period of the beginning of ideal formation, both through partial identifications, deferments, anticipation, and an increase in opportunity for outer-reality experience and testing. (d) As a corollary to the third stage, there is a reinforcement of the attainments of the oedipal struggle by social influences. Teachers, neighbours, church, and group leaders become supporting parental figures, and the family code and flavour are augmented or diluted by other social influences. Especially during this stage, character traits which have already developed fuse with the ideals in so far as they are approved of, or become a matter of further conflict if they meet disapproval.

The individual conscience fuses more or less successfully with the social conscience.

In considering the general influence of anatomical structure on superego formation, one might attack the problem at its very beginning, viz., the strength or weakness of the somato-instinctive urges of infancy which would affect that earliest root of character development, the stage at which the incomplete separation of the infant from its mother and from its surroundings seems to produce the expectation that what the infant feels within his own body toward the outer world may also be returned to it or visited on it by the outer world: the 'I want to bite—I may be bitten' stage of development, which Melanie Klein (1) stresses in her conception of superego development. This strength of the early urge comes partly from the constitutional make-up of the child, and partly, even very early, from the experiences (cultural or at least environmental) to which he is subjected. These may provoke and intensify those urgencies whose raw material is provided in the child's own body. Investigation of somato-instinctive urges would next be extended into the second stage of the struggle for mastery of particular needs —especially for food and for elimination. Such a study, for which there is an enormous amount of experimental investigation reported in the literature, would perhaps be the most valuable of all. But it is exceedingly complex, involving the most careful scrutiny of variations in physical constitutions at and before birth and a meticulous study of the interplay between the constitutional physique and training and experience.  I am not myself prepared for such a comprehensive undertaking, and will deal with only a few of the aspects.

This chapter will be confined to a consideration of how much the child's ego character and superego may be influenced by his reaction to his own body structure, especially with reference to certain gross variations between the sexes, viz., in the genital organs themselves, and the difference in general peripheral muscular development. It is hoped that this may be of interest as supplementing somewhat both the psychoanalytic observations already made and the numerous psychological reports of studies of differences in character traits. The latter have been, for the most part, compilations of observations at different ages with comparatively little detailed study of causation beyond consideration of sociological implications, or not very satisfactory postulations of correlation with hormonal variations (2, 3).

Certain basic factors in the child's reaction to his own organs will be discussed first; then his reactions to the organs of the opposite sex, further resulting in modifications of his reactions to himself; and last of all, the reactions dependent on general body form and musculature. To take the most obvious first, the male organs are exposed and external whereas the female organs are almost completely invaginated. This is of considerable significance. It means that in the male throughout life the genitalia may be seen and palpated and are appreciated in this quasi-external way (4), and this sensory appreciation through vision and palpation tends to an intensification of awareness of the organs, combining with any endogenously aroused sensations in the organs themselves. The manual palpation of the organs which is definitely greater in gross body surface in the young male than in the young female also tends to set up a tumescent reaction making for additional accentuation of organ awareness both through the hand and through the organs themselves. Appreciable stimulation of the boys' genitals by friction with clothing, bedding, and in the process of bathing is inescapable. Some degree of fear of injury in the male must arise from this simple fact of exposure.

In the female infant the situation in somewhat different. The hidden invaginated position of the major portion of the sex organs means that the female never sees her own organs in any way comparable to the male's, neither can she touch them to the same extent. Thus there cannot develop the same definiteness of awareness. The surface, especially, is less clearly defined in the central image or in the concept formed. The organs remain somewhat mysterious and unknown throughout childhood and in many women, often to an amazing degree throughout the entire life. It is indeed a dull boy who does not find his own genitals in the random hand explorations of early infancy, and later, manipulation becomes obligatory in the performance of urination. The female child's position, however, is further complicated by the fact of their being two main zones of focal sensitivity more or less separate, the clitoral and the vaginal. Whether sensitivity in these areas develops simultaneously, or whether one precedes the other, is not yet precisely known. Much of the literature assumes that clitoral sensitivity develops first and vaginal sensitivity later. How much this is intrinsically so, how much it may seem to be so because the clitoris, like its larger male counterpart, is more exposed and more readily stimulated than the vagina, and how much the literature may be influenced by the fact that most observations have been made by men from a male point of view, is not quite clear.

From my own work in analysing female patients, and from earlier observations on psychotic patients, I am inclined to believe that in some female infants at any rate there is a vaginal sensitivity very early. The stimulation does not occur by external friction or contact, and least of all by manual manipulation, but may occur spontaneously by an overflow of central stimulation in states of extreme excitement, frustration, or distress. It is my belief that the early genital stimulation by frustration, which may cause a readily observed erection in the male infant, causes a vaginal stimulation more often than a clitoral one in the female. This is clearly evident only in states where it is so strong as to set up an autoerotism by thigh pressure.[1] Where such overflow vaginal stimulation occurs but is not sufficiently strong to produce obvious masturbation, it may still conceivably cause vaginal sensations and some sort of central registering of the vagina, presumably then producing an intensification of this part of the female body image. This may appear then as an 'intuitive' knowledge of the vagina on the part of the child who has neither explored it manually, been told of it, nor seen it. At any rate, where appreciable vaginal stimulation occurs, whether or not it is accompanied or followed by clitoral stimulation, the vaginal sensations seem generally to be described as

---

[1] I am indebted to Dr. George S. Eadie of Duke University Medical College for the interesting observation that among the snake-manipulating religious cults of North Carolina, in which the snake demonstrations are generally performed by men, the women get into states of extreme excitement and, masturbating openly, appear to show a vaginal rather than a clitoral type of masturbation. While there may certainly be a clitoral participation in the erotic frenzy, it is apparently the vaginal which dominates.

full but diffuse and to lack the sharpness of the clitoral pleasure sensation. With the clitoris, and even more in the case of the vagina, it is evident that the awareness of the organ on the part of the child herself lacks the degree of firmness and consolidation of the combined senses, which is inevitably true in the male child. One might sum this up by saying that the male child *possesses* an awareness of his genitality more clearly, directly, and intensely than does the female child.

The emotional attachments of the child during the first five years of life are also more complicated for the female than for the male. Children of both sexes are first predominantly attached to the mother in the warm organic ways of early infancy, this attachment gradually merging over into some degree of separation from her, but still with a dependence on her to fulfill their physical needs and comfort. The father is an accessory figure in the life of the very young infant. For the boy, the attachment to the mother may remain the dominant one throughout his early years, until it mounts into the crisis of the oedipus struggle, and the process of renunciation, deferment, and displacement onto other female love objects sets in, accompanied by identification with the father as indicated. The girl child, however, turns from the mother to the father for leading emotional attachment; or at least there is some sort of division of the attachment between the mother and the father in a way which is quite different from the boy's. She remains dependent on the mother chiefly for immediate fulfilment of her bodily comfort and care, a kind of security-love attachment, but develops a sharp attraction to the father, so evident in the coquettishness and blandishments of the five- to six-year-old girl. It has seemed to me that in understanding this preliminary stage of the oedipal period in the girl, too little attention has been paid to the fact that the mother continues to be the prime food giver and body warmer and that inevitably the little girl cannot afford to give her up too completely. Again the situation is more complicated for the girl than for the boy, and not as firmly defined and unified. It is quite possible that this may be the source of some of the girl's later tact, indirectness, and lack of simple forthrightness.

Another factor in this situation is worthy of mention at this point. In girls, due to the configuration of the organs, there is some confusion subjectively and intellectually between the female groove and the rectum. By contrast, in boys genitality is more often associated with the urinary function because the same organ is actually used for both functions. It is an interesting question, whether the female confusion between vagina and rectum may be due to incomplete central neuronal localization, a continuation of the earlier cloacal state as a result of which some vaginal stimulation may occur in the course of feeding, especially in those infants in whom feeding readily induces lower bowel activity. This is the more suggested by the observations of infants of a few months, who frequently show a puckering of the mouth as they begin to have bowel movements. If this is common, it would be an additional agent in furthering the mouth-vagina identification in aggressive as well as receptive acts. Such identification is readily detected as prominent in many women. This is also related to the condition described by Lewin in which oral incorporation is displaced to the skin (5, 30, 32). Aside from this, however, since in the whole process of toilet training, unseemly or inappropriate defecation is more sternly condemned than is enuresis, it may be that female genitality gets a further repressing blow from this source.

Which possible character traits that later either directly fuse with the superego or, through the need to struggle against them, set up areas of special conscience reaction, result from the differences outlined? Terman's chapter on psychological sex differences in Carmichael's *Manual of Child Psychology* (6) contains a review of recent experiment and observations along these lines. One may be critical of the findings in some reports whose authors appear to have arrived at conclusions by inadequately controlled or scant statistical methods, or from obviously biased points of view. Still some conclusions are repeated so often from such varying sources that they give the impression of validity. Such, for example, are the observations that boys are more direct, more truthful, more blunt, more concerned with material things, with experimental projects, and with science than are girls (7–15). One author says that boys show preference for things, and girls for people (16–19). Another, putting this differently, states that girls tend to be concerned with personal relations, and boys with causal relations.

Boys tend to link fantasy with reality in the way of mechanical and scientific experimentation whereas girls have more romantic fantasies without immediate realistic attachment. In school work, boys excel in mathematics, mechanics, and experimental science. Girls are expected to be clean and tidy earlier than boys and, in point of act, often are. How much this arises from anal-vaginal confusion and how much from social mores, perhaps still with this nucleus, is not at all clear. Searl (20), commenting on this observation, thought that differences in urination played a part in that the girl was all good or all bad in the matter of urinating at the proper places and time whereas the boy, with greater urinary finesse, might be quite skilfully and maliciously bad. In adolescence, boys like adventure stories and girls like emotional fiction (21-25). And so it goes.

It is not implied that these character traits are based wholly on the relation of the child to its genitals in the ways already indicated, but rather that there is a suggestive correlation and that this relationship may be a definite early factor. If one doubts that the differences in genital and excretory functions in the two sexes, in themselves implicit in the very anatomical structure of the organs, influence and are even transposed onto other activities of the individual, let him think of such simple things as that boys spit, whistle, and throw balls with so much more precision and aim than do girls. At least the spitting and whistling is probably due not so much to any difference in the sexes of the shape of the officiating organs (mouth and lips) as it is to the patterning of the upper body function after a lower genital one of urination. In the case of ball throwing, the difference in muscle development is probably also a factor. It is clear, of course, that all of these activities are reinforced by identifications, which generally combine with social permissiveness and opportunity for practice.

In considering the effect on a girl of observing the body of a boy, it will not be possible to go into great detail concerning how reaction varies according to age (stage of development), and the situation in which this occurs. The psychoanalytic literature has dealt rather extensively with this subject, and only such articles as seem pivotal for this discussion will be mentioned. Freud (24) always seemed impressed by the poor organization of the feminine superego. He was admittedly tentative in his findings and realized that he observed from a masculine point of view. He emphasized that the difference in superego between the sexes was due to the difference in the relation of the castration complex to the oedipus complex which resulted in a greater degree of resolution of the oedipus complex in the boy than in the girl. His conclusions in brief were that the boy's oedipus attachment was destroyed by the fear of castration. This became a verifiable fear when at this stage the boy observed the little girl and realized that she appeared to be castrated. Consequently the boy renounced his oedipal wishes and his masturbatory activity in the interest of the preservation of his organ, and the post-oedipal superego development was thereby set in motion.

Freud considered that the girl does discover her genital zone 'at some time or other' but that the first important step lies in her discovery of the boy's greater gift of a penis, and that this reaction of the girl to the boy occurs earlier than that of the boy to the girl. 'She sees it, knows she is without it and wants to have it.' Penis envy arises and the feminine type of castration complex ensues: she tries to deny her inadequacy, makes substitutes for the penis, and finally must accept that she is without it. This acceptance loosens her tie to the mother whom she blames either for not having given her the organ or for having taken it away. Her acceptance that she is without it, however, favours the development of her positive oedipal attachment to the father. This in turn is attenuated by inevitable frustration, but is not so decisively dealt with as in the boy.

The castration complex thus prepares for the oedipal attachment (to father) in girls and decisively destroys the comparable attachment (to mother) in boys. Freud considered that these developments were at the basis of the difference between the male and female superego. He characterized the feminine superego as showing less sense of justice, less readiness to submit to the necessities of life, more jealousy, and more influence of judgment by feelings of affection or hostility (bias) than in the case of the masculine superego. While there have been criticisms of and additions to this exposition of the superego development, the main points in regard to its structure are still generally accepted.

Certainly it is commonly apparent and substantiated from psychological as well as from psychoanalytic findings that women are more jealous and more envious than men (20–26), and it seems likely that this character trait is primarily derived from penis envy. In the superego reaction formations against it one may see in some women the imprint of a struggle rather comparable in force to the males' struggle against a basic muscular aggressiveness.

The fact that the girl accepts castration as an accomplished fact, and the boy continues to fear it, seems also to exert powerful influences on the character and superego formations in the two sexes. The girl's attitude seems generally to imply that she has already been castrated, and sees it as punishment. This is frequently hypothecated as having resulted from past masturbation, since it is often in a situation of masturbatory arousal that the child is forced to recognize her plight. This in itself seems to me sufficient to account for the greater struggle against masturbation in girls, although the practice itself may be less established and consistent than in boys. This hypothetical sin, for which punishment (castration) has already been meted out, further means an enormous enhancement of later guilt feelings in situations of conflict, as though she thereby has a fund of guilt from which she readily overpays. It seems that from this source may spring some of the marked and rather diffuse or aimless conscientiousness and worrying tendencies of girls, which may accompany paradoxically an unreliability as to fact, i.e., a tendency to lie (27). Such conscientiousness, while part of the superego structure, is to be distinguished from the firmer, more condensed conscience structure more characteristic of the male.

Among the many psychoanalysts who have written of the female castration complex and its relation to the superego, several (28-32) have mentioned the probable influence of early vaginal sensations in the girls' development. Although Freud originally also noted in *The Three Contributions to the Sexual Theory* that the vagina might conceivably be the primary locus of female sexual stimulation, he later largely ignored this possibility and assumed that clitoral stimulation preceded the vaginal. Sachs (28) postulated that in the attempt to renounce the oedipal wish toward the father, the girl child may regress to the oral attitude which she has earlier felt toward the mother. In this later situation, however, there might also be a displacement of vaginal sensations upward. He further thought that many girls continued to hang on to the father with this oral-vaginal incorporative desire. In so far as this attachment was not threatened, the feminine superego was not strengthened by the oedipal renunciation as in the case of the boy. Müller-Braunschweig (29) stated definitely that he considered the vaginal sensations as primary, that the girl was from the first more passive than the boy, and that this very passivity gave rise to castration anxiety (fear of destruction) comparable to the boy's.

Jacobson (30) and Lampl de Groot (31) both indicate the possibility of some sort of vaginal feelings playing a part in the girl's genital awareness. They emphasize especially, however, the earlier onset of the superego development in the girl than in the boy, concomitant with the first phase of the oedipal struggle (that toward the mother). Jacobson observed that the inner vaginal feelings promoted the illusion of an inner penis which the girl sometimes passionately desires to find and to see. These feelings may also further the development of pregnancy fantasy and expectation in the second oedipal period (toward the father). Searl (20), in an article which in some respects parallels the intention of this present chapter but is limited to psychoanalytic conceptions and is focused especially on the problem of abstract thought, stresses also the mystery of the girl's organs in comparison with the boy's, and the possible relation of this to the girl's sexual reserve and secrecy as well as to other traits.

Returning to the reactions of the girl and the boy to awareness of their own bodies, another difference which is derived from the castration complex is of special import in girls. Under the influence of penis envy and in her effort to deny the lack of such an organ, the girl rather regularly goes through a kind of hallucinatory assumption that she has such an organ. This is promoted by clitoral sensations, but is in opposition to vaginal sensations which may also have been strongly aroused even earlier. This may set up a state of inner confusion which I have seen reproduced very clearly in at least two cases in the course of later analyses to an extent that it was a factor in disturbing the sense of body reality. Stated in another way, there is a marked discrepancy then between the primary central body image and a subsequent strong fantasy image based on wishful observation of the boy. Sometimes this is revolved through a displacement of the illusory penis to the 'inside' as described by Jacobson.

In the struggle of the oedipus period, children of both sexes must give up immediate sexual urgencies in favour of immediate actual realistic possibilities in other spheres and defer their sexual hopes for a grown-up time. In the boy there is, as already stated, a decisive struggle of renunciation of the mother in the interest of the preservation of his own organ and the growing sense of its later value in relation to some other woman. In the girl, however, the deferment is accompanied by the knowledge that she can have the child, and the possibility of a child within is a recompense for the lack of the special visible organ outside. Still there is no visible token of all this: she simply has to wait and take it on faith. Even the breasts which are the specialized organs of the mother are not developed and the boy has as much to show there as she has. Penis envy not infrequently gives way to breast envy. And so there is a greater sense of deferment without tangible proof, contributing possibly to a greater tendency to endure, to idealize, to fantasy in peculiarly diffuse ways and to prevaricate fancifully, for all of which she is often admired and condemned.

To turn next to the reaction of the individual to another set of factors inherent in anatomical structure, namely, the development of the skeletal musculature of the body as a whole. Here there are definite differences between the sexes—with a rather wide degree of variation and yet with certain fairly consistent elements. Most important is the greater development of the neuromuscular apparatus of the extremities and of the shoulder girdle in the male. His muscle development is fitted therefore for considerable centrifugal motor aggression—for

TGP-F

running, the chase, fighting, etc. In the female, on the other hand, the greatest muscle development is concentrated in the pelvic girdle. While she has the other peripheral muscular equipment similar to the male's and is not totally incompetent in his pursuits which she may further develop with practice, her centrifugal or extravertive aggression is more tempered by the need to receive, to hold and to carry, and probably her greatest centrifugal aggression is the act of childbirth itself. These differences appear to be a factor in various activities, attitudes, and conflicts which are different in the two sexes.

There are very many early factors of development which are not readily understood, such as the much higher rate of male fetal deaths than of female, and the fact that in the first year of life the female is strikingly more resistant than is the male.[1] In spite of this, and in spite of the fact that the female infant's skeletal development is farther advanced at birth and remains in advance until puberty, boys are heavier, have greater vital capacity and greater peripheral muscle strength consistently throughout childhood. In some respects we might say the young female has greater durability and the young male greater energy capacity. Terman emphasizes these contrasts a little differently. He says, 'The significant fact is that the obvious central tendency toward male superiority in such traits as size, strength and motor ability tends to set standard patterns of dominance, aggression, and energetic activity for all males and contrasting patterns for all females.' These differences in neuromuscular activity are apparent early, even though the body proportions are not yet strikingly different. Boy babies are reported (33) to react more to external stimuli than girls, and at the nursery school level a variety of behaviour differences is reported; boys are observed to be more active in play (6), to show somewhat greater frequency of temper outbursts, and, in general, more aggressive behaviour than girls, except for verbal bossing (34–37). Later, boys show a preference for and greater ability in mechanical, scientific, and mathematical pursuits, all of which are based on precision and,

[1] In 17 of 18 diseases most frequent in the first year of life, the male morbidity and mortality is strikingly higher than the female. Only in whooping cough is the reverse true, perhaps due to the lesser vital capacity of girls.

in the first two, coupled with manipulative skill. Boys are reported as afraid of kinesthetic catastrophes, whereas girls fear social mishaps. Even at the nursery school age girls show more responsible concern for other individuals than do boys, who, on the other hand, are more angered by interference with toys and possessions (38).

This enumeration of traits and characteristics is not exhaustive and may not be precise, but there seem to be certain trends which differ in the two sexes and are of a nature to influence values and standards and become part of the larger superego structure.

It seems probable, and I think it is borne out in our analytic work, that the struggle with aggression, except oral incorporative aggression (30, 32), is greater in the male than in the female, and leaves a more varied imprint on his character structure. The nature of these conflicts are determined not only by the strength of the aggressive urges, but by the social milieu and what is permitted. In this general connection, it is interesting that certain conditions such as muscle tics, stammering, and left-handedness in which a muscular ambivalence (sometimes akin to the conscious-ridden compulsive character) are more common in males than in females; also that certain muscle diseases, for example, tetany, are reported as more frequent among males.

Other possible connections between these anatomically determined traits and conscience development suggest themselves. Thus, in the boy, the dominance of peripheral muscular skill and the exposed position of his genital organs tends for a specially strong masturbation struggle. It might be said that the girl has the greater struggle against masturbation, and the boy the greater struggle with it.

This masturbatory struggle in the boy may in fact be displaced onto the permitted manipulation of tools and small toys, and enhance the mechanical skill which is in process of developing anyway. Indeed, such a sequence is often suggested in the symbolic residue in dreams of male patients. In the girl, on the other hand, her greater concern with social relationships and with responsibility may be derived in a small measure not only from the lack of a ready-made toy (penis) to play with, but with the special nature of her oedipal struggle. She must remain dependent in a very intimate body-comfort fashion on the mother at the same time that the beginning rivalry with the mother and the attraction to the father is setting in. She needs indeed a fine sense of social value to maintain a balance between the two, and with a greater natural ambivalence to the mother with whom she must presently identify in order to achieve a growing femininity. This necessarily grossly incomplete separation from the mother in the pre-oedipal period repeated in another form in the oedipal attachment to the father, recurs again in the characteristically ragged and disturbing mother-daughter struggle of adolescence.

In the matter of formation of ideals, there may be some difference. Girls are often said to have higher ideals, though less clearly goal-directed and less power-driven, and to have vaguer overreaching ambitions with less connection with external reality. The relation of this to the problem of deferment, without even token representation in the female, has already been mentioned. It seems apparent that this, like other character differences between the sexes, may be influenced in some measure by the fact that the boy has a more intact body image in which all his senses concur, while the girl has a mysterious, partly silent, unseen, and not directly palpable area of which she is dimly but not clearly aware and which stimulates her imagination without much chance for reality testing.

## CHAPTER VIII

# CONSCIENCE IN THE PSYCHOPATH*

THE faulty structural development of the conscience in a group of patients within the larger one generally designated as *constitutional psychopaths* or *psychopathic personalities* will be discussed in this chapter. This diagnostic classification has tended to be a catch-all for patients who show repeated evidence of antisocial behaviour without symptoms belonging to the classical neurotic or psychotic pictures. The behaviour of the patients here described is primarily characterized by impulsiveness and marked irresponsibility, intense but labile emotional states, and generally quixotic and superficial love relationships. These patients are not deliberate offenders; they lie and steal impulsively, especially under pressure. They sign bad cheques or impulsively forge another's name, marry on the spur of the moment, and as often impulsively run away from a marriage or a job. Characteristically, they appear to live in the moment, with great intensity, acting without plan and seemingly without concern for the consequences. Indeed, the lack of practical appreciation of time and the inability to learn from experience stand out as cardinal symptoms. They are the living antithesis of the saying, 'A burnt child dreads the fire,' since they repeat the same fiascos time and again in an impressively self-destructive fashion. There is usually poor tolerance of pain. Alcoholism, drug addiction, polymorphous sexual perversions may be associated secondary symptoms. Homosexual tendencies appear in a high percentage of cases, and there appears to be a special predisposition to homosexuality inherent in the very structure of the personality. This group was formerly described as moral imbeciles.

The cases which I have especially scrutinized belong to the private patient group; they are all patients seen in consultation or in private psychiatric hospitals with which I was associated.

---

* Reprinted from *The American Journal of Orthopsychiatry*, Vol. XV, No. 3, July, 1945.

While this is obviously a selected subdivision of the entire group, and may not be generally representative, it is one which presents better opportunity for investigation because there is a higher degree of co-operation and less concealment on the part of both the patient and his relatives than in groups composed of patients who are hospitalized because they are already in practical conflict with the law. Further, the psychopath seen in private practice generally comes from a relatively secure economic background, and there is not the same mass of socioeconomic factors forming a back drop and complicating the picture, factors which, in my opinion, are generally secondary reinforcing involvements, which may be used as rationalizations by the patient; they assume an undue prominence in the patients seen in city hospitals and court clinics.

All private practitioners of psychiatry see a few psychopaths in consultation. Since they generally are not amenable to treatment, they pass from view fairly quickly and it is seldom possible to study them intensively. Psychoanalysis rarely has turned its microscope upon them as they generally have neither patience, willingness, nor emotional capacity to be analysed. The present study utilizing freely psychoanalytic concepts and knowledge, is based on the investigation of the detailed biographical records of fourteen patients, the data being given by relatives, friends, and the patient.

It is my intention to indicate the essentially defective character of the conscience of these patients, and to point out the location and origin of the special defects, coming as they do from a pervasive infiltration of certain unfavourable products of the earliest narcissism, which distorts the sense of reality and devitalizes and degrades the conscience in characteristic ways.

If one examines from a purely descriptive angle the irresponsible behaviour of the psychopath, one is struck not only by the unplanned-ness and lack of deliberation of the untoward behaviour, but especially by the total practical disregard of consequences even though these are clearly known to him. He behaves as though such consequences were meant for the other man, but not for him; as though he will in some way be exempt, or will be miraculously saved. He seems to live only in a series of present moments, without real consideration for past or future. Such consideration as is expressed smacks generally of lip-service and lacks emotional tone, depth, and conviction. This same lack of emotional depth, the substitution of the symbol of gesture or word for the accomplished act seems to characterize the behaviour throughout. Such patients are frequently verbalistic, plausible, and charming. They commonly make a very good first impression but lack perseverance and become impatient. They behave repeatedly *as if* they had accomplished some intention and are offended or non-understanding when others do not accept the intention as the deed, especially if it has been accompanied by the gesture. For example, such a patient, who may have 'borrowed' money without asking, states that he intends to repay, and then acts exactly as though the restitution were already accomplished, and is righteously outraged when he is called to account. If punished, he not infrequently regards the punishment as unfair in view of his having behaved so properly and is no way deterred from a repetition of the same situation. It is characteristic, too, of such patients that they rarely deliberately evade punishment except by flight, though they cleverly talk themselves out of many predicaments by their plausibility.

It has been said that the conscience is the heir of the oedipus complex, that is, with the relinquishment of the demand for sexual gratification from the parent at the beginning of the latency period, the process of incorporation of the parental standards which has been going on for some time is giving a special integrative impetus, through the identification with the parent of the same sex, and the more definite formation of ideals based on the parental images. All this occurs at a time when, with the first experiences in school, there is some practical separation of the child from the parents and the addition of a new set of adults, chiefly teachers, as quasi-parent figures. This, too, is the time when conspicuously there is a special reinforcement and vitalization of the child's concept of the future, of the relinquishment of immediate satisfactions in the interest of future gain. This is an area in which there is special damage to the future psychopath, damage resulting not alone from the traumata or other unfortunate influences which may befall the child at this time, but also from the reaction of these on an already specially distorted sense of reality and impaired emotional reactivity.

Obviously the conscience does not spring fully formed from the oedipus situation. Children, long before the age of five or six, have some standards of right and wrong, of property possession, of restraint in activities which will harm others, and in other particulars. Probably the main sources of the pre-oedipal conscience lie first in the almost automatically established control of uncomfortably large amounts of infantile aggression, and second in the semi-organic conception of code and order which is crystallized in the formation of habits, especially those meeting the bodily needs of ingestion and of excretion. The early roots of the conscience in the erection of threatening fantasy parental figures countering and reproducing the young child's own increased aggression was indicated by Freud when he stated in *Civilization and Its Discontents* that 'the original severity of the super-ego does not—or not so much—represent the severity which has been experienced or anticipated from the object, but expresses the child's own aggressiveness toward the latter.' (This was early indicated in the analysis of Little Hans.) We can understand this as stemming from a time in the infant's development when its realization of its own separateness from the mother is incomplete, and as part of this the operation of the introjection-projection mechanism is prolonged and strengthened.[1] Any influences which tend to increase the quantity of the infantile aggression (such as illness, discomfort, frustration, and restraint) or to delay the sense of separateness will then tend to strengthen this original root of the conscience. As has been pointed out by Melanie Klein (14) and others, these

---

[1] Gesell has noted that children between two and one-half and three and one-half, at first tentatively, then with considerable elaboration often develop imaginary companions, sometimes human, sometimes animals, and that these serve as alter-egos, genuine scapegoats on occasion. This seems to coincide with the child's own definite awareness of his own identity, which is not accomplished, however, without regret and recapitulation of the past, as though he had to reassimilate the fact of his growth from babyhood to this stage. (Cf. Gesell, Ilg *et al.*, *Infant and Child in the Culture of Today*, pp. 210–211.) Interestingly Gesell also remarks that this is a time especially when authority about any specific situation should not be divided between father and mother.

primitive parental images are monstrous and terrifying and arouse in themselves great anxiety. 'They call out violent defensive mechanisms—which are unethical and asocial in their nature.' I would agree with Klein that this heightened aggression of earliest childhood with its reflected severity of primitive threatening figures is of the utmost importance in the development of schizophrenics. I believe that it may also be one of the important contributing factors in some psychopaths, only, however, if it combines with certain later elements which form the essential nucleus for the character deformation of the psychopath. One must quite clearly recognize that these reflected or projected images are at the time of their inception in no way a conscience, but are reacted to by the child as though they were totally outside of himself. Their strength, however, does influence the intensity of that part of the later conscience development which is based on the fear of punishment and of authority. These primitive conscience roots will be further dealt with in this chapter in the discussion of the feelings of guilt of the psychopath.

While disturbances of character formation springing from attitudes developed in response to toilet and feeding training may occur in the psychopath, and seem in some instances to determine the special form of sexual perversions, they are not in themselves more characteristic of the psychopath than of many other psychic disturbances.

In reviewing the life stories of a number of psychopaths, certain configurations of parent-child relationship recurred with considerable frequency. I shall attempt to give first a kind of composite picture, and then illustrate them with specific clinical examples.

It is a little startling to note how many of the psychopaths seen in private practice come from families in which the father or the grandfather has been an unusually prominent and respected man. This is strikingly obvious when one compares a group of psychopaths with a similar number of schizophrenics or of manic-depressives. I think, therefore, that this observation is of true significance and not merely an artefact due to the selectiveness of private practice in contrast to the situations of the public clinic or hospital. Indeed, among the parents or near forebears of these patients are a large number of people whose very work or professions put them in positions of conspicuous public trust and authority, as clergymen, judges, heads of schools, civic leaders, or in humbler walks of life, policemen, detectives, truant officers. They are the 'fathers' to their communities as well as to their children, and stand out as symbolic collective paternal figures. An old proverb that ministers' sons and deacons' daughters come to no good end is probably a general recognition of this frequent occurrence of the irresponsible child in the families of the conspicuously righteous.

Further investigation of the biographical data generally reveals marked discrepancies and conflicts in the parental attitudes in regard to authority, independence, and the goals of achievement. In my experience there is most frequently a stern, respected, and often obsessional father who is remote, preoccupied, and fear-inspiring in relation to his children; and an indulgent, pleasure-loving, frequently pretty but frivolous mother who is often tacitly contemptuous of her husband's importance. While there may be a different distribution of character traits between the parents, there is generally a marked discrepancy or definite conflict in the parental ideals and attitudes toward the child's immediate experiences. The contrast, too, between the brave façade presented to the world and the conflict and misery behind it is often most conspicuous.

In such family configurations, generally both parents are highly narcissistic in their more than ordinary dependence on the approval or admiration of their contemporaries. There is further basically a poor relationship between the parents and the infant from its earliest days. Pride, or its dark counterpart of shame, plays too big a part between parents and child, and substitutes for or counterfeits love. In the groups of patients whose biographies I studied, it was appallingly evident that these children were not greatly loved, and that what might appear as an excess of love was generally an excess of indulgence or solicitude.

Both the inner and outer psychic situations of the parents, with their overvaluation of external appearances, tends to promote a kind of show window display role for the child, with a premium on formally good behaviour for the sake of reflecting favourably on the parents. Where, as is often the case, the mother has an even deeper narcissistic attachment to the child, essentially regarding it always as though it were still only a part of and manifestation of herself, it is obvious that the sense of separateness and individuation is delayed in the child. In consequence of this there may be a strengthening of the introjective-projective stage of development and (seemingly paradoxically) an intensification of the externalized punitive figures as already indicated. The longer the child is treated as though only a part of the parent, the greater will be the aggression against the parent, reflected commensurately in exaggerated fear-inspiring parental figures. This aggression of need for separation is different in origin and probably in quality from the aggression arising in response to early physical discomforts or illness. The family situation I am describing tends to increase very much the exhibitionistic component of the child's narcissism, to exaggerate grotesquely its fear and awe of the parents, and to dilute or stunt the development of healthy love impulses.

Further than this, the actual position of the father in 'typical' situations tends in reality to comply with and verify the frightening images which the child has raised, inasmuch as the father is often distant, awe-inspiring and something of a frightening demi-god, lacking the substance and vital warmth which are part of good object-relationships. Such children are treated as though they must not fail. They are habitually on show, and failures are either denied, concealed, or explained away. Thus they are robbed of the full measure of reality testing,[1] and performance even in the earliest years becomes

---

[1] Aichorn has described well the way in which the indulgent mother protects the child from reality, out of self-indulgent vanity. He further mentions almost precisely the configuration I have described of the stern father and the indulgent mother, and the way in which the child flees from one to the other to escape reality and ends by rebelling against both. (*Wayward Youth*, p. 203. Viking Press, 1935.)

Wall, Heaver and Allen, working with psychopaths treated in hospital setting have also been impressed with this family configuration and its resulting influences.

Wall, James H., 'A Study of Alcoholism in Men,' *Am. J. Psychiatry*, Vol. 92, 1936, pp. 1389–1401; Heaver, W. Lynwood, 'A Study of Forty Male

measured largely by its appearance rather than by its intrinsic accomplishment. One sees in miniature the attitudes which later are so characteristic of the psychopath, *i.e.*, what *seems to be* is more valued than what *is*. This characteristic, together with the essential emotional impoverishment, tends to create a very thin stage-property vision of reality in which the façade at any given time is the prime consideration.

Under these circumstances a highly ambivalent attitude toward the parents and toward all authority inevitably develops. The magic father is feared by the child but at the same time there is an extension of the magic overvaluation to the child himself, and the frequent actual exemptions from consequences of his behaviour because he is his father's son; or on the positive side, his acceptance as his father's son rather than because of attainment of his own. Here again actual experience may promote and seem to accede to just those narcissistic fantasies of magic omnipotence which have already grown to undue proportions.

The degradation of the sense of reality by the opportunistic need to be pleasing seems in these children to develop early a charm and a tact which gives the semblance of responsiveness and consideration for others, but which generally later is unmasked in all its superficiality, and may be the foundation of a later adroitness in managing people which savours of blackmail.

The oedipus period is a particularly vulnerable time in these developing personalitites. The contradictory maternal indulgence and paternal austerity tend to bind the child unduly to the mother and at the same time to promote the formation of peculiarly unreal and gauzy ideals. The psychopath generally has very 'high' ideals but they are especially expansive, and utterly detached from reality. There is an unsuccessful effort on the part of the boy to identify with the father, but this is not possible because of the severity and remoteness of the paternal image, and tends to promote a bisexual identification. At the same time the boy remains in

Psychopathic Personalities,' *Ibid.*, Vol. 100, 1944, pp. 342–346; Wall, James H. and Allen, Edward B., 'Results of Hospital Treatment of Alcoholism,' *Ibid.*, pp. 474–479.

a prolonged emotional subjugation to the mother and never clearly comes through the oedipus struggle. Many psychopaths, in their later life, seem to be repeatedly re-enacting this stage of their life in one relationship after another. Even so the apparent oedipus struggle is conspicuously superficial, presenting a kind of surface show, simultaneous or alternating with strong homosexual tendencies, reproducing the inverted elements in the original oedipus situation. All this is quite striking in the clinical examples which follow.

The bisexuality of these patients has been thought by some to be due to disturbances of the sexual development arising at a time when there was already awareness of special pleasure from the genital area, but when appreciation of the anatomical differences between the sexes was not yet secure (the protophallic stage of Jones). This may be true, but the biographical material which I have does not contain sufficiently detailed data to warrant a conclusive interpretation of this as a primary site of disturbance.[1] Certainly, so it seems to me, children with a delayed sense of separateness from the mother, may as part of this general condition, have also a delayed and uncertain appreciation of sexual differences, the prolonged confusion on this score being part of the broader based disturbance of reality differentiation between *what is I* or *what belongs to me* and *what is his/hers*, or *belongs to him/her*, which includes others than the mother. I believe, however, that such a confusion is very

---

[1] Wittels develops this as the central point of the psychopath's sexual pathology, and believes that there is a secondary fixation in the oedipal phase. He considers the disturbances of behaviour as desexualized displacements. His presentation is persuasive but his interpretations seemingly are arrived at largely by theoretical deduction, and since his illustrations are almost exclusively from characters of literature or mythology which he considers as exaggeratedly 'pure' examples, there is little detailed supporting clinical evidence. His paper is 'based on the principle that the structure of the sex life gives shape to the neurosis and also to the psychopathy.' It seems to me rather that the psychopathy like the psychosis is given shape primarily by the distortion of the ego development and that the structure of the sex life is accordingly disturbed and then gives rise to additional complicating factors. My findings differ from Wittels' in respect to the latency period. He states that the latency period in the pure protophallic psychopath shrinks almost to nothing. My cases differ from this. I was, in fact, impressed with how smooth the latency period was or seemed to be in many cases. (F. Wittels, 'The position of the Psychopath in the Psychoanalytic System,' *Int. J. Psa.*, Vol. 19, 1938, pp. 471–488.)

much increased and generally gains significance by the difficulties of identification mentioned and which were uniformly present in the cases I studied.

CASE I

This was a young woman of twenty, in her second year of college. She had made a suicidal gesture by taking a nonlethal overdose of sedatives. This occurred when the patient felt rejected and gossiped about in connection with a homosexual triangular affair with two fellow students. She was unusually attractive, obviously bright, quite animated, and at the time I saw her only a day or two after the suicidal attempt, she was not really depressed.

The patient had been recognized as presenting especial problems since about her sixteenth year, when she had been expelled from preparatory school for a rather harmless prank. This was the only point on which she showed her contempt for the school authority. She had had the sympathy of her family at this time as her mother and sister felt the punishment had been overly severe. In the boarding school where she next went she made a brilliant record scholastically and was a class leader. She graduated at eighteen. In this period she experienced her first homosexual arousal, which appears to have come about spontaneously; at least, not through seduction. After a few months at college, which she chose in order to be close to her best girl-friend (with whom there had been no overt homosexual relationship), she ran away with a boy from an adjacent college, intending to marry him, and representing herself as having done so. The upshot of this was that both were expelled from college and were married shortly thereafter. A few months later the patient had a brief intense infatuation for her husband's best friend, and divorced her husband.

All this died down quickly and the following fall she reentered college. Here, while she did quite good academic work, she launched into a homosexual affair with a conspicuously masculine girl, then changed to another homosexual partner, and at the same time carried on an affair with a young doctor by whom she became pregnant. During the summer of that year (she was then 19) she attached one man after another. She conspicuously chose married men, and seemingly preferred men who were married to her female relatives. At one time, then, she took an overdose of sedatives in a suicidal attempt. On returning to college in the fall, she found her two earlier homosexual partners united in an alliance from which she was excluded. It was in this setting that she made the suicidal attempt which caused her to be brought to me. This was a repetition of the suicidal attempt a few months earlier.

I next heard of her a year and a half later when she again made a suicidal attempt. In the meantime, she had developed a sudden infatuation for a paternal cousin, who was then living with another woman. She succeeded in displacing this woman and set up an establishment with her cousin, spending more than half of a recent inheritance to furnish their place. She showed more attachment to him than to any of the previous men, stayed with him for more than a year in spite of some discomforts. She made two suicidal gestures, one by attempting to throw herself into a river, and the other by cutting her wrist, when she was piqued and made jealous by this man's waning interest in her.

This girl was the younger of two sisters by six and a half years. The parents were outstanding. The father's family contained several members who were sufficiently well known that the surname itself brought some recognition. The father was a brilliant man, an educator who had attained an unusual position of trust and respect early in life, but had somehow not sustained his early promise. He had thrown over a position of considerable prestige in a fit of pique, and not long thereafter withdrew from his marriage with apparent suddenness, divorced his wife, remarried, and died, all within the course of a few years.

The mother was a brilliant, aggressive woman of a substantial family. First a teacher, she later became interested in educational psychology. During our patient's early childhood the mother was building up a position of considerable note in well-publicized but creditable efforts to bring precise scientific methods into child psychology.

Our patient was a healthy baby, active, pretty, and precocious. She always had to be coaxed to eat, but otherwise was not thought to show any early problems. She talked early with remarkable facility. According to her own recollection, she did not see a great deal of her busy mother except in the evening. During her fourth and fifth years her father was away at service in the first World War and she missed him greatly, especially as she felt she was his favourite rather than her exceedingly brilliant older sister whom she imagined her mother preferred. From her third to sixth year she was a special visitor in the first grade of a school in which her mother was interested. She was both proud and jealous of her sister, whom she tormented consistently in a way which the parents considered cute. She was photographed much, and was frequently used as illustrations for her mother's lectures. Later, in temper outbursts, she spoke in frank resentment of feeling she had been displayed 'as a guinea pig.' Always in the background were her godparents, a childless couple who were her own parents' best friends. At nine when she was vaguely ill (coincident in time with the more obvious disruption of the home) she was taken care of by this couple, but their home was not any warmer than her own. The godfather, a man of considerable repute as a scientist, was capricious, erratic, and rather uncertainly stern, while his wife was a worried, indulgent, fretful woman, unhappy with her husband and overprotective with the child.

The following year her own father seceded from the family and she saw little of him afterward. When the patient was thirteen, her mother received considerable public notice because of certain attainments, and almost at once collapsed in a severe melancholia which was to last for some time. The child was again sent to the godparents to be cared for, but her unhappiness there caused her to be placed in a boarding school. It was here that her overt rebellion against authority began. It should further be mentioned that the patient's father died very shortly before her elopement with the college student, the beginning of her frantic series of sexual alliances. While she herself did not express any awareness of the connection between these events, the time relationship was striking.

This history is given in great factual detail in order that it may speak for itself in regard to the emotional impoverishment of this girl, overlaid by display of attention which really promoted her exhibitionism and made it, perhaps, her most dependable adaptive function. The indulgence and austerity were not allocated so precisely to mother and father, respectively, as I have somewhat schematically described in a 'typical' situation, but the contrast was there, involving the character of both parents and reinforced by the quite 'typical' godparents. The further complete collapse, not only of the parental relationship but of the parents themselves during the girl's adolescence appears as a tragic enlargement of the shadowy part of the earlier picture. Especially striking, too, in this case, is the triangular character of the sexual relationships in which the patient became progressively involved, and in which she generally ended as the excluded third member.

### CASE II

An unusually handsome young man in his late twenties came to psychiatric attention because of periodic alcoholism, especially marked during the preceding four years. In addition, he seemed unable to hold a job beyond a few weeks or months, habitually borrowed money which he did not return, and on a number of occasions removed money from the cash drawer wherever he happened to be working. He had held jobs varying in character from ditch digging to clerical work, had never been able to support himself, much less his wife and child. He had married his wife in an elopement while drunk, but seemed fond of her and was considered to be extremely devoted to his young son. In general he was genial, easy going, optimistic, made friends readily, but generally lost them through 'borrowing' from them. When he was drunk he talked about leaving his family and sometimes of killing himself, but made no gesture of carrying it out. After the birth of his child, he became more irresponsible.

His irresponsible behaviour was the more striking in that he was the son of a father who was interested in all aspects of education. The father, a quiet, thoughtful man, showed in his statement about the boy that he had a pretty clear but detached descriptive idea of the boy's shortcomings, but surprisingly little thought of their origin. The patient was the youngest of a fairly large family, 'spoiled by the mother' and, according to the father, had never developed any serious purpose in life, had seemed always to have things made easy for him, and expected to have things done for him. He seemed to have an unjustified confidence in his own ability, evaded rather than lied outright, and was a chronic procrastinator. He was respectful to and afraid of his father, and very much attached to his mother who felt the bond between them was so close that each could sense how the other would feel at any given situation. The father had been especially severe with his son in order to counteract the mother's indulgence, but it had never done any good. The father was now inclined to resort to the old explanation that the boy had a congenital deficiency of character, had been born soft, as it were. One felt from the father's account, that he had long been disappointed in his son or that he was himself an habitually withdrawn, emotionally detached man. The mother, on the other hand, was a voluble, fulsome woman, rather exhibitionistic in appearance and in the vivid dramatic quality with which she gave her account of her relation to her son. The biographical facts given are put together in chronological form from the statements of all three: mother, father and patient.

The patient was a healthy baby. His mother prided herself on her abundant maternity and clung to his babyhood especially as he was the youngest. A rather sensual appearing woman in general, she spoke directly of the very special pleasure which nursing gave her and of her efforts to prolong his nursing for her own gratification. She had frequently appeared nude before the boy since he was a baby and encouraged him to do likewise, regarding this as evidence of their freedom from any unhealthy inhibitions. When he was about five, the patient had a period of nocturnal enuresis. When he wet his bed, he would then get into his mother's bed, cuddle up to her and attempt to nurse. She repulsed him, insisted on his staying in his own bed, and the enuresis cleared up. During the years until he was twelve, the family travelled much, and he went to many different schools both here and abroad. The mother felt 'that it was a liberal education for the boy simply to be his parents' son, as there were always so many distinguished people around and that to be able to go to a man like his father and ask questions was to get a sensible education of real value.'

The emptiness of this conception is further emphasized by the facts that the boy was chronically afraid of his father's sarcasm, and that he was not permitted to eat at table with his father until he was twelve, after which he was sent away to school. His later retaliative exploitation of these cultural advantages was clear when on one occasion in his early twenties he telephoned his parents who were then entertaining the President of the United States at dinner to tell them that he had stolen a hundred dollars from the cash drawer of his employer and was in immediate danger of apprehension. In the period from age six to twelve there was no conspicuous trouble with this affable charming boy except that he was indolent. On being sent to a rather formal school at twelve, he began to truant. He was then sent to a boarding school, where he became attached to both the headmaster and his wife.

He had respected his father, but stood in awe of him. His mother had disciplined him by spanking even up to age fourteen. For major offences he was sent to his father whose scornful sarcasm he dreaded. In preparatory school he made quite a good relationship with the headmaster whom he found both fair and approachable. It was the one place he liked to return to later. In this period, he barely passed academically, but did somewhat better in the extramural activities, dramatics, and athletics, which were more akin to his mother's interests. He did not really care very much for any of it. He failed his first year in college, and was withdrawn and 'put to work.'

Then the underlying instability began to flower. He truanted from work—loafing or sleeping instead, began to drink somewhat and frequented rather low saloons. Sexually, he was rather prim. At nine he had been made the subject of a sexual demonstration by a little girl of twelve. In his preparatory school and college days he was less experimental sexually than most of his classmates. He had many very thinly veiled incestuous dreams about his mother toward whom he regarded himself as so commendably free. She dissuaded him from an

engagement at twenty which she considered socially inappropriate. When he married, it was only accomplished under the
influence of liquor. In his marriage, he was a cunnilinguist,
and this seemed to him so much the height of sensual pleasure
that he believed any man who said he did not do this was a
liar!

The special neurotic shape of the symptoms, with the fixation on the oral sucking interest is glaringly obvious in this
patient's history. I am more concerned now, however, with
the broader influences of his relationship to his parents which
seems to me to follow quite typically the pattern which was
indicated at the beginning of this paper: the fear-inspiring
remote father, the indulgent, extraordinarily vain mother,
who not only indulged this boy but used him as a kind of
specially provided organ for her own gratification; the complete façade of the emotional relationships to both parents
and the ridiculous mockery of education which resulted.
While this situation undermines the capacity for love relationships, and in so doing further defrauds the sense of reality and
impairs the development of the conscience as already described,
one must also realize that these influences exist continuously in
the patient's life from his earliest days until he leaves his
parent's home. The character changes which have their
inception early are generally fostered by the continuation of
these very same influences later and there is no need or even
opportunity for change until the patient feels it from the
encroachment of the world's demands. It might be said that the
charming opportunistic versatility of this type of psychopath is
the best adaptation possible if the world consisted only of his
own parents. Quite often his overt disturbances of stealing,
lying, etc., appear in troubling proportions only when he is
forced by growth or accident to make a pretence of responsibility. In this respect this group of psychopaths differs from those
in which there is a larger schizoid element, with the predomin-
ance of early semi-organically aroused aggression and a different configuration of the conscience, due to a greater reaction
to the underlying sense of guilt.

This brings us to the consideration of the sense of guilt.

It is not my intention to deal exhaustively with the complicated subject of the sense of guilt or to try to trace out all of the source of the neurotic and psychotic guilt feelings, which like anxiety form the centre of so many vicious circles of psychic disturbance; but rather to limit my discussion so far as possible to what seems to me characteristic of the group of psychopaths I have described. It has been said that the psychopath has no guilt feelings, no conscience (the potentialities of a conscience have never been internalized and what remains is only a fear of external punishment), and no psychic mechanisms of defence; some descriptions state that he has no anxiety. If all this were true, I believe that the psychopath would not live very long, but would explode from the force of his own primitive aggression. It would seem that these characterizations may be due to attempts either to place the psychopath too precisely as a clinical entity in psychiatric nosology and psychoanalytic theory, or to see a special group as representing the whole group; and in general to therapeutic discouragement on the part of the doctor with a consequent retreat to a descriptive point of view. Certainly many psychopaths behave at times as though they had almost no conscience, no defence restraints, and no anxiety. In my own clinical experience I have yet to see the patient who was as completely primitive as such a conscienceless fearless creature would be.

The sense of guilt presumably is a product of and roughly commensurate with the strength of the self-critical faculties of the conscience. These in turn, are based on the internalized controls (commands, punishments, and rewards of discipline) reinforced by the primitive fantasies, which had appeared originally as projections of the child's own aggression before the precipitation of the conscience. The origin of this very early aggression has already been described as coming from the somatic discomforts and frustrations of the infant, but especially in the psychopath from the increased need for separation from the mother due to the specific type of maternal narcissistic attachment to the infant. The very attitude of the mother which arouses this aggression also tends to retard and impair the internalization process. Consequently the psychopath often has vivid and fantastic threatening authoritative figures which are only comparatively little internalized with which he seems to play hide and seek both inside and outside himself.[1]

There are two other very early conditions which seem to influence the formation of the conscience and especially to promote the tendency to the formation of strong guilt feelings: (a) the predisposition to anxiety which heightens the anxiety pitch in the later vicissitudes of life; and (b) a special negative narcissistic relation to the parents which *is* prominent in the histories of many psychopaths. These two factors sometimes co-operate, though it is the second which is most characteristic of the psychopath. In regard to the first, the same conditions of somatic frustration and discomfort in early infancy which produce such a heightening of infantile aggression, may produce also a degree of infantile tension which subsequently combines with current anxiety in disastrous proportions. Anxiety in itself carries with it the psychic element of anxious anticipation, which in these cases then becomes expanded into a kind of expectation of doom, as it is amalgamated with guilt feelings. One sees this commonly in the psychotic, both the depressed patient and the schizophrenic who confess themselves the greatest sinners on earth. More characteristic of the psychopath's guilt feelings is the factor of the negative narcissistic relation to the parents. Where this is true, the child is also overly attached to both parents, especially to the mother; but instead of being a specially favoured part or organ of the mother, it is regarded by her with shame and as evidence of her guilt. The child seems to imbibe this from its earliest days and takes over this guilt and generally both rebels against and succumbs to it.

This was quite clear in the cases of two young women patients who were psychopathic prostitutes. Both had been the object of shame on the part of their mothers, and reproach from their fathers; in the one instance because the father knew, and in the other because he suspected that the child was not his. In both cases the mother indulged, favoured, and

---

[1] It is interesting, too, that under fever or intoxication the psychopath readily breaks down in delirious episodes in which such primitive figures run rampant.

defended, but was indubitably ashamed of the little one in a way which built up a striking but dark counterpart of the magic distinction so clear in the second case given in detail in this chapter. In one instance the father was a detective and, in the other, a court bailiff; both were alcoholic. Thus here again was the exaggerated paternal authoritative figure, but inconsistent in its rightness, and feared rather than respected.

Helene Deutsch (15), in an article on some forms of emotional disturbance related to schizophrenia, describes several patients who present clinical pictures somewhat similar to what has been described in this chapter. Since her paper deals largely with the nature of the disturbance of the sense of reality rather than with the conscience of the patients, the focus is different. She remarks that the 'emptiness and . . . lack of individuality so evident in the emotional life appear also in the moral structure' and sees the ideals and convictions of such patients as being 'simply reflections of another person, good or bad.' In my patients I have been more impressed by the remoteness and unusability of their ideals than by their changing suggestible character. The ideals seemed reproductions of the fantasies of the magic grandeur of the parent(s) but unattached to the everyday life and exerting no leverage on it. Her description of the disturbed sense of reality in her patients is very similar to my own observations: these patients do not suffer from depersonalization because they have never been really personalized.

A number of recent writers, including Levy (1), Bender (2), Powdermaker (3), Lowrey (4), Goldfarb (5), Ford (6), as well as such older investigators as Healy (7) and the Gluecks (8), have pointed with varying degrees of intensity to the essential early emotional deprivation of psychopaths and delinquents. My own findings verify this. It seems, however, that there may be some differences in the special symptom pictures between those cases where this deprivation was by and large the *main* and very far-reaching disturbance as is the case in children reared from birth in institutions, and those here described who suffer an actual love deprivation even though camouflaged by indulgence.

An article by Dunn (9) gives a good picture of the protean

manifestations of the psychopathic personality and contains a survey of much of the recent literature. Henderson's (10) lectures on the psychopathic states recognizes the primary affect-hunger, but in the broad basis of his description he appears to me to shy away from any deep understanding of the questions which he raises. He does bring up the question of the finely balanced trigger-reaction of many psychopaths. This is outside the scope of this chapter, but it is an exceedingly interesting problem bearing on the relation of some psychopathic states to creative ability.

Cleckley (11), in an engagingly vivid account of his clinical experiences with psychopaths, proposes the term *semantic dementia* for the empty 'as-if' behaviour and especially for the speech of these patients, emphasizing that they make the proper gestures and say the proper things but without emotional depth or rootedness. He does not interpret the origin of this disturbance but appears to regard the state as regressive. While many of his clinical histories suggest the very problems of the parent-child relationship which I have pointed out, his reports do not contain detailed facts of the early childhood, and he seems to have been impressed by the goodness and respectability of the parents without recognizing the high degree of narcissism involved. In his cases, the overt symptoms had been long existent and the more remote history was obscured by the florid events of the recent past.

A recent book by Lindner (12) gives a detailed and enthusiastic account of the hypnoanalytic treatment of a criminal psychopath. His presentation stresses certain early traumata, especially a single primal scene experience before the age of eight months. There was a resultant fear and hatred of the father, overattachment to the mother, and latent homosexuality followed by excessive masturbation and a classical fear of castration at the hands of the father. I cannot agree with all of Lindner's interpretations, nor with the validity of his skipping as unimportant so much of the material presented by his patient. Aside from this, he does not deal adequately with the development of the sense of self (ego development) and its defects, but appears to consider distortions as being due primarily to focal traumata. I think that his emphasis on the

primal scene experience may have importance in the understanding of criminal psychopaths in a different way than the
one in which he has presented it: the patient was exposed not
to a single primal scene experience, but according to his own
account, to a series of them. It has long been my impression
that repeated exposure of this kind in early childhood might be
an additional source of overstimulation of infantile aggression
and so play into other accumulations of early frustration, as
well as causing a neurotic scoptophilia and other symptoms.
How frequent and widespread such experiences are in families
living in crowded conditions is readily apparent when one
looks at the actual sleeping arrangements.[1] It may be an
unrecognized psychological factor in slum life from which
criminals so often emerge.

The monograph of Reich (13) published in 1925 on the
psychopath seems to me still the most valuable study of the
structure of the character of the psychopath. While I would
not wholly agree with some of Reich's differentiations of types
nor perhaps with his statement of the way in which the conscience (superego) of the psychopath becomes isolated, his
emphasis on the combination of the indulgence and severity of
the parental figures and on the practical isolation of the conscience are quite in accord with the character structure which
I have been describing. It appears to me that the isolation and
unusability of the conscience in these patients is due largely to
its gossamer substance, its being shot with magic and being
valued as an adornment rather than for its utility. In other
words it is as much the content of the conscience as its arrest
before it is thoroughly introjected that is responsible for its
lofty remoteness, even though the introjection itself is conspicuously poor.

[1] An unpublished study by Dr. Judith Silberpfennig on sleeping arrangements in the families of adolescent patients on the psychiatric service at
Bellevue Hospital, New York City, reinforces my own impression of the inevitable constant sexual stimulation in the families of children in this social
group.

## CHAPTER IX

# A CONTRIBUTION TO THE STUDY OF SCREEN MEMORIES*

IN an early paper, Freud (6) described screen memories as any childhood memories which are retained into adult life. These isolated islands of recollection were found on analysis to mark the location of and to represent the lost continents of childhood experience. Among these memories some were noted as having special characteristics of brightness or intensity which generally contrasted with their relatively indifferent, innocuous, or patently distorted content. They were not only predominantly visual, but Freud further noted that, in contrast to memories from later periods of life, the rememberer was detached and seemed to watch himself as a child performer. Such memories seemed to be screen memories par excellence. In this early paper the mechanisms of repression and displacement were especially noted and screen memories were likened to slips of the tongue or of behaviour, and the other psychopathological phenomena of everyday life. In his book of this title (7) Freud developed the concept of screen memories further and attempted to classify them somewhat formally as retroactive or regressive, interposing, or contiguous memories according to the time relationship between the retained memory and the events which it was concealing. This classification has not proved especially useful as screen memories are found to draw their strength from or 'feed on' (to use Fenichel's hunger analogy) events which have happened both before and after their occurrence. It is probable that they may even be moulded somewhat and get new increments in the course of years.

In later papers (8, 9), Freud stated that screen memories could be treated in ways similar to dreams and like them were products in which repression, displacement, conden-

* Reprinted from *The Psychoanalytic Study of the Child*, Vols. III–IV. New York, International Universities Press, 1949.

sation, symbolization, and secondary elaboration might all participate.

The relation of screen memories and especially of the screening process to precipitating traumata in traumatic neuroses has been dealt with by Fenichel (3) and Glover (10). Fenichel further discussed their relation to *déjà vu* experiences, the traumatic experiences to which perversions are often erroneously attributed, and to pseudologia phantastica (5). H. Deutsch has described the latter also (1) and has also pointed out that hysterical fugues are sometimes reactivated screen memories (2).

Fenichel especially has dealt systematically with the economics of the screen memory (3). He emphasized that it results from a struggle between denial and memory in which a substitute for the memory of the disturbing experience is seized upon and is utilized as a kind of compromise; and that the gradual development of the ego with an increasingly strong sense of reality weakens the tendency to deny. He further considered that this struggle would naturally be greater if it arose in the immediate setting of already established anxiety. This state of affairs might even create a kind of hunger for screen experience which would facilitate the use of old (remembered), symbolic, or even contiguous experiences as screens for the repressed experiences, this hunger being felt as a compulsion to remember or to test the memory (4). It is possible that the appearance in dreams of special phrases or sentences is a phenomenon also of this order.

In Chapter VI, I was concerned with certain problems which encroached upon the screen memory from a different angle (11). The suggestion was there made that intense and shocking experiences of early childhood, especially those which involved strong visual stimulation, resulted in a reinforcement of some visual components in the superego formation, which might be reactivated later in life in similar situations of stress, and could be regularly observed in the course of analyses of such patients. I was impressed with the observations of Ernst Kris that these light effects—halo or aurora—might be related to the peculiar peripheral luminosity and general intensity of screen memories. It is the purpose of this chapter to examine this situation more carefully and then to consider a special form of screen memory in which there is an intensity of stubborn persistence but without brightness, and in which the content appears factually disturbing and very little elaborated. In the most extreme of such cases the memory appears as an insistent unpleasant scene which is told readily by the patient, a marked degree of isolation being achieved by an almost complete withdrawal of affect. In my experience such memories are related to the central theme of the neurosis, are rigidly defended throughout, resist analysis directly, and connections are made by the patient only toward the very end of the analysis.

A careful scrutiny of the structure of a number of screen memories has led to the conclusion that the special intensity and visual quality depends upon pressures of varying degrees from five different interrelated sources: (a) The strength of the sense of reality dependent on the stage of the ego development. The stronger the ego and the firmer the sense of reality, the better can the young individual tolerate frustration and anxiety and the less need he has for the compromise involved in displacement and screening. (b) The intensity of the disturbing experience which provokes the screening. The more severe the experience, the greater is the aggression aroused, sometimes with accompanying erotization. This severity or intensity may itself cause an overflow in the form of secondary visual excitement even when the primary trauma has not been visual as in the case of the severest pain, concussion or other physical distress. In general, however, psychic traumata of childhood do involve vision directly in greater proportion than in adult years. The severity or shock character of traumata with accompanying visual stimulation may contribute directly to the bright edge and vividness of the screen memory through the process of displacement.

This may be observed *in statu nascendi* even in adult life. In extremely frightening experiences the person often finds himself noticing and stressing some inconsequential detail of the scene which seems inexplicably vivid and sticks in his memory afterward even when the central horrifying part of the experience is not forgotten. The mechanism is much the same as in the screen memory—a deflection of focus from an intolerable horror to something which is reassuringly innocuous and familiar. Analysis to be sure often reveals that the very detail selected is itself a screen for some earlier frightening or guilty experience, the emotion of which has been reactivated by the new trauma. For example:

A young man surprised a marauder as he opened the door of his home one night. He believed the man was armed but was not sure whether or not he actually saw a pistol. He was shocked by the experience and was surprised to find his attention fixed on the doorknob which shone in the light of the near-by street light rather than on the man and the question of whether or not he had a gun. The doorknob was the vivid spot in his memory both immediately afterward and long after. Analysis showed that the deflection of focus to the doorknob served to temper his anxiety at the time. Back of this however lay much earlier experiences of peeping through the nearly shut door of the bathroom to watch his parents at the toilet and of attempting to look through the keyhole to verify suspicions of their activities in the bedroom.

Anyone who has examined witnesses to some shocking event will recognize how unreliable are their observations, and especially how irrelevant and peripheral details may be stressed and even invented with a persistent and even annoying circumstantiality.

Katherine Mansfield's story 'The Fly' (14) is a succinct account of such a horror fantasy, showing this mechanism: An older man in a moment of competitive exultation in life is suddenly reminded of the death of his son in battle. Attempting to conjure up the memory of the boy in a kind of orgy of guilty grief, he finds his attention wandering instead to a fly which has been caught in an inkwell and is attempting to free itself. He watches and experiments in its struggle. With its death, he is seized by a 'grinding feeling of wretchedness' which frightens him. A moment later he calls for fresh ink and blotter and suddenly wonders what he has been thinking about.

(c) The stage of libido development of the child and the degree of general erotic arousal at the time with resultant frustration and anxiety. Thus the utilization of a traumatic experience or event may be markedly different, depending on whether it occurs in the oedipal phase or during the latency period, *i.e.*, whether in the ascendency or relative quiescence of erotic feeling and interest. This certainly is but a restatement with a different emphasis of Fenichel's observation about the hungry condition and quantivalence for screen experience of certain infantile states of mind. It is obvious too that not only the stage of libido development but the specific concatenation of recent experience of the child may determine his point of saturation for frustration and anxiety after which he must resort to displacement and denial as defensive measures.

(d) The genetic stage of the superego development corresponding in a general way but not always proportionately with the ego development, but also influenced by the special vicissitudes of the individual superego formation and its interrelation with other components of the ego. This has been discussed in Chapter VI and it is unnecessary to repeat it here. It seems, however, that the detached onlooker quality characteristic of the typical screen memory may be due not only to the paralysis and temporary depersonalization caused by fright or panic and carried over to the substitute remembered experience, but further and perhaps chiefly to the arousal of the superego functions whose force influences decisively the need to deny and the feeling of general intensity, and which are represented by an actual watchfulness in the screen memory.

(e) The form and degree of sadomasochistic character structure which has already been built up in the person at the time of the event(s) for which the screen memory is substituted. It is to be expected that when there is no severe degree of sadomasochistic character structure, simple, pleasant or tepid events may be used as the screen, whereas in severely morbid personalities really traumatic events may be seized upon as representations of the earliest anxious fantasies or experiences of the child and may be used variously as justification, verification or gratification. This has been presented by Fenichel in his discussion of traumatic experiences which act as screens in traumatic neuroses (3) and in perversions such as voyeurism and fetishism. He emphasized that the way in which a traumatic experience is incorporated into the psychic life and into the memory of the person depends upon the intensity of the unconscious readiness to develop anxieties and on the past ways in which persons have learned to deal with anxieties; that where there is already a strong sadomasochistic character, a new trauma may be felt as a gratification. He mentioned especially people who habitually involve themselves in thrilling temptations to Fate and feel some sort of satisfaction when their latent fantasies come true. An extension of this is the situation in which the trauma is not provoked but is a true accident of Fate and is accepted by the sadomasochistically impaired person as a magic fulfillment of his punishment desires. Fate in this way is the successor of the parents who have often held a prolonged Olympian sway in the childhoods of these patients. All this will be discused in relation to the clinical material of this chapter having to do with the special type of screen memory which I have already described, *i.e.*, one in which the content appears traumatic and unelaborated, factual and isolated, has persistence rather than brightness, and is stubbornly resistant to analysis.

## CASE REPORT

An unmarried medical nurse of 35 came to analysis because of certain instinctual temptations toward both men and women which she could neither accept nor reject and which consequently threw her into a state of arousal, frustration, guilt, and anger, reaching the proportions of a severe panic. She said at once that her sexual interest and enlightenment had been extraordinarily delayed and that only during the past three to four years had she been aware of any erotic feelings, since which she had become involved in a series of singularly disturbed and rather adolescent attachments to both men and women. Although she was an unusually able and intelligent woman she saw nothing odd in this delayed development, regarding it as part of her upbringing and general background. This was the more striking since she came from a rather normal appearing family with both parents still living, and her description of the family life was of warmhearted energetic people in a modest semi-rural community. She insisted that she had had neither interest in nor knowledge of sexual matters until toward the end of her nurse's training. She even believed that she had never seen male genitals until she was in training when the experience was forced upon her in the course of her regular duties. When I indicated that this was unusual especially as the family had lived in small quarters and that anyway there was the probability of some observations at summer camps and bathing beaches where she went every summer, she protested that I did not really understand her background and how protected she had been.

On the fifth day of the analysis, after saying that when she was quite grown-up she had asked her mother some facts about her own birth and that her mother had replied by asking *her* facts about obstetrics, she told me that at eight or nine she had gotten up in the night, had passed her parents' bedroom where a low light was burning and had observed them having intercourse. She could not say whether she had understood the scene at the time or when she had come to realize its nature. She did not even know whether or not their bodies were uncovered. Still the scene had a dreary clarity in her mind and she recalled especially that her father's face looked cruel and unattractive although he was a very good-looking man. Later in the analysis when the scene came back to her as it did rarely, she would repeat it as she had originally, in a dry factual way as though she were including it conscientiously as part of the anamnesis, but she could neither elaborate it nor discuss it. Her attitude at most was that it had occurred, that it might have given her an unfortunate impression of her father and of sexuality, but there the story ended. This attitude persisted throughout the greater part of her analysis even after she had brought out many memories which gradually came back spontaneously, involving awareness of a neighbour boy's genitals at 4, sex play with a girl cousin her own age at around 6, and a wealth of other reminiscences of curiosity indulged in with other children involving farm animals, of mutual masturbation and experimentation followed by profound guilt feelings. Still the patient could not say more about this primal scene experience at 8 or 9.

About two weeks after the beginning of the analysis the patient had a dream, reported as follows:

You were saying to me, 'You have been at this for 4 months and are not getting anywhere.' The idea was that since the therapy was not working, I was to bathe all over in Saline, then soap and leave a coating of soap on.

In association she said that whereas the Saline felt and seemed clean, a coating of soap with a spurious cleanliness, really a nasty disagreeable mess. The 4 months she attributed to the fact that she had been a little over 3 months with another analyst and this plus the time with me would approximate 4 months. She had feared that the other analyst disdained her and questioned whether she was analysable. She felt that the analysis with me would have to bring out a mess or turn into one. She began also to project on to me some of her guilt feelings of uncleanliness, saying that she felt that I too disapproved of her and at other times making indirect criticisms of me and of my office. She could bring out these latter only with the greatest difficulty and on several occasions rushed impetuously from the analytic hour rather than say anything which conceivably could offend me. In other respects, however, she was not at all an ingratiating or subservient person and did not show any positive need to please.

The extremeness of the patient's defences as well as the shape and consistency of the experience defended was forecast by the third week of the analysis when she brought a dream:

I was going in and out of places in Rockland County with the question whether I should stay and work there. I was trying to decide about it.

On the same day she brought me a sonnet written some years earlier, of which I quote a part:

I built a wall of thoughts in even row:
Like bricks they were to be, so firm and strong

Protecting me from laughter and mad song
And echoes of a fear that would not go.

\*    \*    \*    \*    \*    \*

Now bricks have crumbled and the scattered dust
Is scuffed by hurried steps of passers-by
And I shall learn because I know I must
I too can roam the world with courage high.
Build fair castles, place a firmer trust
In golden spires that pierce the sky.

Here clearly the first stanza indicated the rock-like wall of
defence which was to characterize her analysis throughout,
while the last stanza showed the direction of hope for a favourable outcome.

Several months later she presented a dream which proved
to be a remarkably condensed version of her very severe
neurosis:

You were hypnotizing me. I was in another room than this, but
lying down. A young girl in her late teens or early twenties put a
whisky bottle on my chest. I realized you were hypnotizing me.
As part of the process you made faces. Finally I just gave in. Next
I was on my way home and dropped this bottle and broke it. It
seemed then as though I had bought it.

At this time, the patient remarked that she very much disliked having to speak about me or see me even in a dream and
that always in dreams about me somebody was interfering.
Here however the whisky bottle seemed a part of the treatment
and had to do with the hypnosis against which she seemed to
struggle futilely. She further associated the whisky with her
first homosexual contact, in which she had climbed a mountain
with her friend, been caught in a rain storm and on returning
to the hotel had taken whisky and gone to bed to avert a cold;
with the croup of her early years; and with breath-holding
which she resorted to in anger at 4 to 5, reaching a point of
panic and fear of losing consciousness. This was coincident with
another kind of withholding, namely constipation as a spite
against her mother. The making faces was related vaguely to a

period of severe neurosis at 7 to 8 when she suffered obsessive thoughts of guilt toward her mother, necessitating endless trivial confessions, and at the same time had a facial tic with wrinkling of the nose and shrugging of the shoulders. She had recovered from—built a stone wall (of her poem) against— this neurosis on being forcibly returned to school at 8. About this event there was another screen memory—a recollection of herself clinging to the newel post screaming and resisting frantically while her parents cajoled, then forced her to release her grip and go back to school after an absence of several months due to her neurotic fears.

Only toward the end of the analysis when the patient could not be kept from some rather dangerous acting out, could these dreams or the full significance of the original screen memory be understood. One more episode during treatment is an interesting link. Fairly late in the analysis, she reacted with extreme anger and panic when a friend of hers referred to me in a mixture of derogation and appreciation as 'a reliable old percheron,' with the manifest reference to my size and durability—that of a good reliable work horse. The patient considered this an extreme insult, abused her friend, and forbade her to speak in such a fashion again. Mentioning it with hesitant humour to me during the analytic hour, she could at first make no associations, then thought of the painting by Rosa Bonheur, with horses' rumps in the foreground, then of another early screen memory of laughing uncontrollably at 5 to 6 when a fat aunt laced her corsets and 'her buttocks looked so funny.' She next thought of the farm of another aunt where there were work horses, and skipping over the thought of a schizophrenic cousin who lived on this farm and had the same name as her father, she suddenly said, 'I think of father showing me things I wasn't supposed to know about. I don't remember what. I think I would get close to father then and get frightened.' Her next thought was of a charming baby she had seen in the clinic that morning. The probable pun on the word percheron (perch-on-her) did not occur to her even when she spoke of watching in the chicken yard and wondering what the roosters did to the hens.

To go back to the original screen memory, the drearily

clear yet not very specific primal scene observed at the age of 8, many of the components of which must be evident from the dream material already given. The patient slept in her parents' room until 4 (cf. the 4 months in the first dream). During this period she had croup rather severely. After she was removed to another room the croup was better, but she reacted to this expulsion with angry breath-holding to the point of fading consciousness, constipation and smearing, for which she was condemned and punished by being made to sit incommunicado in a chair. She was passionately attached to her father until 6, a fact which she had completely denied at the beginning of the analysis. At that age she suffered a severe sexual trauma in seeing some man exposed and masturbating. From the analytic material it seemed probable that this was the schizophrenic cousin who had the same name as her father, or a foreign handy man who worked around her father's place of business. Both figures appeared frequently fused with that of the father, and it seemed clear that she projected on to her father her reaction to his experience and to an even more severe sexual trauma of attempted rape, to which she was seduced by being given money. She had actually a ruptured hymen which was first discovered in her early twenties and which she unconsciously understood in attributing it to having ridden horseback too vigorously. In her official memory at the beginning of the analysis, this rape experience appeared only projected as a memory that her mother had had a severe operation for gall stones and hysterectomy when the patient was 6. The mother did actually have such an operation when the patient was 10, and this situation must have been projected backward some time after that. The identification with the mother in the primal scene experiences before the age of 4, with pressure on the chest during croup attacks, was now turned around and her own castrating experience of rape was put on the mother in a backward displacement of memory, not finally accomplished until the prepuberty period. Reality was in this way utilized as the basis of projection, which was the patient's mechanism of choice. There was some evidence that before she found the satisfying reality of the mother's operation she used various fantasies of medical procedures, gleaned from a chum who was the daughter of the neighbourhood doctor.

Practically all of these elements are represented in the third dream. The hypnotizing refers to giving in to the analytic procedure, to the fading-out sensations of the croup and of the breath-holding (and probably at a deeper level, to nursing). The whisky bottle is another version of this, as in states of extreme depression the patient would drink to produce the effect of obliteration. But the whisky bottle is a peculiarly condensing symbol, not only representing nursing, and taking an anesthetic, but also being a bisexual symbol. Its breaking meant both castration and rape, which she had brought on herself by 'giving in' for the sake of the bribe. The 'girl in her late teens or early twenties' was of the age at which the patient discovered the rupture of her hymen and so the repressed rape trauma was unconsciously reactivated and redefended. This girl probably also represented my daughter with whom the patient made a jealous hostile identification. The fact that I was making faces, immediately associated with her own facial tic, returns however to the screen memory with which she had begun the analysis, the memory of her parents having intercourse and her father's unattractively contorted face.

It has now become clear that the screen memory held many of the elements which were seen in their dispersed forms in her dreams and symptoms. Although the memory appeared so simple and unmodified, critical review brings up two probable discrepancies. It is unlikely that the door would have been left open, especially if a light were left on. One suspects then that the little girl at least opened the door, and felt somewhat guilty at her own intrusion. The other incongruity is that the father seemed to be on top of the mother, yet in some way she had the impression of seeing his face. This would certainly be unlikely if not actually impossible. It seems likely therefore that this screen memory is really combined with early memories from before the age of 4, in which mother and father appeared more fused and interchangeable. There comes next the question whether the child of 8 saw the mother's face (as I was making faces at her in the dream) or whether she saw very little but on coming to the door of the room, realized what was occurring, and that this in itself was enough to reinstate unconsciously the old primal scene experiences. Certainly there was a displacement from genitals to face. This was apparent in her occasional laments during the analysis when she felt sexually frustrated and would feel like drinking: 'I can't stand a world with people who are just eyes and noses to me.' Again it is noteworthy that she used reality as the basis of displacement, *i.e.*, that the faces may have looked flushed and passionate during intercourse, but that to this is referred the observation of genital changes. It seemed too that this was even more determined by the experience at 6 when she saw the seminal fluid of the masturbating man (the soap coating of the second dream) and experienced the rape with obviously a fantasy of pregnancy following. This latter was repeated later in life with a 9-months' amenorrhoea following an appendix operation.

The question may well be asked whether the screen experience at 8 occurred at all at that time or whether it too was a displacement from an earlier to a later time. This cannot be absolutely settled. The patient believed that there was some definite experience then, most likely that she did go to the parents' room and was aware of something. The utilization of this disturbing screen memory as a defence and as a peculiarly stubborn one fits in with her general methods of defence, viz., withdrawal of affect and displacement of disturbing events into quite similar real ones in which she is less or not at all involved.

If this screen memory is scrutinized in the light of the five forces which have been designated as lending pressure and intensity to such memories, it will be noted that this patient had a *strong ego* development. She was well loved by both parents and seems to have been a happy child up to the age of 4. There was, evidently, an overstimulation both erotically and aggressively by the primal scenes up to her expulsion from the parents' room at 4. She was well-endowed intellectually and learned readily, except for telling time and arithmetic both of which seemed connected with severe toilet training problems at 3. Then her aggression took the form of both constipation and smearing. She took on the punishments of the parents, the father who stormed, and the mother who put her on a chair and did not speak to her. She stormed and then built a wall (of bricks or rock) around this, and at disturbing periods in her analysis would retreat into a really stony silence and almost immobility.

The traumatic *experiences were unusually severe*, the sight of the man masturbating and the experience of rape, both occurring with men who were associated to an unusual degree with her father. It is probable that this patient was really a very seductive little girl, who was predisposed by long exposure to sexual scenes and that she co-operated in the instigation of these experiences. At the beginning of her analysis she always spoke of herself as having been so awkward she was almost deformed as a child. Later she said she thought some change had come over her at 4 to 5, and still later showed me pictures of herself as a very merry young child, but with a solemn lack-lustre look at about 7.

The traumatic experiences occurred at 5 to 6, coincident with and probably under the influence of the oedipus arousal, that *most susceptible of all periods of infantile libidinal development*. The struggle with overly severe toilet training and with her aroused aggression seemed to have formed the beginnings of a severe conscience, and the traumatic intensity of the oedipal struggle intensified this enormously. So far all of the factors mentioned would tend to produce unusually severe repressing forces and one might expect almost blazingly intense screen memories, if any. Actually the child went into a very severe depressive obsessional neurosis, with phobias, and frequently reiterated confessions of guilt, to an extent that hospitalization was considered. The end of this was marked by a sudden wave of repression and a flight into intellectualization and physical overactivity, somewhat comparable to defences frequent in adolescence. The neurosis became encapsulated, behind her wall of rock. The brightness which is missing from the screen memory appears however in the ' fair castles . . . and golden spires that pierce the sky' in the latter part of her poem. As for the screen memory itself, of the drearily clear primal scene witnessed at 8, it was chosen at a time when the patient was already in a stage of intense repression and in the latency period as well. It was largely fortuitous (*i.e.* with less guilt), and fitted almost exactly the original traumata from which the oedipal ones had developed. It was, indeed, a snug and effective cover. The patient here used reality to cover reality, and the screen memory served in part as a reality testing, and in part as a most effective projection. This reminds one that a frank confession often deflects suspicion. Jones (12) in an early paper, ' Persons in Dreams Disguised as Themselves,' describes a similar phenomenon in dreams.

As to the *sadomasochistic* character structure in this patient, it is true that there were evidences of a considerable sadomasochistic reinforcement. This was of a special type, however, in that she had used external reality and ego gratifications as her main defences against her instinctual conflicts. The result was a seemingly productive and too energetic young woman who burdened herself too much but generally succeeded. Only in certain work relationships with men did the full force of the self-destructive combination of competitiveness and need for punishment show up clearly in her daily work. She was quite different from the sadomasochistic type who retreats from reality and uses a traumatic screen memory in repeated self-stimulation and acting out with a constant infiltration of masochistic fantasy into daily activity.

One more question presents itself. It is obvious that screen memories and dreams have very much in common. Yet in general the screen memory is isolated, bright-edged, whereas the dream does not have so clear a periphery, and, as Lewin (13) has shown, may have curled edges that roll under or back. I believe that this difference is on a rather simple basis. According to Lewin the deepest dream screen is the breast and the nursing experience. Here the mouth rather than the eye is the primary receptive organ. The dream occurs during sleep and has as its base the earliest twilight and sleepy states at the end of feeding. The screen memory on the other hand arises in consciousness and seeming alertness, utilizing experiences then in which vision has the primary role and is generally reinforced by the all-seeing function of the superego.

## CHAPTER X

# THE PREPUBERTY TRAUMA IN GIRLS*

THIS study supplements Chapter IX, the study of a special type of screen memory (1) of a sexual trauma occurring in the late latency period, the memory of the event being retained with gloomy clarity and singularly little apparent distortion. An extreme resistance to the analysis of this sort of memory, much more than in the case of screen memories from an earlier period of life, suggested that the memory and possibly the event itself served some special function to the individual. Chapter IX deals largely with the relation of this type of screen memory to the earlier memories and with the general dynamics of memory. The present chapter focuses on the economics of the event itself. It is based on the analyses of four women patients, the rather cursory observations of several patients seen in consultation in the course of clinic work, and the direct knowledge of one young girl in the prepuberty phase where the situation was observed as it arose and sequelae observed through the early puberty phase, namely, the four years following the trauma.

In the chapter on prepuberty with which Dr. Helene Deutsch opens the first volume of her *Psychology of Women* (2), she places the prepuberty period as roughly between the ages of ten and twelve. In the cases which I have studied, the traumatic experience occurred with rather surprising regularity either in the tenth or eleventh year. The trauma certainly belonged to the end of the latency period, but its instigation seemed motivated by unconscious attempts to prepare for puberty which was already being glimpsed by the little girl, especially in the development of older classmates or older sisters, although she herself had not yet undergone even the beginning pubertal changes in the sexual organs, and there was no indication of increased genital drives. The child

* Reprinted from *The Psychoanalytic Quarterly*, Vol. XIX, No. 3, July, 1950.

TGP-G*

precipitated the trauma out of curiosity rather than out of physiological pressure.

Dr. Deutsch defines prepuberty as 'that last stage of the latency period in which certain harbingers of future sexual drives may be discerned, but which in the main is the period of greatest freedom from infantile sexuality . . . sexual instincts are at their weakest and the development of the ego most intense' (p. 4). She further suggests that the increased passivity of early puberty is preceded by a thrust of activity, which is not really an increase in aggression but rather an intensive process of adaptation to reality; and that prepuberty is a period in which there is a tendency to renounce the infantile fantasy life and to launch an offensive against the environment, a turn toward reality (p. 7). It is a time in which there is great curiosity about sexuality, the telling of secrets among girls, singly or in groups, but very little actual interest in the opposite sex (p. 17). The interest is no longer in bodily or genital forms, but in body and genital function. This coincides rather closely with my clinical observations in the four cases analysed.

It is a truism that in puberty there is a revival of the disturbances and unresolved conflicts from the period of infantile sexuality. What I found impressive, however, was the great specificity with which the prepuberty trauma repeated the main disturbances of the pre-oedipal phases of development, so that it seemed very clearly a condensed form of acting out in which the child herself became victimized by the trauma which she had precipitated, and the unhappy event was then used as a dramatic defence against entering into the struggles of puberty. In those cases which I have analysed this has occurred in girls who had had especially severe disturbances of the pregenital phases of development, in addition to severe and unresolved oedipal struggles, followed by more than ordinary masculine identifications, sometimes of a sweeping nature but always involving a stubbornly intense effort to solve the castration problem through the persistence of the illusory penis. The last was the result of varying combinations of (a) particularly severe primal scene stimulation with resultant sadomasochistic fantasies reinforced by disturbed anal functioning; (b) intense penis envy; (c) attempts to solve the oedipal struggle by identification with the father.

A woman of thirty sought treatment for severe inhibitions and emotional disturbances invading practically all phases of her life. Extremely shy, sensitive to the point of constant flight from others, she was unable to work for any length of time, and spent much time in idleness, becoming irritable whenever prodded by her family to do anything. In the second consultation interview she spoke hesitantly but emphatically of an experience at the age of about ten from which she dated her major difficulties. She believed that before this experience she had been predominantly a happy and innocent little girl, but that following it, due to the fright of the experience, she had turned from men and boys, becoming increasingly shy to the point of general incapacity. In adolescence she had drawn irritably away from her father to whom she had previously been conspicuously devoted. Among other symptoms she had then developed two rather strong and peculiar fears: one that she was being followed by a 'Black Presence' which sometimes nearly overtook her; the other that she 'did not want to grow up and wear white stockings.' These were not exactly phobias. They might be described rather as dreads that were so persistent that they had an almost delusional quality, though they were not quite true delusions. When under the influence of the fear of the Black Presence, everything light or white seemed desirably pure; when under the spell of the white stockings, darkness seemed invitingly friendly.

This girl had had almost no relationship with men or boys after puberty. In her twenties there had been a brief engagement with a somewhat strange young man from whose physical overtures, slight as they were, she had fled and broken the engagement, later clinging to it in fantasy. She had subsequently a few mild attachments to women, mostly older, and two very shadowy friendships with older men, but even these relationships were too much for her. If they approached any degree of intensity of feeling, toward which she progressively drove them, she retreated with outbursts of unexpected anger or suicidal fantasies and gestures, but continued to be preoccupied with daydreams of the friendships which she was having to sacrifice.

This case is obviously complex, and to organize the material, it is summarized under headings pertinent to the dynamic themes.

## THE TRAUMA

At the age of about ten the girl was roller-skating in the cellar of her own home when a man entered to read the gas meter. She spoke to him and he offered to show her the meter, thereupon lifting her so that she could see the movement of the little hands upon the dials of the meter. In lifting her he put his hand under her dress and stimulated her genitals. She recalls having become extremely excited, ashamed, and frightened; she squirmed free and the man quickly left. She could not recall exactly how the experience ended; she had the feeling that she lost consciousness or 'went blank,' also that she might subsequently have gone into the next room of the cellar where the laundress was working. The whole incident had been very brief, she had not cried out, and the laundress could not have been aware of anything until the frightened child appeared. Admittedly an unpleasant experience, it did not in itself seem sufficient to be the turning point of a whole life, although it had obviously so served in the patient's estimation. The analysis was to prove that she was right: it had been a kind of condenser and, with one or two subsequent lesser traumata, became the barrier to a reasonably normal pubertal and adult development. In the period just prior to the incident in the cellar, the patient had been caught in a kind of tidal wave of sexual investigations among girls of her acquaintance. There had been repeated sessions of talking about sex with another child, always conducted in the dark, either at night or with drawn shades. There may have been some sexual play and mutual investigation, but the predominant activity was telling secrets about the sexual activities of adults. At a house party there was some actual genital stimulation as her best friend told her about having discovered accidentally the peculiarly pleasant sensations aroused by lying in the bathtub and allowing a stream of water under pressure to play upon the genitals. My patient learned quickly. It seemed, indeed, that it was just the information she was waiting for, and it initiated a form of masturbation which was to continue intermittently up until the time of the analysis.

In the period after the trauma, she did not turn at once from boys; there was in fact a winter during which she resumed relationships with her cousin, a boy about a year younger than she, whom she had last known at five or six. She had had a rather warm companionship with him and two of his friends when they went skiing and hiking together. She enjoyed sports with boys in which she could compete reasonably well; in other games she would allow herself to be tied up as mock torture—obviously a struggle between an aggressive masculine and a masochistic feminine identification. Her being so much with boys at this time when she had previously been with girls was partly at her own instigation but was certainly favoured by the fact that the family had moved and that the only children she knew in the new community were her cousin and his friends. A second turning point in this unstable situation came with a new trauma when she expected her cousin to take her to a children's dance and she overheard him rebel because she had grown taller than he. She was intensely humiliated, and when the family moved to still another community just as she reached the age of puberty, the whole process of withdrawal from reality into fantasy became well launched. During this time the child was occasionally utilizing the technique she had learned of masturbation in the bathtub. That she was anxiously anticipating puberty was evident: she repeatedly observed the shadows of her own body, especially the contour of the breasts, on the wall as she bathed. Her aunt, whose namesake she was, was then pregnant. When the patient disingenuously commented on her aunt's fatness, the mother hushed her up. She reacted toward the baby boy as though he belonged to her, referred to him as her brother, and when it soon developed that the boy was severely epileptic, she befriended him with a horrified fascination.

## THE CURRENT SYMPTOMS

In analysis it became evident that she was concealing, for some time out of shame, underlying disturbances originating from her very peculiar sexual balance. One can only describe this by saying that she seemed to be in an unusual state of chronic tension, due to her efforts to control all of the elements of the polymorphous perverse drives which were constantly in danger of breaking through. She could maintain this precarious balance in a state of triggered tension for some periods of time, but in almost any situation involving appearance in public, any special pressure of accomplishments (examinations), or any special sadomasochistic stimulation (fights or accidents), she would 'go to pieces.' This meant that she had some sudden spontaneous bodily discharge: a vaginal orgasm, a burst of uncontrolled weeping, loss of control of the bladder, an unexpected diarrhoea, or, during her menstrual period, an extreme degree of flooding which once caused severe anemia. In two instances of unusually well-organized acting out the patient, who enjoyed an occasional cocktail, drank two or three at cocktail parties where both men and women were present. This amount, which would ordinarily only cause her to be exhilarated, on these two occasions was followed by a sudden premonition of something about to happen. She made her way to a toilet where she lost consciousness. Her actions excited so much concern about her among the guests that she came to, to find others with her, and she requested that she be carried into the apartment of the caretaker of the school building in which the party had been held. She then rested in the room of the caretaker and his wife, went home after a few hours greatly chagrined, saying she would give up her work rather than face her colleagues.

At the beginning of the analysis, the patient practised two types of masturbation: clitoral masturbation, often initiated by remembering at night in bed the trauma of the tenth to eleventh year; and masturbation in the bathtub which seemed to include both clitoral and vaginal stimulation and usually resulted in a vaginal orgasm.

## THE NATURE OF THE PREGENITAL AND GENITAL DRIVES

This patient was an only child of tense, rigid, overidealistic and unconsciously cruel parents. Until she was sent to school at the age of six she was constantly with the mother with whom she gave evidence of having been early in an almost mystical relation, as though appersonated by the mother. Both the patient and her mother stated that she had been an unusually sunny, docile, cheerful, non-neurotic child; however, the girl reported and the mother verified that, mostly before the age of three, the child had been much spanked with a hairbrush. Neither the patient nor her mother at first saw any contradiction between this fact and her supposedly sunny disposition. The patient obstinately clung to her bottle until she was about three. One of her earliest memories was of violently throwing the bottle down the stairs when her parents were having a party from which she was naturally excluded. She felt sure that she had been spanked for this, which may have been the cause of her giving up the bottle. She was 'successfully' toilet trained extremely early. Whether this was true or not I could not clearly determine. There was some indication of her having lost control of bladder or bowels on the first day of kindergarten. Certainly the patient lived in a state of fear of toilet accidents, always going to the toilet just before leaving the house and having to verify where the bathroom was in each new environment. (Later, in her twenties, she used this as a definite aggression against her mother; whenever they went out together she would keep the mother waiting while she stayed unnecessarily long in the toilet, involved with her bowel movements and with brooding sadomasochistic fantasies.) There was some positive evidence or early severe outbursts of temper which were ultimately controlled by whippings until the patient presented the obligatory sunniness which was then regarded as natural.

Perhaps increased by the maternal appersonation, certainly by the too vigorous romping and tickling by her father, and the stimulation of early primal scenes, she developed an unusual kinesthetic erotism. There were memories of having been swung and tossed in the air by her father until she got into

states of almost frantic exhilaration; and from reconstructed
memories it appeared that these reached climactic states of
genital stimulation but no true orgasm. She was able to reproduce something of this happy frenzy in her early play with her
dog, a large collie. She would go racing through the house in a
kind of competitive romping play of increasing tempo with her
dog who often knocked her down and licked her face as child
and dog rolled over and over on the floor. Sometimes such
tempestuous play ended in accidents, a crescendo of breakage
followed by punishment. Later in life under the pressure of
time, as in rushing for a train, the patient would have other
accidents, as the unexpected discharge of a watery stool or
sudden flooding during a menstrual period (unconsciously
equated); or she might have a spontaneous orgasm with a
muccus discharge. It is my belief, however, that in the pregenital period there were few if any of these organ accidents which
occurred only after there was a further amalgamation of bodily
tensions under the stress of a peculiarly difficult oedipal period.

### THE OEDIPAL PERIOD

This was complicated by three major events: a special version
of the primal scene at the age of five; a fantastic enema ritual
practised by the mother on the child a little later; sharing of
toilet activities at the age of four with an old man. In this
four- to five-year period she experienced curiosity and fantasies
about primal scenes with many memories indicating her desire
and efforts to keep the parents apart. When she was five her
family moved to another part of the country, and soon after
this her father fell ill. The patient first remembered that he
had been sick for a whole year, that he had multiple arthritis,
and that he had been practically encased in a plaster cast.
During this time she was his devoted handmaiden, went each
night to sing a good night song to him. Dreams revived an
isolated memory of going unexpectedly into his bedroom and
finding her mother doing something to her father's genitals.
The fantasy was that she was performing fellatio. Further
analysis indicated that the mother was probably helping him
with a urinal, bottle shaped and made of white enamel. This

fused observation and fantasy gave a special turn to the primal scene fantasies, and verified the sex-urination and mouth-impregnation ideas of the child. On analytic investigation, checked later by the mother's own account, it developed that the memory of the father's illness was vastly exaggerated. He had had moderately severe arthritis, had been sick at the most four months, and the cast had encased only one leg and the pelvic girdle. This distortion of the primal scene led the little girl to reverse and confuse the sexual roles, as the mother was the aggressor, and the father helpless. The extension of the cast to include the father's whole body, and the extension of the time to include a whole year, were distortions of memory representing the child's defence against her intense oedipal wishes, and a projection onto him of the wall of restraint of bodily functions which was occurring in her. The idea of the white cast completely covering the father's body was also a displacement from the white urinal covering his penis.

From the observation of this and other cases, I have come to the opinion that in patients with a very faulty or incomplete separation of the self from the environment in the first stages of ego development a 'wall' of some kind—the glass wall of the schizophrenic—becomes erected one way or another as a protection against the overly strong instinctive stimulation of the environment, but that it is given special form and structure by actual restraint in infancy. In other words, the child's pathological need for protective restraint is enormously increased by the poorly applied disciplinary restraints and converted into a confining wall rather than a helpfully protective barrier.

This patient's restraint was increased by enemas which intensified the reversal of sexual roles and the confusion of genital and pregenital functions. One can only suppose that the mother was reacting with increasingly pathological behaviour to the course of events. She was an exquisitely beautiful woman of finely chiselled features and, on the one occasion when I saw her, gave the impression of the hardness of fine steel combined with a dreamy preoccupation that gave one the feeling of seeing her through a mist. At any rate, when the child started in kindergarten she developed an obstipation, probably a reaction to her fear of not finding the toilet in time. The mother thereupon instituted enemas, given to the child in the bathtub where she was instructed to lie with her legs spread. This seemed clearly to prepare the girl for the later 'water masturbation' which was partly cleansing, and which she adopted so readily in the prepuberty era. As though the encasement of restraint were not sufficient, there was an additional event. The child contracted whooping cough, and since the illness was so protracted as to interfere with the summer vacation plans, the parents decided to go ahead anyway. The trip to the summer lodge was made by car with two overnight stops at wayside hotels. The child was warned that she must not embarrasss the family by coughing or vomiting in hotels or they would be evicted. One suspects that she may have utilized the whooping cough aggressively, and that the parents sensed it; certainly they were parents who could tolerate very little aggression. On the journey she almost but not quite succeeded in complying with their demands and, although the family was not expelled, she felt ashamed, disgraced, a failure, and resented the parents' hypocrisy. It does not seem strange then that there was a retrospective distortion of memory of the father's cast 'up to his neck' when she herself was so encased by prohibitions. The father's cast and her restraint were reinforced by the memory of the white enamelled urinal and the white enamelled tub, in accordance with the body-phallus equation of this kinesthetically stimulated and appersonated child. On this visit, too, she had her first experience of clearly seeing the genitals of her little boy cousin.

It is possible to trace the recurrence of these patterns at puberty and in adolescence when she developed fears of the Black Presence and of white stockings. The former seemed definitely the anally determined elements of the conscience, based on her own body tensions and apprehensions and the ever-threatening figure of the (phallic) enema-imposing mother. The plaster cast and the white legs of the primal scene reappeared in the complementary dread of the white stockings which signified growing up. The dirty masturbation at night was associated with sadistic fantasies, in contrast to the purifying, exciting masturbation in the bathtub (associated by the patient with Charles Kingsley's *Water Babies*).

Throughout adolescence the girl was encased in a 'cast' of defensive irritability and silence directed against her father. In her quite conscious fantasies, she was married to him. When she gave directions for the delivery of goods, clerks in stores seemed to hear her say Mrs. rather than Miss. She fantasied purchasing haberdashery for him and play-acted this for an imaginary audience as she window-shopped. In high school she avoided all associations with boys, but went through elaborate bits of play acting and pseudologia to make it appear that she was sought by older boys or men, superior to the high school boys. She was a little late in menstruating and this initiated an outbreak of new symptoms; an increase of muscular tension, a running, often fleeting gait, spontaneous orgasms, and uncertain control of her sphincters appeared at this time. A pressure of general physical activity and in sports was an effort to deny an approaching menstrual period; the development of intellectual interests, a reaffirmation of the illusory penis. In college, however, where she could not avoid competition with other girls, this fragile compensation broke down. Menstrual flooding took its place among the other climactic body discharges, she became periodically invalided, sought unnecessary operations and started a downward spiral of masochism, spoiling every possible success.

The latency period, up to about the age of ten, had been alleged to be a 'good' period of her development. After the difficulty in starting school, her intellectual development progressed quite well. There was the sexual talk and sexual investigation with other girls, usually in pairs. Her association with boys was freer then than at any other time in the girl's life, often characterized by competitive sport activities. Certainly the period from six to twelve did not approach absolute latency, but the sexual interest until ten was characterized by less intensity and pressure, and apparently less physiological tension than before five or after puberty. It was possible to trace a definite bisexual orientation throughout her development. She had confirmed the fact that she was a girl with the inspection of other girls. Nonetheless she allocated her illusory penis predominantly to the clitoris, the hair—both of the pubis and the scalp—and the stool. This was interestingly acted out in analysis. Whenever unconscious material having to do with the clitoris was produced but not accepted by the patient, she would reach up and pull first at her hair, then at the tissue on the pillow which she would twist into a small roll and, just as she left, drop it into the ashtray in a way suggestive of Abraham's patient who walked through the woods dropping paper behind her.

The greatest increase in anxiety and tension occurred, not with the prepuberty trauma, but with the intensification of the castration complex at the onset of the menstrual periods. The girl seemed actually to suffer from both male and female castration anxiety with shifts and attempts at denial, but with a cumulative burden from both. It was after puberty, too, that the compelling dreads, almost of a persecutory nature, appeared. There was a complete breakdown of the poorly integrated pregenital and genital drives, with the establishment of a kind of democracy rather than a hierarchy among them so that an anxious orgastic discharge might occur in any of the systems involved, with fewer determinants than is usually the case. The spontaneous orgastic relief, which involved so much secondary anxiety, appeared almost equal and interchangeable among the various body systems. This was chiefly characteristic of this patient, not occurring in any comparable degree in the other three of the series.

## THE TRAUMA OF PREPUBERTY

The trauma has already been described. Largely through the analysis of dreams and disturbances of behaviour, the meaning of this experience could be pretty well understood. The child had initiated the experience by asking the man to lift her up and show her the meter which was hung high on the wall. As she was ten years old and tall, this was especially seductive and it contained the unconscious wish to be tossed in the air as she used to be by her father. She was already in a state of kinesthetic exhilaration from roller-skating at the time of the incident.

Most strongly determined, however, was the choice of the

man, who represented not only her father but 'the man down-stairs.' That she twice succeeded in getting the caretaker of the building to carry her into his apartment after her exhilaration at the cocktail parties was in both instances an act of compulsive repetition. The factual 'man downstairs' lived on the first floor of a two-family house in which the patient's family lived when she was between four and five years old. This was a year which right up to the end of the analysis remained more hazy in her memory than the preceding year, when the man downstairs was revealed, first as the memory of a parrot (owned by the family below) with an enormous beak and bleary and wrinkled eyes. This screened the memory of an old man, a grandfather or old uncle, who was a member of this same family. Reconstructed, it appears that the four-year-old child going out to play often passed this darkened apartment where the old man stayed alone in the afternoons when the family was out. More than once she tiptoed into the apartment and found the old parrot (man) there. The stimulating event occurred one day when she ran in, urgently in need of finding a toilet. She asked him or he sensed her need, and helped her, lifting her onto the toilet seat, and afterward urinating into the toilet himself. This exciting experience occurred before her father's illness and her going into the father's room and finding her mother helping him. She seemed to have had a pleasant rather than a frightening affect to this experience of sharing the toilet; only under the influence of later events did it become charged with the anxiety that caused it to be repressed; probably after seeing her young cousin's genital. The associations gave the conviction that the child defecated and the old man had urinated, and that there was in this comparison a confirmation of identifica-tion and contrast, which reinforced one factor in the polarities of black and white, earth and water, male and female—fantasies and symptoms crystallized in her dreads of the Black Presence and the white stockings.

The unconscious aim of the child's prepuberty seduction of the man was to see his genital. What he showed her (the gas meter on the wall), aided by his manipulation, since he inserted his finger into the vaginal introitus, only signified to her the realization of her own castration, a fact which she had certainly been verifying with girls, but which she seemed to wish either to confirm or deny in reinstating the former experiences shared with 'the man downstairs' when they had been so cosy in the toilet together. This series of events and the fact that the gas meter itself had the significance of the female genitals and of pregnancy was quite clear in a dream which she communicated at the beginning of an hour. This dream occurred under the influence of the menstrual period about two weeks after the second of the patient's cocktail-party-acting-out experiences into which she already had some insight. It was a time when the material of the prepuberty trauma was emerging into consciousness. She had glanced anxiously at me and remarked that I did not look well and feared that I might become sick again—a very unusual statement from her. As she lay on the couch she stated that the analysis seemed to have taken a new turn, almost like a new chapter, and related this dream.

I was on a bus in New York City. I had to get off because I knew I was going to be sick. I crossed the street to a theatre or movie and I seemed to have been there before. The place was dark. I pushed open a swinging door and entered the lobby of the theatre and went toward the rest room. I seemed to know just where to go. Then I saw that the theatre was full of groups of silent girls. They said I could come in. I did not want to because I did not want them to hear me being sick or having a bowel movement in the toilet. I finally did go in. Then there was another part to the dream. I had a little boy, a very small boy, and I was very proud of him. We were out some place. He put some money in a slot machine, and out came hundreds of packages of little cigarettes. I became frightened because the machine was emptying itself. The little boy suggested a bigger boy to my mind. I thought of my cousin. Then I realised he was really too old to have an interest in slot machines and to take so much pleasure in it. I also was concerned with what people would think of the little boy for being so abnormal.

She began her associations spontaneously, saying that on the day before she had seen on the street a very small woman, whom she could not place, who looked very familiar to her. (Note the familiar theatre and the small boy of the dream.) She had tried all day to remember who she was. Perhaps something had happened to her mind that a memory should so completely pass out of it. This suggested having 'passed out' at the cocktail party and having been carried by the kindly caretaker into his apartment. Now she realized she wished to avoid understanding this part of her recent experience. She would almost rather have terminated both work and analysis than face her shame and understand its basis.

The theatre recalled a memory from the age of five when she was with her parents on the street near a theatre called the Alamo. She had begun to read, and spelled out the letters AL-AM-O, singing them crescendo and with increasing rhythm as she ran along. She had then started a game of hide-and-seek with her parents, running ahead of them to hide in the doorways of stores, and jumping out to surprise them as they passed. (This will be recognized as linked with the kinesthetic thrills of early childhood, and further analysis justified the interpretation that it was also an early anal-vaginal masturbation hidden from the parents.)

The swinging doors of the theatre, which opened in the middle, suggested a hotel where the patient used to go with her mother to meet her father in the 'downtown section.' There she would usually take advantage of a ladies' room which had an arched, padded, baroque door, painted black and bright red. At this point the patient became somewhat disturbed, and said that in the morning (following the dream) she had become unreasonably angry at a fellow worker; on getting up from her seat she was aware of some menstrual flooding which evoked the fear that there might be blood on the floor as there had once been when she had thought she saw a clot of blood on the floor (an illusion based on the fear of anal incontinence). She had hurried to the bathroom and arrived in time to prevent an accident.

The slot machine recalled at once the gas meter and the gas meter man. She then first remembered clearly the man's finger in her genitals, and that this had induced in her a state of great confusion. The little cigarettes signified bowel movements, and castration.

It seemed justifiable at this point to interpret the dream as representing her desire to see the genitals, and as a reliving of past conflicts in identification on the basis of genital comparisons, which were discussed with her. She had begun with anxious concern about my health and her own menstruation, expressed in the dream as having to vomit or to have a bowel movement. The theatre primarily represented her concept of the female genitals, with a secondary combination of vagina and rectum: darkened rooms, silent girls, the red and black padded door. For this patient this was not merely a fusion of concept but an actual confusion of stimulation, due to early stimulation of the vagina through the rectum; symptomatically there was a practical interchangeability of vaginal and rectal discharge in excitement.

The little boy who was too big to play with the slot machine seemed clearly to refer to clitoral masturbation, deliberately undertaken, stimulating vaginal-rectal excitement; moreover, it represented the envy she felt of her cousin's penis, and her unsuccessful attempt to restore her own value by reclaiming the memory of the old man downstairs, through the experience with the gas meter man. The patient both confirmed and rejected this interpretation: she shuddered slightly and said, 'I can hardly make myself think of the clitoris now. I am blocked about it. . . . . I didn't like to see the movement of the little hands at the top of the meter. I think I must have got confused.' The following day she reported dreaming that Mr. D., the caretaker of the building, had seen her coming in and said, 'Hello, little girl, are you sick?' which referred directly to the Parrot Man.

A few days later the patient expressed the beginning of some spontaneous insight as to the significance of the trauma at the age of ten and her reaction to it. She had already recognized that she often seemed unable to anticipate pleasure; as longed-for situations approached she would precipitate events which would spoil her pleasure or make participation impossible. On this occasion she had been looking forward to attending a meeting in which there was to be a discussion of literature for adolescent children, a subject about which she felt she knew a good deal. She thought she really wanted to participate. The night before, however, she had a nightmare, awoke feeling distressed, and as soon as possible telephoned to report herself unable to attend on account of illness. The nightmare was as follows:

I went to the meeting (on adolescence) because I should not run away from it. It was in a brightly lighted room upstairs (like our room for smaller children). I saw Mrs. S., a fellow worker, but she had an undressed appearance because she was not wearing her hat as usual. Her hair seemed flattened down and ordinarily she wears high-crowned hats. I left them feeling I should not have come. I felt very sick. I was wearing a silver pin on the front of my blouse. I looked down and saw that the clasp of the pin was broken: two little prongs of the broken clasp were left. It could not be fixed, and really there is only one piece to the clasp. Mrs. M., another colleague, came in wearing fancy black suede shoes. She showed me that they did not fit properly and that she had cut them. I did not like that and I left the meeting.

The patient brought many associations confirming the obvious symbolism and giving specific content to the dream: the reactivated castration fear of puberty, for which the meeting on adolescence gave such a neatly convenient framework. This was the beginning of the patient's deeper and more or less organized insight, though it was repudiated and fought off for some time.

This patient had a much more severe disturbance of sexual functioning than any of the other patients, although all were markedly sadomasochistic. A strongly aggressive attitude sufficient for reasonable happiness was maintained in the latency period with the help of a bisexual orientation and the possession of an illusory penis. It seems that this is stronger throughout the greater part (especially the latter years) of the latency period in these patients than in the average girl child, although in only one of the four patients was there a sweeping masculine identification and a practical abdication then and later of the feminine position. In that patient, described in Chapter IX, a very severe sexual trauma had occurred in the immediate post-oedipal period following which her abandonment of femininity became conspicuous. She also was the only one who became an overt homosexual adult.

In all of the patients the prepuberty trauma was induced

by the child, generally quite clearly under the stimulus of observations of an adolescent or of an older woman, in one instance a sister, in another a mother. Although the traumatic situation was precipitated by the child under the influence of curiosity and seeming preparation for puberty, it represented in each instance a repetition and condensation of one or many pre-oedipal experiences which in a sense the child already knew to be disturbing. While this compulsive repetition may have contained an effort at reality testing, yet the highly defensive value of these traumata, their value as real evidences of the dangers of sexuality (even when, as in the instance cited, the actual danger was not great) was indicated by the regularity with which these children told their mothers or other adults about these experiences and utilized them consistently as defences against sexuality, especially after puberty. That prepuberty is especially favourable for the provocation of such traumata follows the heightened curiosity and the thrust of activity which is physiologically determined by growth processes preceding sexual maturation. It is interesting that according to studies of normal growth and development there is an acceleration of the rate of growth in girls between the tenth and thirteenth years when a deceleration of rate occurs, and the gain in weight follows a similar course (3).

SUMMARY

While the prepuberty period is generally one of the more silent areas of analytic investigation, a particular group of cases is exceptional in the appearance in this period of fateful traumata which were part of the presenting picture of the neuroses when the patients came for treatment. These traumata were provoked by the victims, and were compulsive repetitions of pre-oedipal conflicts influencing the intensity of the oedipal phase and subsequent severity and deformation of the superego. These conclusions are drawn from the analyses of four patients.

The combination of the increased thrust of activity of the prepuberty years with increased sadomasochism derived from pregenital phases and a strong masculine identification during latency favours the occurrence of such traumata. There may, however, be a real element of fate as far as the child is concerned, which turns the significance of the experience one way or the other, depending upon the readiness to response of the person provoked or seduced to aggression. In all four cases the trauma involved experiences with adults : in three instances there were oedipal traumata, in one instance the re-enactment of a primal scene. The utilization of the trauma as a masochistic justification for a defence against sexuality was apparent and reinforced by its communication to others, and sometimes by its subsequent use for masochistic gratification. It is probable that the effect of the prepuberty trauma as a defence is dependent upon variable combinations of the degree of pre-oedipal sado-masochistic development combining with the severity of the later trauma, which is not wholly dependent upon the child herself. Traumata of an oedipal pattern are also more utilizable for defence than those occurring with other children, since the guilt can be the more readily shifted to the adult, and the child's own instigation of the trauma, together with the earlier events which have produced the pressure of provocation, more readily concealed.

## CHAPTER XI

# GENERAL PROBLEMS OF ACTING OUT*

NOT very much has been written about the problems of acting out in the course of analysis, although they are most difficult to deal with, frequently interfere with analysis, and sometimes escape detection unless and until they become flagrant. Perhaps the earliest extensive discussion of acting out appeared in Freud's *Psychopathology of Everyday Life* (1901) under the headings, 'Erroneously Carried-out Actions,' and 'Symptomatic and Chance Actions' (1). Particularly the latter chapter included some illustrations of what was later called acting out. At that time, however, such actions were generally considered from the angle of what other elements in the current situation were being displaced onto and concealed by them, and less emphasis was laid on their significance in relation to the earlier history of the patient. Perhaps the most systematic description of acting out has been presented by Fenichel (2), who defined it tentatively as '. . . an acting which unconsciously relieves inner tension and brings partial discharge to ward off impulses (no matter whether these impulses express directly instinctual demands or are reactions to original instinctual demands, *e.g.*, guilt feelings) ; the present situation, somehow associatively connected with the repressed content, is used as an occasion for the discharge of repressed energies ; the cathexis is displaced from the repressed memories to the present derivative, and the displacement makes this discharge possible.' Fenichel notes that this definition does not adequately differentiate acting out from neurotic activity, and emphasizes that in the former the quality of *action* is in itself especially conspicuous and important, and that it is generally a fairly organized activity, not merely a single movement, gesture, or mimicked expression. He further differentiates that by displacement and by rationalization it is generally ego-syntonic, and that

* Reprinted from *The Psychoanalytic Quarterly*, Vol. XIX, No. 4, October, 1950.

it '. . . shares with transference an insufficient differentiation between the past and the present, an unwillingness to learn, a readiness to substitute rigid reactive patterns for adequate responses to actual stimuli.' Acting out, in other words, is a special form of remembering, in which the old memory is re-enacted in a more or less organized and often only slightly disguised form. It is not a clearly conscious visual or verbal recollection, nor is there any awareness that the special activity is motivated by memory. His behaviour seems to the subject to be plausible and appropriate, although to the analyst and to the patient's friends his actions appear to be singularly disproportionate and inappropriate.

It would seem that in acting out there may be special problems in accepting and understanding current reality either because of (a) specific problems in the immediate real situation; (b) special persistence of memories of earlier disturbing experiences; or (c) an inadequate sense of reality. These also apply to the development of many symptoms and attitudes, but in the case of acting out there is a compulsion to reproduce repetitively a total experience or episode rather than to select some small part of it as a token representation. It may be translated into new terms or forms, but the experience in memory retains its original organization to an appreciable degree.

Fenichel notes the quality of motility or action[1] which pervades all acting out, as the very term states. He speaks of '. . . an allopsychic readiness—perhaps constitutional—to act . . .'' as being one of the contributing factors, discusses the fact that being in analysis favours and utilizes acting out in the transference, and that the analytic process itself may somewhat stimulate acting out in predisposed individuals, in that it educates the patient to produce less and less distorted derivatives of his repressed impulses, while it mobilizes and provokes all repressed impulses. For these reasons acting out is relatively more frequent in persons who are undergoing analysis. It is to be particularly guarded against when it occurs outside of the transference because it interferes with the analysis by discharging tensions in an unanalysable way, and because it may

---

[1] The term 'acting' is used by Anna Freud in *The Ego and the Mechanisms of Defense* (Chapter II) in the sense in which 'acting out' is used here.

create reality problems in the patient's life of far-reaching and detrimental import. It may be useful, however, to differentiate between neurotic behaviour and neurotic acting out. Doubtless these two are related, but acting out implies organized activity which is generally based on a tendency to action, especially in those patients who show numerous instances of acting out during analysis.

In dealing further with the subject of acting out, this discussion is limited to considerations of first, its genesis, and second, suggestions as to technique. It will be necessary to limit the discussion pretty much to habitual neurotic acting out in contrast to psychotic acting out in which the unconscious memories and attitudes take over the current situation so completely that the stimuli of the latter may be scarcely discernible. We would also differentiate isolated, occasional, or really symptomatic acting out during the course of analysis from those conditions in which the acting out is frequent, habitual, or characteristic of tendencies evident in the entire life of the patient. It is obvious that the impulsiveness is based on an inability to tolerate frustration, a special disturbance of reality and of self-criticism, the quality of marked motility or activity often of a dramatic character—all especially characteristic of the extremely severe neuroses, which sometimes appear perilously close to psychoses and the psychopathies.

In the *genesis* of habitual acting out, Fenichel mentions oral fixation with its high narcissistic need and intolerance of frustrations, the heightened constitutional motility, the presence of severe early traumata (producing a repetitive, abreactive acting out similar to the traumatic neuroses) as being factors producing tendencies to action and therefore contributing to acting out. While all of these factors seem to me of undoubted importance, I would add two more: a special emphasis on visual sensitization producing a bent for dramatization (derivatives of exhibitionism and scoptophilia), and a largely unconscious belief in the magic of action. The need for dramatization may be one of the factors which is most influential in turning tendencies to neurotic action into acting out, in that it predisposes to retention of the episode in memory as a scene or an organized memory rather than to the selection of parts of it for repetition. Such people often believe that to do a thing in a dramatic or imitative way—to make it look as though it were true—is really the equivalent of making it true. It is obvious that this works also to ward off with magic activity as well as to produce by imitative approximation.

It may be, however, that the common genetic situation which combines with or sometimes partly produces these character-istics, and the accompanying general tendency to act out, con-sists in a distortion in the relation of action to speech and verbalized thought, arising most often from severe disturbances in the second year and showing its effects in the following months as well. Repeated clinical observations of patients who habitually acted out first led me to consider these relationships of speech and action: (a) Even when the action involved in acting out includes speech, the latter is usually secondary to the action which is the more important function. Sometimes the speech itself seems, through its own motor qualities of pitch and intensity, to participate in the motor discharge of tension rather than through establishment of communication or any distilla-tion of the situation into thought. (b) In many patients who frequently act out in the analytic situation, such periods are characterized by an extraordinary large number of distortions of language—slips, malapropisms, spoonerisms, and pseudo-aphasias, and even a heightened tendency to punning and klang associations. In one patient in whom I was able to work out the origin of this disturbance rather clearly, the acting out in the analytic situation was often associated with a silly-sounding preoccupation with proper names, in various klang combinations, for all the world like the sound-mouthing ex-plorations of a two- to three-year-old child. This had originally been used by the patient to ward off grief and anxiety at the age of four when she lost through death from lockjaw an older male cousin. She had turned to him with a displaced oedipal attach-ment after feeling deserted by both parents subsequent to the birth of a younger brother. Even earlier this child had frequently been taken by her nurse on daily walks to the nurse's home, and had been the passive witness of sexual scenes. She was warned not to tell, and gained much praise from the nurse for

keeping the secret. A precocious and attractive child, predisposed anyway to an excess of adulation, she spoke early, well
and clearly; but under the pressure of keeping the secret, she
developed a special tendency to amusing prattle in which
she made shrewd remarks, doubtless 'half-revealing and all-
concealing' her secret. It seems probable that in this situation
the child, who was thus already neurotically disturbed, incorporated her infantile concept of the disease, lockjaw, into her
repetitive mouthing of variations of the cousin's name with such
a cute effect that her 'mourning' by identification became an
attractive joke, and the cornerstone of a disturbance of character development. She became a great practical joker, punner,
and 'gag' producer throughout her life, and both talked and
acted in order to avoid feeling.

The various types of association of word sounds, their relation to the period in which identity is established (with a
separation of the self from the outer world, and an acceptance
of the existence of two sexes), as well as their connection with
names, and natural functional sounds is beautifully apparent
in a book for children, *The World Is Round*, by Gertrude Stein.
Examination of the psychogenesis of development proves that
this is certainly a period in which speech and other motor
functions, especially those of locomotion and of imitative action
may become subject to special complex involvements. It is my
impression that the motility of acting out comes more from
these than from inherently constitutional sources, at least in
the sense of the congenital constitution. This is a period when
both speech and walking are begun and are gradually being
mastered. The orality of which Fenichel speaks is certainly
important and has generally already been determined either by
constitution or by the vicissitudes of the individual infant experience. It is certainly true that the orally frustrated child expresses
its distress through heightened diffuse motility, and that oral
frustration or special forms of indulgence may produce a general
inability to tolerate other frustrations. It is also true that the
persistence of oral demands may be but the most conspicuous
focus of a general state of emotional tension during the first
months of life, and that this is a source from which heightened
disturbances at any later time occur. The special character of

any early oral trauma may further play into delay, distortion, or diversion of speech functioning.

During the second year of infancy, however, when mastery of speech and of the special motility of walking is being accomplished, sphincter control is also in process of establishment. Not infrequently speech and mouth movements become combined with or influenced by the expulsive sphincter movements of bladder and bowl, and the character of the speech is clearly marked with imprints derived from other body ejecta. General motor behaviour, too, is influenced, but not so often involved in an inhibitory way, by the struggle for mastery of the body excretory processes. Activity seems rather to be increased by the effort to control the excreta, and the first communications in regard to these are generally in terms of gestures or infantile, often onomatopoeic, terms which may persist strikingly well into adulthood.

It has seemed to me, then, that in those patients who tend chronically to act out (a) there was often more or less emotional disturbance in the early months of infancy with increased orality, diminished tolerance for frustration, and a heightened narcissism; (b) speech was inhibited, delayed, or otherwise disturbed in development relatively more than motor discharge which might progress well into walking, and in any event take over the burden of the increasing need for communication because of the greater tensions and pressures of the period of toilet training. It is, however, the disturbance of the function of speech, rather than merely of the form, which is important. In some instances the child learns to articulate very well, but the speech becomes degraded in its functioning, being used for exhibitionistic purposes rather than for communication. This emphasis on the cuteness of the speech with subsequent diminishing of its utility value may occur about equally in children with unclear speech and those with precociously clear verbalization, sometimes based on their amusing imitations of elders. In either event, speech functioning is exploited or even largely diverted into services other than those of communication. In other instances in which any slight uncertainty of speech was derided, an inhibition of speech and an almost complete dependence on action may occur.

Under either set of circumstances, there is an inevitable

increase in rapport by looking. Dr. Anna Katan has verified (unpublished communication) the importance of repeated primal scene experiences in influencing acting out. In her experience, the child who is repeatedly subjected to primal scenes may undergo heightened visual erotization through participation by looking, but not infrequently by its crying excites the anger of the one or the other parent and so is drawn into active participation. This may, if repeated, definitely increase both the scoptophilic-exhibitionistic elements of the character and the preverbal acting into the situation which later contributes to acting out.

Anyone who works much with severe neurotics becomes aware how much their communication is in terms of body language—whether of involuntary body tensions, gestures, transitory somatic changes, as well as acting out. All of these forms of communication, even when they appear within the analytic situation, are peculiarly difficult to analyse and may be obstacles to analysis, probably because they essentially belong to a preverbal form of thinking and represent an actual earlier difficulty in making this transition in the life of the child. The capacity to verbalize and to think in verbal terms seems to represent an enormous advance not only in the economy of communication, but also in a focusing of the emotions which are associated with the content of thought. This, I believe, is a very important consideration in understanding the problems of acting out.

While it seems that this disproportion between verbalization and motor activity is characteristic of most habitual acting out, it is apparent that its importance must vary greatly with the degree and type of acting out. It is always determined in considerable measure by the pressure of the specific content of the individual piece of acting out, which will then be reproduced repeatedly as it is elicited by current stimuli, as though to ward off danger 'by doing it first,' or to repeat the past event as though 'to see it again' and prove it to be less noxious, very much after the fashion of the stages in the development of a sense of reality. Indeed, an incompletely developed sense of reality has appeared characteristic of many of these patients. But chronic or habitual acting out is a repetition of past events and an establishing of transference relationships with too great a burden, from the second year of life. Both are lived out and presented without the sufficient emotional equipment or the methods of communication that belong to later development. This symptom complex is intensified when, in addition, a weak and narcissistic ego persists due to other causes. In most instances this very narcissistic weakness of the ego, with its accompanying over-dependence on dramatic activity rather than on work-directed activity as a means of expression, is associated further with tendencies to exaggerated and somewhat detached fantasies which, in turn, impair the sense of reality or at the very least jade the perception of reality.

In one of his early papers on technique (3), Freud discussed the subject of acting out, in accordance with the technical developments of that period (1914), and advised against encouraging it : 'Allowing "repetition" during analytic treatment, which is the latest form of technique, constitutes a conjuring into existence of a piece of real life, and can therefore not always be harmless and indifferent in its effect on all cases. The whole question of "exacerbation of symptoms during treatment," so often unavoidable, is linked up with this. . . . [For the physician] recollection in the old style, reproduction in the mind, remains the goal of his endeavours. . . . He sets about a perpetual struggle with the patient to keep all the impulses which he would like to carry into action within the boundaries of his mind, and when it is possible to divert into the work of recollection any impulse which the patient wants to discharge in action, he celebrates it as a special triumph for the analysis.'

Anna Freud (4), much later (1936), summarized the increased knowledge to the analyst of the analysand's ego reactions obtained from observations of acting out, but stated that this is peculiarly little usable for therapy, as in the very process '. . . the ego continues to function freely or if it makes common cause with the id and simply carries out its behests, there is little opportunity for endopsychical displacements and the bringing to bear of influence from without.' It seems probable that in these relationships lie the reasons for the therapeutic limitations of such methods as group analysis and the psycho-drama, no matter how much they may relieve immediate strains and tensions. Anna Freud implies that habitual acting out cannot be analysed.

It would seem that the three techniques known for the management of acting out are interpretation, prohibition, and strengthening the ego (Fenichel). These are applicable in varying degrees according to the specific nature of the acting out, the structure of the ego, and whether the acting out occurs inside or outside the analytic situation. Beyond the general prohibition against making important decisions affecting the analysand's life during the course of the treatment, prohibition of acting out is not easy. Analysis would soon become little more than guidance among many prohibitions, provided the analyst were sufficiently astute to anticipate the exact nature of the dangers the patient would encounter; furthermore, since in its very nature acting out is ego-syntonic and the patient is not aware of its destructive nature, it comes to the attention of the analyst in most instances after its occurrence (if at all), and sometimes is not reported or only indirectly.

Interpretation would certainly seem to be the method of choice, but it is inevitably limited to those patients who have reasonably well-integrated egos and those in whom the acting out occurs only sporadically and in accordance with especially laden earlier traumata which are being revived in the course of the analysis. It is my experience, however, that too early interpretation of some of these traumata will reactivate accessory or related ones, and may set in motion a temporary tendency to act out in a patient who previously has not done so. It may then be as much a question of the timing as it is of the accuracy of the interpretation of the specific memory content, the conflictful childhood situation, which is the nucleus of the later disturbance.

Another kind of interpretation is necessary, however, to strengthen the ego and develop adequate self-criticism, which must precede or overlap analysis of id contents in patients who engage in widespread and diverse acting out apart from the analytic situation. Generally such patients reveal these tendencies in their lives before they come into analysis— whether in the frankly impulse-ridden behaviour which is apparent in the history, or in generalized restraint and inhibition which wall off and disguise the latent impulsiveness. Frequently in the latter cases, habitual acting out becomes apparent only after analysis is well advanced. This is especially true in patients who have suffered an infantile psychosis which has become encapsulated. Such patients must have extensive periods of analysis during which id contents are dealt with only as much as is absolutely necessary. Many such patients bring graphic and interesting dreams and seem to have a flair for understanding symbolism. Some interpretations may have to be given which may *seem* to be accepted but are utilized only for narcissistic gratification. It is the narcissism rather which needs most to be analysed. Patients may seduce unwary analysts into working too quickly with this deeper material at a time when it cannot be assimilated by the patient, which only increases anxiety and may even be used as justification for acting out in deeds or talk outside of the analytic situation. Such patients may tend to distort an interpretation into an authoritative direction, or take a dream as a portent.

In Chapter II, Part II (5), I made an attempt to describe my own methods of dealing with a group of patients many of whom showed this tendency to frequent acting out. Adding to the material of that study, the following points of special importance in habitual acting out, associated with poor ego structure, seem worth mentioning. It is usually important that the positive transference should be especially well established before any id content is interpreted even though it may have been presented before. In many cases, there seems little difficulty in gaining a positive transference, as affectively hungry patients will form an immediate but too demanding type of transference and readily sense and exploit a sympathetic countertransference. Other patients will exhibit a rather showy type of positive transference which is, however, shallow and quickly reveals itself as too susceptible to acting out both in the transference and outside. Both types of apparently quickly established positive transference need time for their solidification. Some of these patients certainly can never form a sufficiently firm transference to be analysed.

Interpretation of the patient's *narcissism* must be begun early and pursued patiently. Among other narcissistic phenomena, the inability to distinguish fantasy from reality goals, and tacit reliance on magic are outstanding. The latter reveals itself in a special picturesqueness of language and behaviour (to make it look as though it were true is to make it true), also in overplaying the significance of coincidence. Relatively soon it is possible to acquaint the patient directly with his overreadiness to act, and that this is one of his ways of warding off anxiety. This generally leads to his awareness of his basic state of tension and his susceptibility to anxiety which has been concealed by activity, spuriously rationalized as productive. It will become necessary at some time during the first months of the analysis for the patient to be acquainted directly with the evidences of his very early disturbances, manifest in his body language, symptomatic acts within the analytic stituation and in behaviour outside—not so much to understand at first the fully detailed significance of such behaviour, but rather that he is using this as a way of communication and that it is robbing him of the possibility of a fuller possession of his capacity for expression. While it may be necessary to use an intellectualized approach about just these problems, this is done in order to cultivate the patient's self-scrutiny and self-criticism. If this is accomplished, the patient will begin to make his own prohibitions and much of the battle with acting out will have been won. This is accomplished only at the expense of considerable pain because of the narcissistic wounds and reductions involved, but may be compensated by a definite feeling of growing competence which is appreciated by the patient himself. Only when this is well under way can the analysis of the id be developed to the fullest extent.

There is still the question of how fully the contents of the preverbal period, which have given rise to and are sometimes contained in the acting out, can be converted into verbal (thought or spoken) expressiveness, and so relieved. That the general manner of the patient's expressiveness may be changed from acting out to verbalization has been proved in my clinical experience. Some patients may always have to guard against tensions too great to be tolerable, never getting relief by working through the traumata of these earliest months to a degree

comparable to what may be attained for those whose patho-
genic conflicts have occurred in the period of verbalization.

One further consideration has suggested itself from the angle
of the analyst's reaction to the patient who acts out. Fenichel
mentions that some analysts provoke, enjoy, or encourage
dramatic acting out in their patients and overstress its possible
benefit as abreaction, rather than really analyse it. This seems
quite occasionally the problem of young and inexperienced
analysts, but may also occur among analysts who themselves
tend to act out, either directly or in an inhibited form, and to
enjoy this vicariously in their patients. This may be of greater
frequency and importance than one might at first think. It
occurs among analysts who display no overt acting out but who
react as some severely restrained adults who enjoy and tacitly
applaud the impulsive behaviour of their children who dare to
do what they themselves have not been permitted. This is seen
strikingly in the parental attitudes which form the background of many impulse-ridden psychopaths. An attitude of
overanxiety on the part of the analyst about the patient's
acting out is frequently sensed and reacted to by the patient,
who then unconsciously gratifies his sadism as well in the
acting out and gets a spurious sense of power and independence
through it. If the analyst behaves in either of these ways to any
appreciable degree, acting out will continue no matter how
much its specific content is interpreted.

A final question, which may only be posed, is the relation
of acting out to conversion hysteria. It is obvious that, symptomatically, acting out is very common in conversion hysteria.
This diagnosis is made much less frequently than it used to
be either because the neurosis actually does not appear so
often or because we now tend to see in it a set of much deeper
disturbances than we used to, and tend to group these cases
rather with the narcissistic neuroses. It is a subject worthy of
further study.

# SPECIAL PROBLEMS OF EARLY FEMALE SEXUAL DEVELOPMENT*

THE sexual development of women is complicated by the presence of two main zones of erotogenic pleasure—the clitoris and the vagina. The most generally accepted theory of development of sexuality in women, as stated by Freud is substantially as follows: the two sexes develop in much the same way until the onset of the phallic phase. At this time the girl behaves like a little boy in discovering the pleasurable sensations from her clitoris and associates its excitation with ideas of intercourse. At this stage the clitoris is the centre of the girls' masturbatory activity, the vagina remaining undiscovered to both sexes. It would thus seem that the children of both sexes are at this point little boys—the girl being the littler boy, considered from the angle of body sensations. With the change to a feminine orientation under the influence of the penis envy, the girl repudiates her mother and renounces clitoris masturbation, becomes more passive and turns to the father with the oedipal wish for a child, a state which may persist well into adult life or be only partially dissipated. Freud believed that the failure to make this feminine identification and the development of the masculinity complex in its place was largely due to constitutional factors: the possession of a greater degree of activity, such as is usually characteristic of the male. He believed further that there was, strictly speaking, no feminine libido, in so far as the female function was essentially passive from a teleological point of view and that Nature's aims (of reproduction) being possibly achieved through the aggressiveness of the male with little or no co-operation from the female, the masculine function is, from a teleological angle, more important and the female function correspondingly less differentiated (3). In his chapter on the psychology of women

* Reprinted from *The Psychoanalytic Study of the Child*, Vol. V. New York, International Universities Press, 1950.

in the *New Introductory Lectures on Psychoanalysis* (1933) from which I have summarily quoted, Freud left the mechanism by which transferral of erotic sensation to the vagina was accomplished pretty much undiscussed. That it might be anticipated by the wish for a child from the father, with a clearer idea of the child from within, and a clearer conception of intercouse seemed possible—only to be accomplished in many instances, if at all, by the actual experiences of intercourse is implied rather than expressed. That such a course of development occurs with relative frequency and that often no transferral of sensation to the vagina is accomplished is also the experience of all those who deal with the intimate problems of women. Freud considered that what he said about the psychology of women was incomplete and fragmentary. This chapter is based on the closing admonition of his chapter. 'If you want to know more about femininity, you must interrogate your own experience, or turn to the poets, or else wait until Science can give you more profound and more coherent information.' From all three sources, I would proceed.

The material of this chapter is drawn predominantly from cases of pathological sexual development and as such may be open to criticism as the basis of deductions regarding normal female sexual development. Only in a few instances has it been possible to supplement it by observations on girl babies and children, and from the experiments and observations of other investigators. It is necessary at the very outset to establish these limitations, and present the material as problems of female sexual development rather than attempting any consistent theory. It seems, however, that pathological conditions often are the source of much stimulation for deductions and observations regarding normal conditions, and it is hoped that this presentation of problems may serve ultimately therefore to extend our knowledge of the normal as well as of the disturbed sexuality of women.

As has been repeatedly indicated in previous chapters, it is my belief that genital stimulation may occur much earlier than the phallic stage, and that it occurs in situations of extreme or general stress to the organism where there is a diffuse surcharging of the neuromuscular equipment and a consequent utilization of all mechanisms of discharge. That such discharge tends to be mediated first through the organs whose functions have already matured is evident, but under conditions where relief in this way is insufficient it appears that there may be a diffusing into systems not yet quite matured, and a premature functioning which might conceivably then promote their anatomical and physiological maturing in the way indicated by Langworthy (13) in his investigations, if the strain is not too great. That such a forced premature functioning may occur and become established at a moderately stable but vulnerable level is quite apparent in the common experience of bowel and urinary training which is accomplished before the neuromuscular development has reached its optimum state.

In the investigation of the development of female sexuality the relation between two main erogenous zones, the clitoris and the vagina, must always be considered. It may be, however, that the progressive development does not always follow so regularly the sequence outlined already as we have thought. In this same chapter on the psychology of women (p. 161) Freud states, 'It is true, that here and there, reports have been made that tell us of early vaginal sensations as well; but it cannot be easy to discriminate between these and anal sensations or from sensations of the vaginal vestibule; in any case, they cannot play a very important role.' It is only with this last conclusion in regard to the importance of the observations that this chapter would wish to bring further evidence, *i.e.*, in regard to the question of the significance of such early sensations—and as a part of this problem, their peculiar relationship in time and in meaning whether in contrast to or in amalgamation with clitoral sensations.

The material here will be discussed under the following headings:

(A) Indications and conditions of early vaginal sensations; (B) Evidences and frequency of prephallic clitoral sensations; (C) Clitoral stimulation during the phallic phase; (D) Early situations in which a bipolarity between clitoris and vagina occurs; (E) Later sequelae of bipolarity between vagina and clitoris; (F) Conditions of vaginal dominance; (a) through special accentuation of vaginal stimulation; (b) through by-passing of clitoral stimulation and (c) through repression of clitoral sensations; (G) A special elaboration of the penis envy and castration complex in which the struggle is reflected on to the breast-testicles—'the Medea complex'; and, finally, (H) A review of the literature.

### INDICATIONS AND CONDITIONS OF EARLY VAGINAL SENSATIONS

For many years I have had the impression, based wholly on clinical observations, that vaginal sensation does not develop by any means uniformly secondarily to that of the clitoris, and certainly does not always await actual intercourse for its establishment, but may be concurrent with or even precede clitoral sensation. In deeply regressed psychotic women patients it is noted that autoerotic sensations are of a vaginal type in an unusually high proportion of patients. This was obvious to me during my years in psychiatric hospitals in the direct observation of masturbatory practices as well as in the bizarre hypochondriacal complaints and delusions of such patients. Thus the genital orgastic explosions complained of by some schizophrenics as annoyingly produced by others seem more often located in the vagina than in the clitoris, even in women who have been vaginally frigid in the prepsychotic conscious sexual lives. The automatic orgasm of latent psychotic patients or those in a state of prolonged panic is more often vaginal than clitoral. Here the orgasm occurs spontaneously without the manipulation or conscious fantasy, and literally overtakes and bewilders the patient who is sometimes unaware of what stimulus in the environment has set off the discharge. According to whatever clinical investigations I have been able to make, this particular type of vaginal orgasm seems to occur in patients who have suffered long, severe and early anxiety and who show other autoerotic discharges as well. I have thought that it occurred then as part of the revival of an intense polymorphous perverse period in which the incapacity of the weak infant to endure the overstimulation to which it was subjected caused a diffuse and disorganized general response with discharges through many channels, including the genitals even before genitalization had become a well-focused phase, as already mentioned.

Fitting in with this is the fact that such spontaneous vaginal orgasms rarely give adequate relief and are felt by the patient as being shallow, and not so sharp as the clitoral orgasm nor so full as the more regularly aroused vaginal response.

It has appeared, however, that there are also vaginal sensations derived from early rectal and anal stimulation—a fact clearly recognized by Freud, in the quotation already cited. It is to be remembered that in the girl the lower rectum and the vagina have actually been fused into a common opening, the cloaca, until relatively late in fetal life, and even at birth it may be that this differentiation is incomplete in the central nervous system localizations—in other words that the fetal central registration, or body image, weak as it probably is, may still persist. The fact that in many infants a stimulation of the mouth through feeding produces a readily observed lower bowel stimulation (which may in the girl communicate itself to the vagina as well) gives us an additional understanding factor in the mouth-vagina equation universally present in women. That this is not on an intellectual visually symbolic basis was amply evident to me in the analysis of several women patients. One patient, at a time when she suffered from a severe paroxysmal cough, awoke in a coughing fit to find herself in a simultaneous vaginal orgasm, associated with a dream which showed quite clearly the mouth with entrance to lungs and oesophagus equated with the genital groove with anal and vaginal openings, I have also recovered evidences of similar states in childhood in patients who had then suffered from severe whooping cough.

In some instances there is a special linking of the activity of the musculature of the vaginal introitus with anal sphincter activity and with the acts of suckling and swallowing. This seemed possibly the situation in the case of the patient with the audible vaginal tic, mentioned in Chapter II, Part II, 'Predisposition to Anxiety' (6). It may not be a mere figure of speech to refer to this condition as a kind of smacking of the vaginal lips associated with air swallowing. In cases where there has been much oral stimulation in infancy associated with strong anal sphincter arousal, or where this latter has been accentuated by early constipation and the use of enemas and suppositories, the vaginal introitus itself may become involved in the anal sphincter sensitization and vaginal sensations from this area become well marked and strong. Such rhythmic vaginal contractions, clearly felt as comparable to swallowing, are described occasionally by women patients and may be observed directly in the course of gynecological examinations. They are associated with subjectively felt erotic sensations in varying degrees, sometimes being quite detached. This specially strong sphincter responsiveness favours the development of vaginismus, which further promotes and is in turn determined by the development of severe castrating desires as part of the penis envy problem.

Just as oral stimulation may produce lower bowel (and vaginal) activity in the infant, so oral frustration may produce a special form of active response, evident in the erection of the male infant—in Halverson's experiments (7)—but not readily visible in the female infant. This may produce sufficient stimulation to set up a masturbation by thigh pressure and/or a vaginal discharge. It should be noted, however, that such a local response, even if not apparent grossly, would promote genital (and if I am correct, generally vaginal) sensation which would be registered somewhat in the central body image of the infant. Here again I must differ slightly from Freud's idea that children of both sexes know nothing of the vagina early. I am impressed in the course of analyses that in some female patients there has been some kind of vaginal awareness very early, hazy and unverified though it is. This may occur quite definitely even in patients who have not had extreme early stress. This has also been noted by a number of other analysts whose observations will be discussed later. Vaginal awareness is further increased in those female patients who in infancy have been subjected to repeated stimuli of the rectum and anus, and when this stimulation has occurred before the phallic phase, a strong oral-vaginal response occurs in reaction to primal scene observations.

## EVIDENCES AND FREQUENCY OF PREPHALLIC
## CLITORAL SENSATIONS

Clitoral sensations do occur in some children earlier than their regular appearance with the phallic phase, but, in my experience with analytic patients, are much less frequent than vaginal sensations. At first thought this might seem peculiar inasmuch as erections in the male infant occur quite frequently and are especially noted under conditions of stress. Further consideration and comparison of the anatomical relations in the two sexes presents a reasonable basis for the clinical observations. In the female the greater connection between the vagina and the rectum may mean that the vagina is readily stimulated by anal discharges and, since this mechanism matures earlier than that of the clitoris, the vagina thus regularly borrows stimulation earlier, and the clitoris would only receive such stimulus as could not be discharged at the earlier level. In the girl child, bladder distension seems to merge in sensation and stimulus with the rectum and vagina while irritability of the urethra may sometimes combine with clitoral sensations but more often with sensations from the vaginal introitus. The urethra is actually closer to the vaginal opening than to the clitoris. Examination of a sagittal section of the pelvis shows quite clearly how distension of the excretory organs, bladder or bowel, would produce mechanical pressure stimulation on the vagina more readily than on the clitoris, which is rather surprisingly isolated from the other organs. In the male, on the other hand, urinary functioning causes a direct stimulation to the penis, and since there is only the one organ of genital pleasure discharge, this alone can be available also for channelling diffusion responses from central stimulation.

In those patients in whom clear clitoral sensations seemed to have occurred in the prephallic phase, I have suspected and in some instances had definite evidence that there had been direct manipulation of the clitoris by the mother or nurse in repeated overanxious cleansing activities, in the effort 'to break up adhesions' around the clitoris—one form of the so-called female circumcision which used to be advised by doctors as a cure for or a prophylactic against masturbation, which it actually promoted. Since the clitoris is extremely variable in size and degree of exposure—although commonly it is fairly effectively embedded—these facts alone must influence the amount of casual stimulation to which it is subjected, and the latter vary accordingly much more than in the analogous stimulation of the penis.

## CLITORAL STIMULATION DURING THE PHALLIC PHASE

That the maturation of the clitoral sensitivity to stimulation in the phallic phase causes it to be the site of spontaneous masturbation in the girl is probably the usual but by no means the universal story, in this way differing somewhat from the boy where the constant inevitable stimulation of the penis by bedding and clothing and the permissiveness to handle the organ in urination cause a uniformity of response to the heightened sensitivity initiated by the phallic phase. In the girl, however, the masturbatory clitoral stimulation undoubtedly becomes fixated when the little girl at this particular time and under the influence of awareness of the pleasure of her organ, sees a contemporary boy either urinate or masturbate. The very focused quality of pleasure to the girl then becomes the occasion for intense jealousy of the boy and envy of his organ. This susceptibility to penis envy remains heightened, I believe, until and throughout the oedipal period because of the inevitable frustration in the wish for the child and the relatively recent phallic discovering in herself. Under the influence of the disappointment about this, the regression to the wish to have a larger pleasure organ is obviously easy and increases the masculinity complex. All this may be very much heightened if a younger brother is born at this time, in which case the girl's masculinity takes the form of a particularly heightened masculine maternity or of a frank identification with the masculine sex through the adoption of the illusory penis—the assumption that she has a penis which is not directly visible.

Thus the castration guilt so typical of the girl may be quite short-lived, and very quickly surmounted by the establishment of the illusory penis on the very basis of the clitoral awareness and the peculiar reinforcement of the penis envy under these special circumstances.

### EARLY SITUATIONS IN WHICH A BIPOLARITY BETWEEN CLITORIS AND VAGINA DEVELOP

Some degree of bisexual identification probably occurs in most girls at some time during the latency period, unless the girl remains almost exclusively under the domination of prolonged oedipal striving. However strong the masculine identification may be in conscious or unconscious fantasy, still there is a reality knowledge supported by body image from reality sensations which does not permit the girl to abandon completely her feminine identification (except in those rare and extreme states of psychotic development where fantasy takes over). Quite occasionally in the course of analysing women, however, symptoms may be encountered which have arisen from an unusual balancing of the masculine and feminine identifications with a continued localization of genital sensations in the clitoris and in the vagina, the two never being harmonized—resulting in a confusion which has affected the sense of reality, especially the sense of identity, and interfered with the thinking. This clearly may contribute to states of depersonalization. Such a marked degree of polarization of feeling between clitoris and vagina occurs, in my experience, when there has been (a) very early vaginal stimulation in any of the ways already mentioned followed by (b) a strong phallic phase, reinforced by observation of masturbation in a contemporaneous boy, this combination of affairs resulting in an especially strong penis envy and establishment of very intense fantasy of having a penis. It is noted from clinical study that situations of early anxiety which have contributed to the overflow of stimulation to produce an increase in vaginal reactivity, produce also an incomplete development of the sense of reality, with a prolongation of the tendency to primitive identification with others in the environment (in other words, an incomplete separation of the self from the environment) and an increase in the tendency to magic thinking and fantasy. These very concomitants of the predisposition to anxiety would tend, therefore, to strengthen the intensity of the illusory penis with its primary locus on the clitoris if exposure to comparison with a boy has occurred during the stage of clitoral masturbation, to circumvent castration guilt. The displacement of the illusory penis to the 'inside' certainly occurs in many girl children, utilizing the vaginal and upper rectal sensations. But under other conditions, especially if reality exposure to penis rivalry continues and clitoral masturbation is prolonged and is followed in the oedipal period by an especially poor resolution of the oedipal conflict with resultant identification with the father, the clitoral illusory penis persists with great intensity. It is also noted that if a strong oral-anal-vaginal stimulation has occurred before the phallic phase, the girl under the influence of the oedipal disappointment regresses not only to the clitoral pleasure, but in just those cases of the birth of younger brother at this time there is not only the increase of penis envy, but a further regressive tendency increased by the breast and oral envy from the sight of the baby nursing. Under these conditions an extreme polarity of oral-vaginal and phallic clitoral sensitivity may develop. Looked at from another angle, it might be said that both pressures are so great that there is a real conflict between the body image based on the actual experiences and the fantasy phallic image which has its nucleus of reality in the clitoral sensations.

## LATER SEQUELAE OF BIPOLARITY BETWEEN VAGINA AND CLITORIS

When both vagina and clitoris excitability have been established in an early, strong and mutually antagonistic way, the clitoris may be the site of a persistent and practically hallucinatory penis, and this is maintained generally throughout the latency period; *i.e.*, the masculinity complex is particularly strong and this element plays a part in the overwhelmingly severe reaction to puberty. Such girls are frequently unusually aggressive during the latency period and may participate actively in all sorts of investigations, sexual and otherwise, but at the same time carry on secret fantasies of great elaborateness concerning passive and masochistic activities. The condition of phallic hallucination involves not only a visual hallucinatory state but a combination of this with hallucinated tactile and tumescent sensations, derived not only from clitoral tumescence but especially from the over-plastic body responses and 'body suggestibility' of children whose first stage of ego development in infancy has been impaired. It does not preclude the girl hanging on to the father with an oral-vaginal babyish grasp which alternates with her phallic strivings. There is then actual conflict between the hallucinated phallic genital image and the actual body image arising from the endogenous vaginal sensations which may not be as sharp but have a longer history and the greater force of reality than the phallic ones.

This conflict between the two images of the genital self sometimes results in constant pendulum shifts from clitoral to vaginal orientation or may give rise to a state of unreality with the abandonment of the problem and a flight into thought of a characteristically vague and airy kind. This is most frequently seen in a well-developed form under the influence of further anxiety generated by the onset of puberty, especially the appearance of the menses. Such girls may then frankly 'founder on the rock of puberty' and break down, or retreat into unproductive intellectuality and philosophizing.

Sometimes, however, one zone is disowned or suppressed in favour of the other. Probably the clitoris wins out more often, partly by virtue of its special capacity for sharpness of sensation; the repression of vaginal awareness being furthered by the female castration problems at puberty, which have previously been repressed or successfully defended against in the infantile period, especially when associated with actual experiences causing a fear of pregnancy and childbirth. A strong (latent) homosexuality develops with particularly stubborn vaginal frigidity. These patients may present superficially the appearance of the beginning of a sexual development resembling the ordinary sequence described by Freud, but transferral of sensation to the vagina does not occur under the influence of real experience with intercourse.

## CONDITIONS OF VAGINAL DOMINANCE

The condition in which the vagina, whether in its upper segment or in its introitus, appears as the leading or practically the only source of genital pleasure to the girl comes about (a) through an accentuation of vaginal awareness not balanced by the development of a strong illusory penis; (b) through situations causing either a bypassing of interest in the clitoris or (c) the repression of clitoral interest and pleasures after its development.

The general conditions promoting premature awareness of the vagina, viz., conditions early in life, in the prephallic eras, which cause an overstimulation of the infant and the need for total discharge reactions have already been discussed. Such conditions, especially when combined with prolonged oral stimulation, with or without states of urinary or bowel retention but without marked anal sphincter stimulus—and especially in those infants in which there is not any definite synchronization of the responses in the entire gastrointestinal tract (5)— may promote a strong vaginal stimulation in the prephallic period. Stated in another way, the receptive-distensive elements of the early disturbance are increased but in the absence of strong anal sadism. This is presumably due not only to the special vicissitudes of the infantile life but to differences in body constitution, involving proportionately different peripheral muscle and visceral reactivities. If, on this basis, penis envy is especially delayed due to the girl child being totally surrounded by females as occasionally happens when all the siblings are girls, or for other reasons girls are in the dominant role in the environment, then the vagina may take over and remain the leading erotic zone. The late competition with boys which follows lacks the keen personal rivalry so apparent in girls who have had an earlier penis envy with strong castrative desires or with definite illusory penis formation. No true masculinity complex seems to develop, and the competition is either genuinely lacking or takes the form of a withdrawal from boys' activities and a singular disregard of them. Such girls may be somewhat competitive with other girls, but even there the competition is not characterized by the sharp pressure which so regularly occurs among girls, in whom it is derived essentially from an earlier penis envy. It is my belief, based, however, on a very limited experience with this type of woman, that other functions may become patterned after this essential genital one, and that such women may appear vague, lack force in social and intellectual pursuits, but are not necessarily unproductive. In the one case that I worked with most thoroughly, there was a kind of withdrawnness which was not primarily a reactive introversion, but which gave a superficial impression of a princess complex, though without haughtiness.

In this case there had been a practical ignoring of the clitoris, probably due in part to its being small and deeply embedded, as well as to other conditions which did not induce its being especially favoured, as it was discovered by the child under humiliating circumstances when she was not yet at the phallic stage. Clitoral interest was then inhibited, and this became chronic—promoted by the actual anatomical smallness and protection of the organ. It should be noted, however, that clitoral sensation was not repressed, *i.e.* there was no clitoral frigidity, only its participation in erotic pleasure was never demanded.

It is conceivable that there may be a real failure of development of clitoral sensation due to a bypassing of the organ and a failure of stimulation. Such a case has, however, never come under my observation and it seems more probable that there is regularly some degree of clitoral sensitivity which develops by the spontaneous maturation of the phallic phase, and that this subsequently meets with repression. In those patients who presented a history of no clitoral sensations, deeper psychoanalytic investigation generally revealed that there had actually been a very intense clitoral phallic phase, which had occurred simultaneously with exposure to penis envy together with open threats from parents or nurses who observed the girl's clitoral masturbation. The latter may be so completely repressed that the clitoris remains frigid thereafter and is eliminated as the site of phallic strivings, the girl then either develops an especially severe castration complex with resultant masochism, or reallocates the phallic desire to other parts of the body determined by special narcissistic and/or erotized foci, of which the vagina may be one. In such cases vaginal dominance takes, over, the penis envy struggle sometimes resulting in a complete frigidity.

## THE MEDEA COMPLEX[1]

There is a form of deformation in the sexual development of some women in which there may be an exaggerated semblance of femininity coupled with great narcissism and a desire for extreme revenge when the woman loses her mate through death, or especially if she suffers rejection at his hands. The analytic experience I have had with this type of woman leads me to believe that there is a rather special constellation of breast and penis envy with the severest form of castration complex, reflected in a breast-testicle comparison which allows the girl a specious expectation of superiority after puberty.

The basic situation which seems to favour this is the birth of a younger sibling before the fifteenth to sixteenth month, that is in the preverbal era. The envy and jealousy of the baby, especially the baby at the breast, is felt by the little girl with an extreme oral intensity, and possibly can be compared to the terrible jealousy evident in some animal pets when a baby is born. If the baby is a boy or if a boy sibling is born within the next two to three years this original oral and visual envy is augmented by or converted into penis envy at the third to fifth year. The castration complex is extremely severe and the child may retreat to an oral craving for the mother or have especially pronounced oral components in the attitude toward the father. The primitive sense of deprivation and of being an outcast is very tenacious and forms a more than ordinary basis for the

[1] According to the Greek myth Medea was a resourceful woman who helped Jason to seize the golden fleece by giving the dragon knock-out drops. She had fallen in love with Jason and quickly eloped with him, delaying her father in his pursuit by slaying her younger brother and depositing his bones where the father would find them and be distracted by his grief. Returning thus with Jason to the court of Pelleas, his usurping uncle, she bore Jason two sons and succeeded in poisoning Pelleas. Jason, still unable to seize power for himself, fled with his wife and two sons to Corinth. The tragedy of Euripides begins with the period in Corinth. Jason, the weak and boastful husband, resented his guilty indebtedness to his wife. He decided to marry the Corinthian princess, excusing this on the basis that this marriage would consolidate his position at Corinth and he could then pass on the protection to Medea and the children. Medea's possessive and single-minded love for Jason turned to hate and revenge. She poisoned the Corinthian king and princess with poisoned gifts; and completed her revenge on Jason by killing the two sons who were dear to him.

typical feminine guilt feelings of the developing castration complex. The image of the breast seems especially strong back of that of the penis, and the compensation 'I will have better and bigger ones when I grow up' may finally be achieved in the post-oedipal period of superego building.

Such children often clearly eliminate or disregard the penis and fixate rather on the testicles, while the breast is exalted over *any* male genitals. They delay any adequate solution of the oedipal disappointment or the penis envy problem until puberty. Until then they feel deprived but hopeful. One patient of this type told me of an early memory from the fifth- to sixth-year period when the chauffeur's son had 'shown her his testicles.' When I asked what had happened to his penis she at first said she simply could not remember his having had one, and then quickly brought another memory of another boy, also considered inferior but socially of her class, who in school stood in front of the blackboard beside her 'holding his penis in his hand, because he was probably ashamed of it.' What a neat way of dealing with her envy of the boy's masturbation!

The oral visual incorporative drives toward the male genitals are especially strong where several younger siblings are born in the patient's early childhood—sometimes with a phase of hope of growing male genitals in this way, the hope being apparently abandoned but actually sustained in the reinstated idea of the breast as already mentioned. A considerable intensity of various drives may permeate the latency period, but become consolidated at or just before puberty, in the expectation of breast development, under impact again with the castration complex and the onset of menstruation.

Such women are extremely fastidious in their dress and body form. There is a somewhat specious femininity, however, both male and female genitals being represented in the breast. These young women often have an appearance of maturity and may be very beautiful, but do not ever achieve a healthy integration and individuation. They are narcissistically lost without a man even for a brief time; but they often marry childlike or weak men. Their attitude toward their children conspicuously lacks tenderness. They may be very proud of them, are generally conscientious toward the children but not infrequently show a hostile type of anxious worrying. If the marriage is disrupted the attitude toward the children may be uncovered in all its rawness, from spiteful possessiveness to revengeful abandonment. The increase in tenderness and appreciation of the individuality of the child is lacking. In the sexual response such women show sometimes a vaginal response (probably based on the extreme orality, with or without clitoral participation). It is possible they may be frigid, depending on other vicissitudes of development.

### REVIEW OF THE LITERATURE

One is impressed with the general awareness of complexity of the subject of female sexuality in the minds of most writers, and with the relatively few theories advanced, together with the large number of clinical reports indicating variations from or exceptions to the recognized theories. I have, in this chapter, added to this impression of complexity and variability in sexual development in women. I do not feel sure, by any means, of the frequency of the occurrence of the different types of feminine sexual organization which I have presented in this chapter in the development of the more ordinary neuroses of women, having to recognize that my own practice has included a rather disproportionately large number of cases of severe neuroses and latent psychoses and that my earlier psychiatric experience of nearly fifteen years was predominantly with psychotic patients.

I shall make no attempt to make a systematic review of *all* of the literature or to present the historical development of different points of view regarding female sexual development, but attempt to stress rather that which has special pertinence to the points which I have raised in this chapter, viz. (a) the possible early vague awareness of the vagina, which however is not subjectively adequately differentiated from the rectum; (b) the influence on vaginal awareness and reactivity by states of oral stimulation or frustration (which may be registered at the lower end of the gastrointestinal tract as well), by direct stimulation of the rectum and anus, and by a surcharging of the organism by massive stimulations greater than can be cared for through appropriate channels of discharge, so that immature discharge mechanisms may be prematurely stimulated. As a corollary to this, there is the implication that there may be distortions of the regular sequence of pre-oedipal development, or in the extreme, different types of pre-oedipal organization. This leads to (c) the consideration that clitoris and vagina may have varying relationships to each other, with a patterning which has a far-reaching influence on the sexual response of the woman and a deep, sometimes decisive effect on her character and even sometimes on her intellectual functioning.

I am inclined to question whether these differences in organization may not be the bases of some of the opposing points of view expressed by theorists, where the observations of some one type of organization may have been quite impressive and diverting and yet not really worthy of a complete controversion of the basic theory.

Freud's basic theory regarding female sexual development as stated in his *New Introductory Lectures* (1932) has been summarized at the beginning of the chapter. In his paper the previous year (4) he gave a somewhat more explicit account and raised more clear-cut questions on which my own presentation has bearing. In this paper he was greatly concerned with the pre-oedipal developments in the girl, emphasizing that the early attachment to the mother both in intensity and form lent much to the subsequent oedipal attachment to the father, that this attachment to the mother did not terminate as early or as decisively as had been thought, but continued on into the phallic phase when it might be found as part of the girl's phallic strivings toward the mother—and that in some cases was never relinquished, the woman treating her husband as she had previously felt toward her mother (rather than her father). While he commented here as in other papers on the number of investigators who believed little girls did have early vaginal sensations, yet he seemed rather to dismiss this again and stated categorically that 'we may justly assume that for many years the vagina is virtually non-existent and possibly remains without sensation until puberty.' Again in the same paper, however, he commented on his own difficulty in exploring adequately the early development of female patients because (with him) such patients 'have been able to cling on to that father attachment

in which they took refuge from the early phase' and he believed
that women analysts were 'better able to apprehend the facts
with greater ease and clearness because they had the advantage
of being suitable mother-substitutes in the transference-situa-
tion with patients whom they were studying.' In a paragraph
in which he discussed the girl's phallic wishes toward the mother
and the way in which children react with passionate rage toward the giving of an enema by the mother and then reverse
the proceeding with the wish to attack her, he stated that he
had understood their peculiarly passionate fury when Dr. Ruth
Brunswick had interpreted this as comparable to the orgasm
following genital excitation; and that the accompanying anxiety
should be construed as a transformation of the desire for aggression stirred up, 'and that on the anal sadistic level the intense
passive excitation of the intestinal zone evokes an outbreak of
desire for aggression, manifesting itself either directly in the
form of rage or, as a consequence of suppression, as anxiety.'

It has seemed to me, although I am by no means completely
sure of the situation, that in these severe enema situations of
early childhood the reaction is even more complex, dependent
on the amount of actual pain involved and on the attitude of
the mother, and that the fury represents indeed a phallic attack
sometimes associated with clitoris stimulation, but consists
much more in the excitement which cannot attain full orgasm
—it leaves the child exhausted rather than relaxed. One en-
counters this, I believe, even more intensely in boys than in
girls. In girls, as I have previously indicated, it seems that the
clitoral stimulation is associated most with the extreme sphincter
stimulation, whereas the rectal stimulation itself may cause a
reaction in the vagina which reaches an orgastic-like climax
and relief with the discharge of the bowel contents. In such
situations both vagina and clitoris may be stimulated and do
not act in harmony. Certainly the situation is by no means
entirely simple or clear, and deserves further study.

It is noteworthy that a number of analysts, Lampl de Groot
(12), Jacobson (9), Sachs (16), Müller-Braunschweig (14),
Payne (15), Brierley (1), have all noted the primary appearance
of vaginal sensations, but this has been studied largely as part of
a situation involving castration anxiety and beginning superego

formation, earlier in the girl than in the boy. Freud's own comment concerning Melanie Klein's (11) displacement backwards of the oedipus complex to the beginning of the second year, and Fenichel's objection to it, is an extraordinarily valuable one. Although stating that Klein's deductions are not compatible with his own reconstructive findings in analysis and especially with his observations regarding the long duration of the girl's pre-oedipal attachment to the mother, still the apparent incompatibility might be softened by the realization that what is demanded rigidly by biological laws and what is subject to shifting under the influence of accidental experience is by no means easily distinguishable. It is exactly in the varying developmental speeds and combinations which may be promoted by accidental or forced premature functioning and/or by the linking of different body systems in stimulus and discharge situations that I believe there may be varying pre-oepidal configurations established, of particular import to the girl because of the two zones of genital reactivity.

The observations of Ernest Jones, expressed in his 'Early Development of Female Sexuality' (10), have considerable significance in regard to the content of my study.[1] At this early time (1927), Jones had already noted that in women with an extreme attachment to the father this had generally been preceded by an equally extreme fixation in regard to the mother, definitely connected with the oral stage. He indicated further that following the oral stage there tends to be a bifurcation into clitoris and fellatio directions—'with digital plucking at the clitoris and fellatio phantasies respectively: the proportion between the two naturally differing in different cases; and this may be expected to have fateful consequences for the later development.' He believed that in the normal heterosexual development the sadistic phase set in late, neither oral nor clitoral

---

[1] Jones' remark, 'There is a healthy suspicion growing that men analysts have been led to adopt an unduly phallo-centric view of the problems in question, the importance of the female organs being correspondingly underestimated. Women have on their side contributed to the general mystification by their secretive attitude towards their own genitals and by displaying a hardly disguised preference for interest in the male organ,' reminds us that anatomical structure promotes these attitudes: the man's organs are central and visible, whereas the woman's are mysteriously secreted.

stage receiving any strong sadistic cathexis, and that therefore the clitoris did not become associated with a particularly active masculine attitude, nor on the other hand was the oral sadistic fantasy of biting the penis at all highly developed, that rather in the normal heterosexual development, the oral attitude is largely a receptive sucking one and passes into the anal stage. The two alimentary orifices thus constitute the receptive female organ. According to Jones, ' *The anus is evidently identified with the vagina to begin with, and the differentiation of the two is an extremely obscure process, more so perhaps than any other in female development.* I surmise, however, that *it takes place in part at an earlier age than is generally supposed.*'—'This mouth-anus-vagina represents an identification with the mother.'

Although I have found evidence of the degree of oral sadism described by Klein and Jones, occurring only in adults and exceptionally impaired infancy (mostly in latent psychotic individuals), the emphasis on the early oral-anal-vaginal anticipates very much the findings which I have described and believe to be relatively frequent. Ruth Brunswick in her paper on the pre-oedipal phase of libido development (2) called definite attention to vaginal sensitivity arising early, associated with anal stimulation, but considered it probably minor. Hendrick (8) reported a direct observation in which a three-year-old girl was obviously aware of pleasurable sensation from both clitoris and vagina, and in which the behaviour suggested an association of vagina with anus, yet a definite differentiation from it. It is possible that a careful scanning of the experience of pediatricians would bring much more evidence of this kind to light.

### CONCLUSION

The importance of the present study, incomplete and sketchy as it is, may lie in its indicating not only the probability of varying configurations in the bi-zonal female sexual development in the pre-oedipal phases rather than merely by the different degrees and routes of the resolution of the castration and the oedipal complexes, but especially in the further indications of the existence of different types of interorganization of the pre-oedipal phases in general, whether male or female.

## CHAPTER XIII

# RESPIRATORY INCORPORATION AND THE PHALLIC PHASE*

A LITTLE boy of four years played with a feather impris-oned between his cupped hands. He opened his hands, waited for the light summer breeze to take it away, joyfully recaptured it, and began the play over. Occasionally he helped Mother Nature by blowing on it himself. The child played in this way, teasing the feather into recurrent activity for several moments; then turning to his mother he said with comical infantile sagacity, 'Do you see what I've got here, mummy? It is a devil, and it is going way, way through the air and it's going into Midge's mouth and then she will be a devil!' Midge was his eight-months-old sister. This makes us think of the broken bits of glass which got into Kay's eyes in the Andersen fairy tale of the Snow Queen. This child was a wistful, pre-cocious little boy, who until the birth of his sister had been the sole focus of the love and attention of both parents, perhaps the more so in that they had to travel much and the endearing child was the pivot of all home activities to them. He was now distinctly at the phallic phase, interested in his organ, of which he was proud. When he drew pictures of people he put a small penis where the legs joined the head, even though he omitted the body. He had undoubtedly heard some talk of church, God, and the devil from his religious grandmother, and distinctly placed God in the airy medium of the sky. When someone re-marked that something smelled to high heaven, he asked in surprised tones, 'Do you mean God?' He was clearly fascinated by movement, and was constantly seeking explanations. 'Look at that!' he said to his father with intense curiosity, pointing to his own little penis in a state of partial erection when he arose in the morning, as though he had not seen it before. He watched the trees, the clouds, the flowers as they bent in the

* Reprinted from *The Psychoanalytic Study of the Child*, Vol. VI. New York, International Universities Press, 1951.

breeze. 'Are they alive? he would ask. 'What makes them move?' This had gone on for some months, and at the time of the feather incident he was well aware that an imperceptible force, the wind, God, or the devil, gave apparent life or movement and activity and took it away again. In his pretty feather fantasy he was certainly enacting his own hostile feelings toward the intruding Midge, feelings which he loosed, recaptured, reloosed, etc., before finally letting them gently forth to invade the unsuspecting Midge. At other times he blamed the wind for his own misdemeanours; when he knocked down a small table and its contents he offered the grave excuse. 'The wind blowed it.' It was clear that the wind was the spirit, the breath, the unseen force of life for good or evil, and on its way to taking a place in the constellation of the conscience. As might be expected, this same child was fascinated by his own voice, and the voices of others, especially by singing, and by the sounds and sensations of flatus. This last was clearly shown in the fact that, when he passed flatus, it was not always easy for him to tell whether he had begun to pass a bowel movement or whether this was only air. The flatus was, as it were, the ghost or spirit of the stool. It is quite possible that our little boy would have liked to blow his little sister away or back where she came from.

This reminds us of an old story about the late Chauncey Depew and the late Mr. William Howard Taft. Mr. Depew was a slender man and Mr. Taft a conspicuously obese one. Mr. Depew, when introducing Mr. Taft at a banquet, referred to Mr. Taft's wisdom and foresight in many matters, and concluded his remarks with the pleasantry of referring to Mr. Taft as 'the pregnant Mr. Taft,' whereupon Mr. Taft replied that he thanked Mr. Depew for his appreciation of his (Mr. Taft's) creativeness, and wished to say that if the child was a girl he would certainly name her for the revered Jane Addams, and if the baby turned out to be a boy he would name him for the honourable Theodore Roosevelt, but if, as he suspected, it turned out to be merely hot air, he would call it Chauncey Depew. The story may not be literally true, yet it is a good and valid one.

A clinical excerpt from the case of a severely sick patient

illustrated a pathological version of our little boy's experiences. On an extremely hot day in summer, some ten to eleven months after she had first consulted me, this young woman came into my office and quietly lay down on the couch, but before she could speak she burst into the most extreme sobbing. Shaking with terror, she pointed in the direction of a pedestal electric fan which was so placed that it would circulate air freely over the couch; she burst out, 'I don't know why, but I seem to feel you are insulting me, and I can't stand it.' Her terror was so intense that I turned the fan off at once and only said that since it bothered her so much there was no point in our using it, and that I only hoped that sometime we would learn why this fan had frightened and insulted her so. There were certain things in this young woman's history which naturally gave me some clues as to the source of her terror, but I was not to get the detailed story for many months, and only then pieced together through many bits of analytic work.

This patient had come to me in an acute state of panic late in September of the previous fall. Her disturbance was so severe that I had thought at first that she must be hospitalized, but as she had made an immediate clutching rapport with me and was a valuable woman still carrying on her work in spite of overwhelming symptoms, I decided to keep her and work with her as long as I felt her hold with me was sufficient to protect her from the intensity of her own pressures. The story at this time was briefly as follows: she had suffered marked anxiety without apparent cause in the summer and fall of the year before she consulted me. Her elderly parents had both suffered mishaps; the mother had had a very mild cerebral accident, with a brief facial palsy which had cleared up completely after a few days, and in August, just before I saw her, the father had cut his finger rather severely on an electric revolving saw while working in his basement shop. The patient had been at hand and had helped in both accidents, and had been shaken and anxious afterward. She was an overconscientious unmarried woman, a cautious rather than an aggressive spinster, docile, unable to bear any show of hostility in herself or others, and I naturally saw at once that her panic was due to the enormous aggression and castration guilt which was aroused in her; and she herself

very soon realized that the revolving blades of the fan had reminded her of the electric saw which had injured her father.
That the air played a part, however, I was sure, because of
certain symptoms; she was pathologically sensitive to the
slightest change in timbre of voice, was fantastically aware of
odours, and like a dog could often tell which of several patients
had preceded her in the room. Then there were certain elements in her history; she had had minor panics between the
anxieties accompanying the accidents to her parents and her
coming to me on the twenty-third of September; she had been
especially distressed over a labour organization which was increasing its membership in the offices where she worked, and
on Labour Day itself she had had a severe panic with depersonalization feelings while walking from her office downtown to the
Pennsylvania Railroad Station. The first time that she had
been seized with terror and unreality feeling was on noticing
the bridge of the Metropolitan Life Insurance Company, but
she had pulled herself together and continued uptown only to
have an intense recurrence when she saw the same sort of
bridge at Gimbels' store. She had seen both of these many
times before, but on this particular day they reduced her to a
state of terror. Her birthday was on the twenty-first of March,
and this, together with the fact that there had been, the year
previously, a panic late in September, and that now her culminating anxiety had reached its extreme at September 21–22, led
me to hypothesize that she made some cosmic identifications in
which the wind and air played a conspicuous part. More will
be said of this case later.

The thesis which I would present, to which the foregoing
clinical anecdotes are an introduction, is this: That the phallic
phase (especially when there has been an early overly strong
oral stage), existing as it does between and merging with the
anal and the genital (oedipal) phases, has certain characteristic
contributions to symptom formation and to the superego, which
is in process of crystallization; it is a period of autogenous
genital stimulation, and with or without masturbation—with
or without earlier marked awareness of-the genitals—it is characterized by a sense of inner power contributed by the inherent
positive genital sensations, a sense of genital life especially

exaggerated by its contrast with the profound oral-receptive or incorporative influences of the early months; an expansion of vitality without corresponding material, corporeal, visible change. The oedipal attachment already in process of formation gets a new element of positive aggressive pleasure. Whereas the earlier stages of libido development have been definitely attached to developing and concrete visible shifts in the dominance of body drives and their gratification and mastery, the phallic phase is characterized by an increment in body sensation and a sense of new force—a reinforcement of positive identity. This is not accompanied by any special mastery to be accomplished, but rather by a feeling of expansion and anticipation, in the sense of life.[1]

Because of its special relation to and overlapping with the anal phase, this period favours certain preoccupations with death as well as with life. The regular giving up of the stool, the acceptance of the consignment of a part of the body to a watery grave, leads inevitably to ideas of death. Especially is this contrasted to the stirring phallic impulses. Naturally the idea of death will be coloured by the child's actual encounter with it, but there is rather uniformly a need to distinguish between what is living and what is dead, whether on the basis of motion, growth, or the attitude of adults of interest or

[1] The story of the Snow Queen tells of these same forces in the following excerpt: After the grandmother had compared the snowflakes to white bees swarming, the children Kay and Gerda asked if there was a Snow Queen as well as a Queen Bee. 'Yes, indeed,' said the grandmother. 'She flies where the swarm is thickest. She is the biggest of them all, and she never remains on the ground. She always flies up again to the sky. Many a winter's night she flies through the streets, and then the ice freezes on the window panes into wonderful patterns like flowers.' . . . 'Can the Snow Queen come in here?' asked the little girl. 'Just let her come,' said the boy, 'and I will put her on the stove where she will melt.' . . . In the evening when little Kay was at home and half undressed, he crept onto the chair by the window and peeped out of the little hole. A few snowflakes were falling, and one of these, the biggest, remained on the edge of the window box. It grew bigger and bigger, till it became the figure of a woman dressed in finest white gauze, which appeared to be made of millions of starry flakes. . . .Still she was alive; her eyes shone like two bright stars and there was no rest or peace in them. She nodded to the window and waved her hand. The little boy was frightened and jumped down off his chair. Then he fancied that a big bird flew past the window. Two days later the thaw came, and after that the spring and flowers.

abandonment. The stool is dead, is killed, is relinquished. This, together with the force of the muscle control and the magic power (to offend) of the discarded feces adds to the lively phallic or clitoral stirrings and gives increased sense of power over life and death. Preoccupation with killing and being killed follows regularly, influenced, naturally, by whatever the child's own experience with death has been: Is it lack of movement? Is it that which lies quietly dead? Is it bloodiness, violence, mangling?

Time and space have become appreciable factors in experience. The child no longer moves by crawling or by merely horizontal walking, but jumps and skips and becomes aware of the birds that fly.

The sense of smell is still important. Contact through speech is well established and mediated through the air. Looking is through the air. Past events can be recalled, and there is a definite awareness of memory and of thought. The image is now important, as well as the direct experience. Thus, although the child may still eagerly confuse fact and fancy through the intensity of his wishes, still he does not generally do so. He has come to know the representation of the object when it is not there. He even becomes capable of simple lying, and regularly goes through some stage of infantile philosophizing, about the thing and its airy representation.

As part of the concern about what produces motion, and so what lives and what dies, the enigma of passive motion arises, and gradually the awareness of the breeze and of the wind, which is so closely related to the blowing out of the child's own breath. The secondary meanings of inspiration and of expiration are very significant. The air that is drawn in and makes one feel light, buoyant, and powerful is the inspiration; that which is thrown out to be abandoned, lost in all the other airs of the world—that is expiration. It is something like an airy representation of the stool. Especially at this time the child may become entranced with his own flatus. Here definitely is a ghostly representation of the object. From the body sensations alone, it may not be easy for the little one to detect the difference between the flatus and the stool, and he shows surprise and pleasure in passing flatus. At this time too there is quite regularly an interest in the motes to be seen in a sunbeam, in the casting of beams of light, and in the activity and change of shadows. It is not to be indicated that these interests are limited to this period; they have certainly existed in some degree back into the second year. But they have now a certain speculative and conceptual value to the child. Freed from the greatest intensity of concern with his own body excretory functions, he is ordinarily infatuated with the *mysteries* of his surroundings as well as their objective existence. To a certain extent this period picks up the positive and negative hallucinations of the first and second years—but cannot use this capacity so immediately, since time and space are now to be dealt with also. I believe, however, that many of the experiences of the first to the second year of life may receive a special further elaboration at this time; under ordinary conditions it is a kind of forestage for the formation of ideals, which will become so essential in the solution of the oedipal disappointment. Under unusual conditions this phase may contribute special attributes to the later character structure, with a special emphasis on the uncanny, the weird, the sense of telepathy, and the predilection to religiosity.

### CASE HISTORY

The patient whose concern with the breeze has already been mentioned has repaid me generously for long work with her through her contribution to my awareness and understanding of these problems. When I first knew her, she was thirty-five years old and in an acute panic. She felt, however, that she had probably never been very easy or relaxed since her childhood, perhaps never at all. Five years earlier she had been through a few months of depression, when, living away from home, she became lonely, felt she could not keep her apartment clean, and avoided having any guests. This state had followed the marriage of the young woman who had shared the apartment with her and the termination on her own part of a mild friendship with a young man. She felt she had rescued herself from her loneliness by becoming an air-raid warden, a job which brought enforced contact with others, especially strangers.

In the present era of disturbance the initial events, in addition to those mentioned, had had to do with the birth and care of babies. The mother's stroke had followed her going away to be present at the birth of the first child of the patient's brother, B., sixteen months younger than the patient. A few weeks later the patient got into an especially tense state over the plight of an unmarried mother who must place her baby for adoption. She suffered a panicky claustrophobia, felt periodically as though she were losing her senses; felt inefficient, then worked compulsively in what she called 'a spiral of intensity.' This culminated in her fainting while travelling in an airplane, attempting to work at the same time. On this trip she had also stopped to see her brother, D. (incidentally, an air pilot), who was five years older than she. She had not been really friendly toward him since childhood and had been inwardly hostile and critical when he married after a pre-marital affair during which his fiancée feared she was pregnant. Just before the acute anxiety which brought her for treatment she had been irritable, unforgiving and self-accusatory of her attitude toward this brother's oldest child, who had visited during the summer.

The first hours of her treatment were characterized by an extraordinary break-through of old memories. She could not say how deeply these had been repressed. Some she seemed to have 'completely forgotten,' others she 'just had not thought of for years.' She brought these out with great shame, rather as though she were in an intense struggle to get rid of stored-up disgusting things. These consisted of sexual interests and experiences conspicuously belonging to the oedipal and pubertal epochs of her life.

At four and a half there was a noteworthy event, when she had undressed with a little boy in the bushes near the church, and having stripped first, was quite nude when his mother suddenly appeared, grabbed her, and whisked her across the street before dressing her hurriedly and taking her home. She could not recall the end of this experience, only that the woman was rough and she recalled especially her long brown 'stiff' stockings and being humiliated that these were put on for her instead of her being allowed to do it herself. She also recalled being hot with frustration and shame, and that the coolness of the breeze on her skin had been soothing. The memory of this experience had never been completely banished. She remembered the humiliation as a continual warning to herself, probably in accord with the kind of superego which was already forming in her. (It appeared later in the analysis that this memory was retained also as a screen to another one concerning her older brother, which was tenaciously hidden.) Each year she congratulated herself on being farther away in time from this unholy episode. Only the intense bodily desire of the experience, later expressed in erotic exposure to air, and the equally intense curiosity concerning the boy's genital and excretory apparatus, represented in the brown stockings of the memory,[1] were missing and were re-enacted in fantasies and experiments with cousins during summer vacations of the latency years.

It is interesting that after the initial telling of this incident in the fourth hour of her analysis, and repeating it a day or two later, the patient did not mention it again until exactly nine months later. Then she developed a laryngitis with hoarseness, fever and general malaise. On her return to treatment after a short absence, she remarked that it was just nine months since she had begun treatment, commented that she felt changes in herself, a new hope and a sense of a new outlook on life. She then referred again to the incident with the little boy at four and one-half but followed it now with an account of masturbation fantasies derived from it, but now visualized as though she were the onlooker and not the main active character: a delicate young woman on a pirate ship whom the pirate captain would undress and attack, 'though of course she was willing.' Another fantasy would be of a woman nude and out-of-doors, wicked and licentious, attacked by a mythological creature like the Sun God.

Almost at the same time as the undressing experience, for she could never be sure which had occurred first, she had been sleeping in a twin bed in the room with her mother when

---

[1] As was shown later in the analysis, this was clearly also a representation of her earlier reactions to unusually severe toilet training when her stool was taken away, rather than, like the stockings, forcibly given back to her.

the father had entered. 'He gave me the impression of a strange being, an It. He got into bed with my mother. I heard some heavy breathing, and there was an atmosphere of struggle—then He or It got up and went away again. I did not brood over it, but it seemed strange, and all this took place without any words.' The It creature thus reappeared as the exalted mythological Sun God, and the two events were brought together. At thirteen, a few months before the onset of menstruation, she had a kind of love affair with her dog, fantasied about his being human and talking to her, and attempted mutual genital play with him. When he failed to co-operate she felt humiliated and disgraced, even in the sight of the dog. Later on in her twenties when she was very lonely she spent her last cent for a sheep dog, who seemed a combination of this puberty Airedale and her early blanket fetish.

The patient was unusually aware of the erotic nature of her early attachment to her father which had been transformed into extreme embarrassment at puberty. It was, in fact, her overconsciousness of this attachment and the peculiar extent of the expression of it that constituted some of the clearly pathological elements in her present state. Thus she would not touch her father's clothing, as 'that seemed too personal,' and was angry when as part of her household duties she had to handle his underwear, or even if the laundress hung his night clothes next to hers on the line. She knew in a quite clear yet inadequate way that this had a sexual meaning to her, but nonetheless there was something very close to a magic in the intercourse of the clothing, through the laundry, and her awareness of the sexual meaning of her phobias only reinforced rather than diminished their intensity; they took on a delusional force.

She was not nearly so aware of the nature of her reactions to her brothers or the intensity of her attachments to them. She had had a number of fantasy attachments to high school and college boys, obviously patterned after the brothers, but was unresponsive or frightened at a direct approach. A young minister held her attention for a time, and again a singer, whom she described as 'a young man of unusual presence, with a wild—no supernatural or ethereal, no I guess I mean strange and exotic—manner.'

This girl had a history of prolonged fetishism: an early hanging on to a blanket and putting her face into it was supplanted in the post-oedipal period by a fetishistic attachment to a stick or a stone. These were lucky pieces of great magic value, so that she had been definitely anxious if they were taken away from her; and especially she could not be persuaded to leave home without one. This fetishism lasted from five to nine, when it went into eclipse under a special airy wave of interest in the heavens, the sky, the stars, etc., but recurred again for a short time at fourteen, after the onset of menstruation. Then she especially carried stones to church with her.

This patient accepted no sexuality whatsoever when she gave her superego a say in her attitudes; yet she was in a continual and almost constant struggle with her erotic masturbatory, genital and pregenital impulses and drives, which she expressed seemingly in every part of her body and clothing, detached and depersonalized yet vivid, or projected in the transference. She spoke of her body impulses directly and precisely, using the dignity of exact language in the service of warding off emotion from the subject she was mentioning. Thus she spoke of her body parts as though they were detached and personalized acquaintances or children being greeted by their proper names.[1] In reporting masturbation she might say, 'My clitoris aroused me because it was awake and wanted to be rubbed,' or 'My hand felt that it wanted to touch,' etc. Similarly, in speaking of the incident of undressing at four and one-half, she always referred to 'my experience with Sylvester Ebenezer Wilson, Jr.' I had at first thought this a sly defensive humour, but soon realized that it was her way of encapsulating the experience with dignity, perhaps comparable to her clinging to the fetishistic stone.

The expression of bisexual interest was also strikingly apparent in her dress. At first she frequently wore, on alternate occasions, two hats which were identical except in colour.

---

[1] A few homely childish words crept into her vocabulary. The genitals had been called 'the bridge,' and the stools were called *getchens*, a corruption of *dejections*, the old English word used by her prim father.

They were brimless hats of 'pillbox' shape, but came to a slight point at the centre of the crown where there was a button as decoration. One was of a brown-beige and the other a grey-beige colour. These predominantly represented breasts, sometimes testicles; and individually, penises. (She dreamed frequently of pairs or twins, usually almost alike but not quite.) She frequently wore a kind of chiffon scarf, which quite clearly represented the foreskin or the labia in her fantasies. Sometimes her clothing representing body parts appeared, very slightly disguised, in her dreams, and she was continually having to make choices and renunciations.

The first dream, several days after the beginning of the analysis, was as follows:

I had a terrific need to get some relief. I got into a tub to use water. I had on some brown beads but just ripped them off and got in.

This dream initiated her telling me of her masturbation, which had occurred since puberty, by dripping water on her clitoris while bathing. It was not regarded as a problem, 'only as a fact;' she told also of her experience with the dog at thirteen, which she thought she had not recalled in the intervening twenty-two years. 'But it came back as soon as I began to talk.' She spoke of the incident with the little boy at four and a half (but this time did not mention the brown stockings), and she told of her depression at thirty when she felt utterly unable to keep her apartment clean. She spoke of having been bathed with her younger brother until seven or eight, of the difference between his genitals and her father's, her fear of subway exhibitionists, of a movie called the 'Ten Commandments,' seen at ten, which 'showed how to break them all, the Children of Israel looking lustful while waiting for Moses, and a man feeling a woman's breast.' Toward the end of this single hour she spoke of both her brothers, of a homosexual experience at twenty-two, and of her friendship with the male church singer, who offended her by bringing her flowers, but especially by his poor physique: 'He was short, homely, colourless, wore glasses, had a poor complexion, had an excellent tenor voice and drove a car upholstered in royal blue.' The almost explosive catharsis of this hour, with its atmosphere of voluptuous religiosity—probably sedately represented in the brown (Rosary-like) beads—was striking.

During the first year of her analysis she poured out quantities of dreams, mostly vivid, frequently in colour, and often quite stark in their open symbolism, which she understood in a kind of detached profitless way, and seemed under a compulsion to repeat. (I regarded this as representing her resentful submission against her very early, strict toilet training.) A few months after beginning treatment, she brought a dream, which anticipated the visit of her younger brother's wife and child:

I was in a second-story kitchen. At my left and in front were a beige-coloured hat or beret, gloves to match and a white scarf. I was supposed to choose either the scarf or the cap and gloves. Also still in the same place, someone suggested that I was entitled to have natural gas pumped into the kitchen as a facility. This privilege seemed to represent an indemnity that was owed me by someone like a Prince. But it wasn't clear what all that was to be used for— it really didn't seem a valuable or useful privilege.

The kitchen *was* a kitchen but without visible appurtenances of a kitchen; it reminded her of her brother D.'s third-floor apartment immediately after his marriage, the apartment in which his first child (whose troublesome visit had preceded her initial panic) had been born. On her visit there, her sister-in-law had remarked that the patient's father, although deaf, could hear when he wanted to; also she herself had overheard the sexual activity of her brother and sister-in-law, and this had reminded her of her parents at five. She did have a beige beret in high school and gloves to match, and her mother almost always wore beige gloves; but the white scarf belonged to the patient and to her alone—her mother had never worn anything like that at all.(In subsequent associations the white scarf was foreskin and wedding veil and external labia.) For the natural gas, she had an image of a pipe coming up like a drain pipe in reverse; the arrangement did not seem a good one for the natural gas, as the pipe did not make good connections at either end. The Prince suggested her older (disliked) brother D., and in some vague way she was sure he owed her a recompense for something he had done. It seemed perhaps the gas might come in a different form, but whoever was telling her about it never told in what other form it might be. Her older cousin had recently told her that in childhood she had idealized D., but it was hard for her to believe this, although she had tried to think of him and his wife as an ideal couple when they first married; and he still was trying to put up a smooth line of talk about himself. She thought all in all the natural gas was the hot air of talk.

It seems quite plain in this dream that her excitement at seeing the little daughter of the other brother aroused memories of the older brother, the handsome one, whom she had idealized and distrusted, and whose oldest son had annoyed her so in the weeks before her breakdown. The pumping of the natural gas, which is clearly the devaluated pretentious smooth talk (of the brother and probably of the analyst), represents the ambivalent hope of intercourse similar to what she had overheard with her parents and with this brother and his wife, as well as the reclaiming in gaseous form of the lost stool-penis. But the incident for which the brother owed her indemnity was, as we were to learn definitely late in the analysis, his flaunting his genitals before her in a teasing way early in their childhood, and even urinating and masturbating in her presence. It was clearly portrayed, however, in the dream of the following day, of which only a part is quoted:

D. and I were on a sailing ship. (She had actually travelled to Europe with her younger brother B.) We were talking about a girl who stood near the rail, and we talked about the way she had arrived at her marriage—I was on an upper bridge of a gunboat in the night. It was a dark blue night with stars. As it passed down the bay, the gunboat was shooting upward into the sky silently. A state of war was on; anything might happen. The gunboat was aimed at atom bombs and was trying to hit them while they were still in the sky.

But at this time she gave no associations, by-passing this part of the dream altogether.

A striking characteristic of this patient was the precision of her unconscious sense of time. Exactly a year later the patient brought the following dream:

TGP-I*

A raft of children came to see about buying our canoe. None of the adults knew what the price should be or what the original price had been. D. had something written on a scrap of paper—torn from a newspaper but with lines on it—giving his private accounts from long ago. It was square-shaped. He was facing me and holding it low, so I would not see it. Then he showed it to the adults—so they would know.

Next I was talking to Uncle Jack, and had in my hand a softish fish and banged him in the right eye with it. He was not offended and I was surprised at myself.

I discovered that I had a double. There had been an air warden's class that I should have attended but had not. Lillian insisted she had seen me there. I then realized that I had a double and felt like a smarty.

Here we can recognize at once the ship is reduced to the size of a canoe. The accounts still have to be straightened or 'squared' according to the dream. The paper appears in place of the sail of the earlier dream. (This appearance of the square or oblong form or paper appeared repeatedly in her dreams. Only much later did she bring associations of oblong sheets of paper with obscene drawings on them or dirty words. In one dream, where 'the edges of two oblongs came together,' she associated this with the fly of the trousers.) The upper bridge with the gunboat seems now represented by the question of the air raid. There is presented the whole idea of a lie or an illusion in the double, which here also includes the question of breasts rather than illusory penis. The patient brought the associations that they had indeed had a canoe in which she and two little girl cousins went paddling in childhood. The fish was like a dried or stuffed fish that her uncle had high on the wall of his camp, only now it had become soft and round like a big muffin. 'It hit Uncle Jack in the eye, as though it made him look at something. About D., it sounds like his hiding an exposure. I seemed to know so very definitely that I was not supposed to see it.' (I remarked that she made uncle see something—the muffin—while denying that she herself had seen the private accounts of D.) She then continued that her friend Lillian suggested me—she thought her voice had the same kind of intensity. Recently she had been very much troubled by varying intensity in my voice, sometimes it seemed compelling to her, like Lillian's saying she had seen her. She then went on to give an account of various trivial spying activities in my household, accomplished when she had gone to the bathroom in my apartment— thus verifying the theme of what she had seen. About the double she said only that as an air-raid warden she had been permitted to go around at night opening doors and turning lights on and off. When I remarked 'and looking,' she added quite serenely, 'It *would* be pleasant to have a double' (1). While the scoptophilic elements in the dream were those most emphasized by the patient and interpreted at this time, the illusory self, the misrepresentation through this; and the wish to establish superiority by having two (breasts) and hit the uncle in the eye the way D. had done with her is very clear. The main focus of the dream had referred to a prepuberty period (9 to 10 years) when she had spent the summer at Uncle Jack's with much surreptitious peeking at the boys, and open looking at each other's genitals by the three girl cousins. The devaluation of D.'s genital to a stool, hidden behind the square of the private accounts (possibly also representing toilet paper) and her aggression toward it are also obvious.

The next few days brought further amplifications of these themes, and then suddenly uncovered a whole period in the patient's life which she had never talked about in the analysis, although she was not conscious of deliberately withholding it. This was introduced through a dream about an analytic hour, in which through what I said to her she realized that I already knew about her elaborate fantasies of childhood. It was a characteristic way for her to divulge things, *i.e.*, with the sense that I had already almost read her thoughts; and indeed there were times in which this idea presented itself strongly to her almost as a conviction; at other times it seemed that her withholding was like a lie.

This was a period of disturbance which had caused her to be taken out of school and tutored at home between 9 and 13. What was divulged in her dream were fantasies she had indulged in that people carried on a battle of colours, engaged in armies of colours, that each army changed the other's colour by touching, like a game of tag, or by spray or by spilling or 'by anything else that might come off of them.' Also that I realized that this had begun in infancy when she and her younger brother, B., had been bathed consistently in the same tub and the spray had influenced them both, so that they were so close that they were really the same flesh and blood. So much for the introductory dream.

This period of illness could not be accepted as such in retrospect by the patient. After the informative dream, she told me only that she had been withdrawn from school because the redhaired teacher had punished the whole class of pupils by making them sit with their hands behind them, and that her parents took her out of school because they disapproved of this punishment. She did not believe that she had been nervous or upset by the punishment and saw nothing strange in the fact that she had remained at home on this account for nearly four years— she regarded it only as a statement of fact. There were other fantasies, too, which she now recalled, from the same period: one was an image of an enormous reptile which opened its mouth and another reptile was inside that and another inside that, etc., *ad infinitum*; a third was of a huge apartment house alive with people, the apartment house itself having a somewhat phallic body form (like the Russian dolls); a fourth was of being inspected, as she lay in bed, by bad creatures who came and hovered over her, waiting for an excuse for an attack, which could only be warded off by complete immobility.

On Hallowe'en of the same year she had gone into a panic at a children's party when, believing an evil spirit was in the hall, she insisted on having the light on, and the door open 'for ventilation.' On awakening in the morning, she thought she saw her mother materializing out of steam escaping from a radiator and taking the form of a witch. At other times she thought an It creature was lurking at the end of the hall. After each new admission she would repeat her fantasies in the transference with a temporary delusional force. She thought that I suddenly changed size, grew thinner and fatter. Her own body parts again became detached and assumed independent personalities. She was oversensitive to my voice, and developed hoarseness herself, explaining that 'her larynx wanted it that way.' She weighed herself from day to day; and was anxious because her brother B.'s young daughter was sleeping in the same room with the parents. On hearing that I was to read a paper at a meeting, she decided to attend, then became anxious lest I should be quite literally exposed before the entire audience. Actually in the auditorium she was able to see that I did have my clothes on, but the clothes took over elements of the body. She saw me as wearing a brown hat with something sticking straight out in front and this frightened her so much and she left so embarrassed in my behalf that she left the meeting shaking. It also seemed to her that I looked voluptuous and not quite myself.

At different times throughout the analysis it developed that the battle of the colours and other fantasies had existed since the age of 5 or so, and gradually faded during early adolescence. They were coincident in time with her stone fetishism. She believed that she had some visual difficulty which had been discovered also about the age of 9, and had then been cured with glasses. It was startling, however, that her myopia had been exposed when her mother noted that the patient, on meeting an elderly man on the street, referred to him as a little girl. It was a very long time before she could understand that this was due to misinterpretation and not to myopia. Other symptoms similarly, as they emerged from her amnesia, nearly always by direct presentation in dreams, were obviously denials, reversals or un-doings of more positive symptoms. She recalled having written hymns on the sidewalk in front of the house, so that people would see them and have good thoughts. When I suggested that she might previously have seen other words there, she was sure she had never heard such words, but was amazed soon afterward to see the very words written in various places, almost as though I were magically convincing her.

During the period out of school, she had managed to keep up with her class and even make up an extra grade at school, in spite of the fact that she could not sit still for more than a few minutes at a time; and to relieve her tension would run out into the garden, where she swung back and forth, as high as possible into the leafy trees, talked to the clouds, built fairy houses, communed with the Sun, or whispered to the flowers. She read omnivorously, mostly the standard children's classics, myths and fairy tales, and the Bobbsey Twins books. At one time when she was trying to understand this period of her life she had the following dream, during a brief attack of laryngitis:

I wanted to go to a certain high place to hear 'the Voices'—a superhuman phenomenon which existed. But it seemed too much of an undertaking, and meant climbing up and then staying overnight. Father did not want me to go. Still he suggested my wearing a grey bathing suit which would not be spoiled by the rain. But I found old stained brown corduroy clothes, different from anything I have ever had. We drove out on Long Island. B. and his girl were in the car. Mother was in the back seat driving. I don't know which seat I was on. We got out beyond civilization, on a rough and rutted road. Finally we got out and saw this massive mystical tower rising, like a Shangri-La phenomenon. There was mist around it, but it was square in shape. We climbed up farther but did not hear the unearthly voices. We heard a clock strike or the bells of a clock ring. The feeling about the voices is indescribable. I had a yearning to hear them, but still it was frightening.

*B.'s girl friend* suggested a girl with a boyish haircut, but otherwise femininely attractive, whom her brother had briefly loved during his college days. The *tower* was like an ancient thing, a Greek oracle, also the tower of Babel. Its shape was Babylonian. The London conference failed because people could not understand each other. The tower also looked a little like the Chrysler building in different weathers and a haze (obviously the penis); *climbing up* means growing up, and understanding adults. Father's reluctance—he tries to avoid understanding things. The girl, not the mother, seemed to be driving the car—patient was not sure really which it was, nor where she herself was in it. Anyway, the girl disappeared—she was probably only a friend and not a sweetheart of B.'s, perhaps the patient herself. *The voices themselves?* She could say little—my voice, the analytic work. The clock suggested the clock of the Metropolitan Life Insurance tower which she hears strike often (and it was the bridge at the Metropolitan Life Building which played a part in her early panic). Although the patient was not ready to see it at this time, this represents so clearly the attempt at spiritualization of her masturbatory drives and the intense phallic worship accompanying it. (From associations at other times, I was inclined to think that the striking of the clock represented clitoral stirring like the ticking of the clock in the dream of Freud's female paranoid patient (2).) It is interesting in this connection that later in her life the patient developed a compulsive playing of the piano, ending in improvisations during which she felt uneasy and 'in too much communication' if her father came near her.

This patient presented many other picturesque variations of the basic themes. But to return to the problem of the fan which had produced the minor panic in my office, early in the analysis; between two and three years after this panic the memory of this incident was again brought out by the patient. In answering her I remarked that she was probably referring to the time she had been frightened by the pedestal fan at the foot of the couch. To my surprise she became quite angry, and said that the fan certainly had not been at the foot of the couch and had not been a pedestal fan but a table fan which was at the head of the couch. I remembered the incident quite clearly, and had some notes about it also; but she was adamant in her anger, became tearful and said it almost made her feel that she could not continue to work with me if I could not remember details more clearly and was going to make mistakes and mis-statements of this kind. I indicated that there had been a table fan at the head of the couch at a later date, but the original offending one was on a pedestal and she had been frightened and had later referred to seeing the blades which had reminded her of her father's saw. This too, she denied, emphatically and emotionally, saying she did not *see* the fan at all, but had only heard it and it was clearly at her head and only the noise had disturbed her. Again it was weeks before the fan reappeared. Only then could I get her to see that the very emotionality of her denial indicated some great need to defend herself against admitting this sight. What ultimately developed was that it was the pedestal of the fan that had reminded her so of the intolerable sight of the penis, and that the whirring at her head was not only a displacement upward, but the noise of the primal scene in the dark, and the whirring in the head which these early experiences produced, associated also with the mother's stroke, which occurred so close in time to the father's accident with the saw before her major panic.

Another version of these experiences, fusing eating, smelling and breathing together, and the wish to touch fused with the wish to see appeared in a particularly distorted dream at the end of the second year of treatment.

A little boy, vaguely in our dining room, a fair-haired, blue-eyed boy, my brother or my nephew (*i.e.*, D.'s son) was eating chocolate. Father said he should not eat it but could have it as a backlog. Then he put his thumb and index finger on either side of the little boy's windpipe to make him choke it up. . . . Mother said 'I will give him this for a backlog' and hurled something into his mouth in a way that it went straight up into his nasal passages. I saw that this was dangerous, and I shook him in such a way as to dislodge it. It fell out, and I saw it was a pair of eyes with part of the bridge of the nose between (which reminds me at once of dolls' eyes). It was bad of mother to throw that that way.

Here she thought the child was about four years old and the father looked like her brother D.; that the child, although a boy, made her think of a neighbour child whose name was the same as mine, and whom she had recently dreamed was going to be put in a cast for a long time. Also that the *eyes* further suggested fish eyes and roe, or seminal fluid. In the Eskimo Twins book which she had read in childhood the twins considered fish eyes an especial delicacy—the backlog, it seemed ludicrous and farfetched she said, but it suggested stool. (And then suddenly) 'Isn't it a sporran that the Highlander wears hanging down in front?' Her beadwork thing (cf. the beads of the first dream) was in that position, a little low for the navel and a little high for the pubic hair.

In this dream there is seen a state of apparent confusion, in which everything is glued to everything else, subject and object are not differentiated, and the function is also represented by the organ, while the dream itself is pervaded by a sense of violence. Such dreams occurred quite frequently premenstrually, and in this instance the menstrual period was reported the next day. It appears that under the impact of the castration anxiety of the approaching menstruation there was rearoused the infantile state of panic associated with the main infantile traumata, the allusions to which are quite decipherable in the associations to the dream, the content of which is so conglomerated.

Much later a dream pronouncement of the patient's preparation to admit her aggressive sadistic wishes toward the phallus was as follows and occurred the day before her birthday.

I stood with some freshly sliced pieces of a man beside me. I had done the slicing and tried to escape. I passed someone who was looking for the man. I realized that it was going to become evident what I had done. I thought the simplest thing was to admit it directly. So I did. I thought it would take the person a little time to come to and realize that what I said was true.

First it may be noted that although this is an introducing or informative dream, she is here preparing to accept responsibility herself and is no longer confusing herself with others including me, as in the last dream given, but is prepared to make her own deposition. The associations began with the fact that she and her father had recently had liver for lunch and she had felt badly that entire weekend. She had watched the butcher slice the liver. The atmosphere of the dream was one of intense reality. Next she thought of having looked into a flat on Rawson Street (a peeking incident from an elevated train reported some months earlier, with especial emphasis on the pun on the name Raw-son). 'I thought of myself like a murderer who cuts people up. It was like a totem amount in the dream.' (Here I asked what she meant by a *totem* amount, to which she replied quite blandly, 'Oh, did I say *totem*, I meant to say *token*.') 'Well, I felt very tired all day— As a child I did not really feel like killing D., but I wanted to do something to him. . . . . I seem to think of father having sliced his fingers in the cellar. I saw that saw the evening before my dream, with its bright teeth. . . . In the dream I had the awareness my crime was going to be found out. In school my technique was to admit guilt to the teacher before she found out, if I was sure she would find out anyway, but I never did do very much. That liver seems also to make me think of a penis. . . . I think I used to think I only got angry at D. or B. if they interfered with me, but I may have had some undercurrent against them. Father again spoke of his pride in me when, at the age of four, I was dressed like a little George Washington. But when I was dressed in a male part anyway he felt especially pleased.' But immediately after this hour with its pronouncement, the patient did not behave like George Washington who could not tell a lie, but like a four-year-old child interweaving fantasy and fact and mixing things up in an Alice-in-Wonderland fashion, which accomplished denial.

These excerpts from the case study document fairly well many of the points which have been described earlier. It is apparent, however, that this four- to five-year-old child was probably not in an ordinary state of firmness to withstand these traumata, which are in themselves not so very rare, and do not always leave as disastrous imprints as they did in this child. It would seem from the total material produced that all three traumata—the primal scene under rather special circumstances, the guilty exhibitionistic and scoptophilic frustration with Sylvester Ebenezer Wilson, Jr., and the overwhelming stimulation by the older brother D.—all occurred in the four- to five-year-old period, but that the latter was repeated during the tenth year, which began the long period of nervousness necessitating her being out of school until thirteen. There was in addition a disturbance at the age of five when the brother D. almost drowned and had to be resuscitated.

But of the period before four, especially of the first two years of life, certain facts were reconstructed, many of which could be checked by a baby book which the patient's mother had kept zealously. That there were both *overstimulation and deprivation in the oral phase* seemed indicated both by dream production and by direct account. The child was a normal-size baby and was breast-fed for three months. The mother then assiduously plied her with the bottle, seemingly believing that weight meant health and impressiveness. By eight months the baby was enormously fat. The bottle feeding and the excessive weight continued until eighteen months, with almost no chance for normal chewing activity as she was given no solid food until after eighteen months. In the meantime the brother B. had been born when the patient was sixteen months old. Her walking was delayed, perhaps because of her extreme weight. After the weaning, she grew in length, became more active and thinned out, so that when she began to walk at twenty-two months she was no longer a fat child. The loss of the weight so relatively soon after the birth of the younger child certainly reinforced the identification with the mother, who was a dominating, absorbing mother, who made the child a veritable part of herself even in the way the patient later seemed unable to separate her identity from those around her and was continually in a state of infantile introjection and projection (or perhaps the terms incorporation and excorporation might be more suitable) to an extraordinary degree. On the Christmas before she was three, she reacted to the Christmas story, chanting often 'I am going to be born.'

In the meantime two other events, or series of habitual events, were taking place. The mother proudly claimed to have trained the child to the toilet by the time she was a year old, but at the same time kept her exclusively on the bottle. It would seem that in this she was accentuating both oral and anal tension with a peculiarly disturbed balance between them. From the time the little girl was twenty-two months old and her baby brother B. was six months old they were bathed in the same tub, which as she said apropos of one of her dreams, 'had made them one and the same, of the same flesh and blood, through the spray of the bath water.' She was never as excited by the genitals of her brother B. as they already belonged to her, but was frantic with excitement at D., who was five years older.

It is interesting to consider the influence on body tensions as well as the effect on body image in this child who was so stuffed by the mother during her own pregnancy; with a falling off in weight, whether due to the weaning or the loss of the mother's major attention after the birth of the younger brother but coinciding with slight delay with the mother's change in form. Changing shape and form, undoubtedly based on concern about the penis, but possibly also due to this unusual shift in body image in herself, and to an early primary identification with the mother, always preoccupied her, as was shown quite clearly in some of her dream-productions, and was one of the themes of the clouds, shadows, steam and mist. Twice later in life, she was to make dramatic shifts in body weight in a way quite clearly patterned after this original one.

It seems probable that the patient whose case is here

described might possibly have become a mystic or a saint, a Bernadette, in another setting. It was not, however, the purpose of this clinical report to present the case structure *in toto*, but rather in sufficient detail to tell the clinical story. A similar symptom constellation with the same basic dynamics may be encountered in somewhat different character structures. It seems to emerge with more or less clarity quite often when special problems of the phallic phase are reactivated during analysis.

A second patient presented somewhat similar symptoms in a more circumscribed form. She was a young married woman, still in her twenties, a successful journalist who came to analysis because of a periodic writing block. Almost at once she began to protest that she did not wish to be a Talking Woman, making many witty and sarcastic comments regarding prominent women colleagues who 'sounded off' as she said, in the press or radio. She was the fourth child and only girl among five siblings, in a family in which the father was distinctly a Talking Man, a popular and liberal educator with a flair for political oratory. The mother was a retiring woman with primarily domestic interests. The parents had been divorced only after the marriage of the patient. Of all the children she was the one indubitably most like the father, and her protesting cry of denial of talking ambitions was part of her being torn in identification between the two parents. Equally important, however, it was a denial of her rather general envy, derived from her early intense penis envy. She fairly soon gained some insight into this, but the imprint on her character in her extreme narcissistic power drive and intellectualization was considerable. The refrain 'I can do anything (he) (she) (you) can do,' rang throughout her analytic work. She was unusually afraid of pregnancy, thought the deformation of the body shameful, and was fearful of the pain and destructiveness of birth. These symptoms represented a very considerable neurosis with outcroppings at puberty of compulsiveness and fantasies of impregnation by immaculate conception, especially through seeing. Now she had become pregnant by an accident, which was influenced by her competitiveness with an old college friend. She felt whatever this young woman could do, she could and must do also.

The material of a single hour during the seventh month of her pregnancy is here presented. This had been preceded by considerable discussion of the time, at the age of four, when her only younger brother was born. This child had been a consolation gift to the mother by the father, in a situation when under the spell of one of his numerous love affairs he was planning to divorce the mother, but felt she should have a child as a last memento. This strange state of family relations had coloured the patient's fear of pregnancy, and linked it with the fear of abandonment and with the idea of the phallic but feminine woman with a child, separate from the father. In the same period as the birth of this younger brother, she had herself had a tonsillectomy, done at home, and had been terrified by the anesthetic and especially resentful of the pre-operative enema which had given her feelings of uncontrollable explosiveness. Also around the same period she had fallen against a radiator while roughhousing with an older brother, had hit and cut her head, and had been rushed to the same hospital where her mother had given birth. At the time, she had thought, 'I will always remember this moment' (typical of the screen memory hunger), and indeed this did screen her earliest pregnancy fantasies of this period.

On the Monday here reported, the patient came to her hour reluctantly, saying that she had a sore throat such as she had not had for years. In the past these attacks had been followed by laryngitis and aphonia. She had heard on Saturday from another college friend, who was pregnant and who had phoned her at the beginning of her labour pains. She thought this friend's voice sounded unusually far away. On Sunday she heard from the husband that the baby had arrived by a breech birth and that no anesthetic had been given. This frightened her, but she thought at once, 'If she can do it, so can I!' That night she dreamed:

I was here in my analytic hour. You said that you hoped I would learn to call things by their right names; that you and your mother had had a campaign to have people call things by their right names, especially in regard to volume, and you mentioned different meanings of volume. I thought I did not use volume except with the meaning of a book. I wondered if your mother was alive. You looked out of the window and saw that it was snowing. You said the snow was wet and came from a different direction than you were used to. I wondered where you came from and thought it must be Pennsylvania. We both started to leave the room, but ran into a Negro girl who had come to see you without an appointment. You greeted her cordially but went on. Next I was in the labour room with my friend. The doctor wanted to give her an anesthetic, but she did not want it and said, 'If Caesar were pressing my brow that would hurt whether or not I had an anesthetic.'

About *Caesar*, she thought at once of a Caesarean operation. The day before, her husband and her mother had worked in the garden with her, and her mother remarked that on Mother's Day she generally planted something in memory of *her* mother. It suddenly struck the patient that it would be strange to have a daughter who in turn would have a daughter, and so she might become one of a long line of mothers and daughters. (In this she was trying to place herself in her biological role but also to find a superiority over the male, who could not be a link in so close a chain.) She had next thought of me, thought she had heard children in my household and wondered if I had a daughter, who had a daughter who might become a mother, etc. *Calling a thing by its right name*— She suddenly burst out, 'Well, I was constipated yesterday, and concerned about it.' As to *volume*, it was only a book or perhaps pitch or sound over the radio. She had been preoccupied with her friend and the baby yesterday and had thought again, 'If she can do it, I can do it also.' The *wet snow* made her think of her friend's husband having said that the waters (amniotic fluid) came early; and her mother had said, 'Poor girl, a dry birth and a breech.' In the dream I seemed to be superior about a dry snow and the patient was defending herself. *Pennsylvania* made her think of Pa for father and the fact that she knew that I had gone to La (Louisiana) the year before; that she herself had learned to spell Pennsylvania from hearing a little girl chant the spelling rhythmically in a movie of 'Tom Sawyer.' In this, the children had gotten lost in a cave, and later Tom and Huckleberry Finn had sneaked into the church, where they listened to the eulogies of their own funeral services. She had once been in a cave with stalactites and stalagmites, like the one in the movie, and one of the girls in the party had become frightened lest she hit her head on a stalactite and injure herself as she had previously suffered a concussion and been told that further injury might be dangerous. In spite of the fear, no injury had really occurred. Also a caller had recently sympathized with the patient for looking tired and had remarked that she was herself tired, as she had not fully recovered from an operation on her head.

In the early part of the analysis the relation of speech to urinary control and the comparison of the speech of the Talking Woman to the directed flow of male urination became obvious. In this hour, however, we are dealing with other elements of the phallic period as well, in which the patient sees the approaching birth as a terrible castration similar to the tonsillectomy at four. The concern with the excretory functions is further evident in the references to the dry birth, the wet snow, the breech delivery, and the Negro girl who came without appointment, this latter referring not only to anal birth and a bowel movement at the unexpected time as with the pre-operative enema, but further to the fantasy impregnation through watching a Negro houseman in his basement rooms at four to five. Of especial interest is the theme of the large or small voice, the question of the anesthetic and the many references to the head, with the displacement of power from the genitals to the magic and omnipotent thoughts—the condensation of all of these themes, occurring in the idea of the importance of the right word and the comparing of the unborn child with Caesar—whereas the word *volume* serves as a key to the ideas of the genitals, of the pregnancy, and of the omnipotent thoughts. My campaign to have things called by their right names, meant not only the analytic work, but especially, like the phrase 'to call a spade a spade,' referred to the fantasy of magic impregnation by looking at the coloured man, which the patient had at this time alluded to many times but not clearly admitted. On the next day the patient brought a dream which was again concerned with the problems of birth and death, and with many references to her having a double—in this instance the unborn child.

Much of what I have described has already been noted by

other analysts, especially during the early golden days of psychoanalytic investigations and reporting. Jones especially in his
book, *On the Nightmare* (3), and in an article on auto-sugges-
tion (4) makes extensive observations along similar lines but in
other terms. Jones says, 'The transference of the ideas connected with the flatus to the subject of the breath and voice is
peculiarly easy in the case of the horse, whose neighing is evidently a sexual process and has hardly any other biological
significance'; and quoting Jähns, 'Since a stallion chiefly
neighs when he feels the impulse to copulate and since pro-
creative capacity and the sense of life are as closely associated
with the idea of light as barrenness is with that of darkness and
death, we have the reason why a lusty neigh counts as a good
omen.' Jones adds that the Teutonic races paid the greatest
attention to neighing, divining future events from different
intonations, and both the Persians and the Irish decided the
choice of their king from the omen thus obtained. And again,
quoting from Jähns, he illustrated the sexual significance of
neighing as follows: 'Girls ride on a broomstick to the door of
the stable and listen. If a steed neighs it means the girl will be
married before Midsummer Day, but if she hears only the flatus
of a horse she will bear a child in the coming year without
being married.' Jones adds that from neighing to speaking is
only a step; mythology and history are full of accounts of speaking horses. Later in the same book he remarks, 'In connection
with the words *Mare* and *Märchen*, it might be added that the
idea of bringing news is obviously connected with the ideas
both of finding out knowledge and of passage through the air.'
He also traces a connection from neighing to speaking, especially in an oracular fashion, and to oratory, declamation and the
beginning of poetry.

In this connection, I would comment that in the development of the child the increase in sphincter strength goes on
simultaneously with laryngeal and mouth (labial and lingual)
co-ordination promoting speech, and roughly accompanies the
perfection of walking. This means that ordinarily from the
end of the first year to the third year there is an increase in the
sense of autonomous periodicity and rhythm in the child.
Whereas the soothing effect of rhythm is present from birth,

but may be largely brought to the child by rhythms supplied from without (being rocked or walked with), the increasing rhythmic capacities of his own body give both comfort and power, and with the mastery of sphincter control and speech, there is quite frequently a period of the mouthing of words with special emphasis on alliterations and primitive rhyming.

Also concerning the neighing of horses, the cat, like the horse, makes special characteristic sounds in connection with its mating, and like the horse it is the subject of nightmarish superstitions of sitting on the chest, especially the chest of the baby and killing it by sucking out the air. It is interesting that in the Fuselli painting, used as a frontispiece in Jones' book, the devil seated on the maiden's chest is catlike in posture and appearance.

Freud's paper on 'The Uncanny' (5) harmonizes with the emphasis in the present description to the extent that he sees its origin in the end of the first and the early part of the second year with the capacity for positive negative hallucination (reinforced by certain fixations in relation to animism). Fenichel (6), too, emphasizes that in primitive thinking the respiratory apparatus becomes the site of incorporated objects in the same way as the intestinal apparatus; that primitive people, psychotics and children sense that by breathing they are taking in substance from the outer world and returning some substance to it; the incorporated substance is invisible and therefore suitable for conveying magical ideas, which is reflected in the equations of life and soul with breathing, which further lends itself to magical use because it is the one vegetative function that can be regulated and influenced voluntarily. (Compare this with the megalomanic ideas developed by some male patients who have in childhood consistently produced erections and orgasm by fantasy alone.) Fenichel further remarks that inhaling the same air as another means to be united with him, and exaling means separation. Respiratory introjection is associated with smelling, i.e., with anal eroticism on the one hand, and with the idea of identification with dead persons—inhaling the soul—on the other. Harnik (8) in an article on the fear of death in early infancy, relates this to a fear of dying, i.e., being suffocated, sometimes originating by forcible early feeding, and that this becomes worked into the superego anxiety with ideas of the breath as spirit or soul.

Melanie Klein (9) hints at the relation of such findings to the conscience and superego, stating that sadistic omnipotence through feces and flatus becomes modified and is often used to inflict moral pain. She thinks that these sadistic attacks being carried on secretly and with great watchfulness and mental ingenuity in guarding against counterattacks of a corresponding character, the original omnipotence becomes of fundamental importance for the growth of the ego. I am not prepared to go wholeheartedly with Klein regarding this last emphasis. At least in those cases which I have seen I would say there was an expansion of the ego, but not in itself contributing essentially to its sound strength and solidity.

Breath-holding attacks of childhood are rather uncommonly described in psychoanalytic literature. In a personal communication, K. Eissler has told me that Aichorn found from clinical observations that they might be followed by pseudo-stupidity. M. Chadwick (10) quotes D. Forsyth as describing children who get pleasure from holding and playing with their breath and hold to the point of cyanosis in anger, and relates these activities to correlated sphincter activities, with pleasure in the clear demonstration of power. It is my own impression from direct observation of such breath-holding attacks, that particularly in children in the phallic and oedipal periods, the child may have not only a power satisfaction, but a peculiar pleasure in the heightening disturbance accompanying the cyanosis, with a relatively sudden letting go at the end in a kind of twilight state which has the curve of an orgastic response and may be related to it. Rank's study, *Der Doppelgänger* (1), clearly indicates the relation of some of these phenomena (mirror reflectors, shadows, and guardian spirits) to the belief in the soul and fear of death. He stated that the idea of the double was originally an insurance against destruction to the ego, 'an energetic denial of the power of death' (compare the fantasy companions of early childhood), and that the immortal soul was the first double of the body; that while the double arises from the primary narcissism it does not disappear with the passing of the latter, but can receive fresh meaning from the later stages of development of the ego, slowly forming a special function of observing and criticizing the self and exercising a censorship within the mind—the conscience. The quality of uncanniness, he said, could only come from the double being a creation dating back to a very early mental stage, and one in which it doubtless wore a more friendly aspect.

It is evident, thus, that most of what I have brought out in the present study has been observed and described in other frames of reference many years ago. Whatever this study has to offer is in its clinical illustration, with especial effort to understand the symptoms in terms of the developmental processes of early growth and changing balances, with especial emphasis on relations to the phallic phase.

# SOME FACTORS PRODUCING DIFFERENT TYPES OF GENITAL AND PREGENITAL ORGANIZATION

THAT the oepidal period is the most momentous era of psychic and emotional organization and the oedipus complex the most significant network of conflicts throughout the entire life has been amply verified throughout the years, since first described by Freud. The crossing of this boundary between infancy and childhood is more perilous even, though outwardly less dramatic, than the somewhat comparable change from childhood to young adulthood at puberty. It is perhaps unnecessary to point out that the way in which one comes to the oedipal phase, however, as much as the circumstances existent then, determines the nature and the fate of this particular period of life with its far-reaching consequences. The experiences which have already accumulated, with the establishment of special strengths, tensions, and patterned expectations form the useful or cumbersome equipment of this part of life's journey, influence the efficiency or failure of the crossing of its frontier, and so affect the entire life.

The description of the infant's organization, on the basis of the sensorimotor growth and relationships of the first five years of life in terms of a fairly regular succession of dominant drives, was the work of the early years of analysis and gave rise to the formulation of the libido theory which has been the backbone of analytic understanding, importantly supplemented to be sure by the more recent work on other aspects of individuation, viz., the development of the ego. It was on the background of the understanding of the libidinal growth of the organism that the concepts of fixation, repression, and regression resulting from traumata, so important in the early work on the neuroses, were developed, and significant patterns of organization in the different neuroses were differentiated.

This chapter is concerned with further observations regarding these fundamental concepts. It is based on analytic work, including the study of a large number of unusually severe neuroses and 'borderline' conditions. Compared with earlier investigations dealing with somewhat similar subjects (1) this presentation puts more emphasis on consideration of the fundamental biological maturation of the infant, while special events of the individual infant's life are examined, rather in relation to their effect on its biogenetic unfolding. This is a point of view always implied by Freud in his stressing of the biological foundation of psychoanalysis. It may however have been less conspicuous in the writings of earlier investigators, when the psychological components of development, the unique carriers of individuated developmental processes were under close scrutiny, as was essential in understanding the psyche and making a system of psychoanalytic therapy. At present, when many observations concerning parent-child relationships are more or less taken for granted by the general public and when the interest in child psychology and the physical development of children has found widespread support, we have at our disposal a mass of data concerning behaviour and growth (sometimes non-analytic in source) but valuable for correlating with, extending, and elaborating our observations from therapy in childhood or from reconstructions from the adult.

It appears that in evaluating the effect of trauma in the young developing organism, it is important to consider not only the maturational phase at which the trauma occurs, whether the specific nature of the trauma is one which tends to reinforce the libidinization of the dominant phase or to reinstate an already developed phase, either by direct stimulation or by encouraging regression for adequate satisfaction; but further whether the specific nature of the stimulating trauma calls for a response in accordance with a phase which is close to maturity or as yet quite immature. In addition to the specific nature of the trauma in terms of its relation to the timetable of libidinal development, the severity and the duration of traumatic conditions are most important in shaping the results. Certain fundamental relationships have become so impressive that they are offered here even without benefit of detailed case studies which must come later. While it may be possible to study precisely the varying combinations of influences during the pre-oedipal years and their exact effect on the genital development in relation to the oedipal situation of the child, for the present we must limit ourselves to a few aspects of these problems, with the hope that these may furnish the bases for further investigations.

The principles of relationship here considered are as follows: (a) The earlier in life severe traumata occur, the greater are the somatic components of their imprints, due to the peculiar emotional-somatic plasticity and participation of the infant before the development of the ego, with the special economizing functions of speech and conceptual memory. (b) Very severe or very prolonged (chronic) traumata may produce so massive a stimulation as to suffuse the organism. (c) The activation of libidinal zones prematurely may produce a precocious but a peculiarly vulnerable development, whether this results from specific stimulus calling for a specific (as yet incompletely prepared) response or from massive stimulation such that the organism is required to respond with all its channels of discharge including those which are not yet matured. (d) Excessive stimulation, whether massive or specific in origin, results in primitive erotization and ultimately in some genital stimulation long before genitalization in its truer sense is developed, *i.e.*, before the phallic phase. It is possible that further observations along these lines may contribute to our understanding of primary masochism. It is at least suggestive that premature erotization culminating in *genital stimulation under strain* might increase the pain component in the pleasure-pain amalgam which is the nucleus of all satisfaction, here linked with genital arousal.

While much of what is outlined in this chapter has been incidentally described previously or at least implied in clinical studies and case reports and may not therefore seem new, I do not know that it has been systematically developed or especially emphasized. It will require much more than the present information to delineate its wider and specific applications fully.

Concerning the question of premature stimulation and its relation to later genital development, it is apparent that much will depend on the degree of prematurity of the special stimulus demand. If the gap is not great between the specific response demanded and the corresponding spontaneous maturational phase, a sounder but less striking precocity may ensue. If, however, the gap is considerable, either libido will be drawn from other functions into the specially demanded one which is then established at any price, or the infantile effort at compliance breaks down and a secondary diffusion and state of general stimulus results, even when the initial stimulus has been repeatedly specific. There is some indication that this state may be subjectively comparable to dissolution anxiety of later rage. A few illustrations of premature demands may help. One such direct and common situation is the occurrence of genital masturbation long before the phallic phase. That this may occur even to the point of orgasm is a frequent observation, and in my experience, is most common in infants who have been subjected to early stress with resultant increase in tension and susceptibility to an irritable body responsiveness. It has been described as early as the eighth month. That it may occur as the result of specific genital seduction is also a common observation. Especially noteworthy are those cases in which an overanxious and sometimes unconsciously hostile and envious mother or nurse repeatedly stimulates the baby boy's genital by daily stripping the foreskin and swabbing for purposes of cleanliness. In such cases, there is undoubtedly a precocious development of genital responsiveness but occurring, as it often does, during the first year of life when the differentiation of the infant from the mother is very incomplete, the genitalization even with erotization, deforms and degrades the later oedipal relationship to the mother and does not merely intensify it. Such early stimulation of the penis may convert it practically into an umbilical stump.

Other common illustrations of precocious and severe stimulation are forced feeding, the giving of enemas early, or very early toilet training. The local erotization of these procedures is a matter of common analytic observation. The fact that some degree of actual precocity of neuromuscular response can be promoted is clearly evident in the instances of extremely early training to bowel or urinary cleanliness, which may be accomplished in the second six months of life. More striking even than this are the fortunately rare, but verifiable, reports of infants taught to perform extraordinary feats of gymnastic skill within the first two or three years of life. Not only is the specific neuromuscular apparatus forced to an entirely premature compliance, sometimes accomplished at the expense of accessory safety measures (over-alertness to feelings of fullness, watchful conditioning to the sight of the chamber pot, utilization of accessory muscle controls, etc., in the case of early bowel training), but the differentiation of the infant from the environment is so grossly incomplete that the whole significance of the giving up of the excreta is greatly blurred. Indeed when we analyse such children later we find quite often they react as though they had been chronic enuretics or soilers because the actual performance has been an incompletely perceived one and because they have had to be so continuously on guard that tension about possible wetting or soiling has developed and formed the substratum of anxiety as markedly as though they had actually been subject to toilet accidents. That a tendency to anxiety accompanies any markedly premature functioning, including the genital, may be true and establishes a subsequent vulnerability of performance with frequently a later breakdown of the compensated activity. It is obvious, however, that where such specific stimulations have occurred, there will be a distortion of the orderly libidinal development and a linking of the precociously demanded libidinal phase with the one which is naturally dominant at the time. It is probable that changing fashions in child care give rise to distortions of this nature which are paradoxically more misleading to direct observation than to careful analytic reconstruction. It is a clinically observable fact that massive stimulation or severe frustration results in genital stirring even in the very young infant, easily observable in the erection of the male. Later in life, too, any stimulation, if sufficiently severe, may produced genital orgasm. What is less clearly observed is that in such instances there is sometimes a suffusion of the entire organism with stimulation, so that all possibilities of relief are tried. In the infant under such conditions, all libidinal zones may be stimulated at once. If this is often repeated, especially in an infant whose discharge capacities are already handicapped the intensity of the suffused stimulation results in a *conglomeration of zonal sensitivity* and a state of disorganization, in which there is a relative loss of specificity of stimulus and discharge. This is reproduced later in life when one response is substituted too readily and inappropriately for another. In such children there is sometimes a persistence throughout the latency period of a variety of autoerotic discharges and defences, with enuresis, thumb-sucking, special mannerisms and masturbation occurring concurrently. In others there may be a thin layer or veneer of compensated behaviour which readily breaks down, however, under new stress and reveals these polymorphous perverse drives very close to the surface. I have described one such case in considerable detail in Chapter X, in which the young woman in situations of stress might have an unexpected bowel movement, an involuntary urination, an unexpected vomiting, a genital orgasm, or a severe menstrual flooding without warning and with less than usual relation to the specific precipitating situation. This was the more striking as this patient had a sufficient intellectual and general social development to be able to carry on highly specialized work, although obviously an emotionally handicapped person. It has been my impression that this conglomeration of drives and loss of specificity of stimulus and discharge is discernable in some schizophrenic patients, particularly in those in whom the schizophrenic processes are developed from an impaired state, with gross special handicaps of a constitutional nature, which form then a basis of intra-organismic strain from birth on.

Less severe states of this kind are seen in patients who, although other conditions of early life have been relatively favourable, have been subjected to general and repeated stimulations of the primal scene, or to acrobatic handling of being tossed, violently played with, and tickled severely early in infancy. In this same general group are those patients showing peculiar emotional-somatic labilities and confluence of instinctual drives, apparently due to the birth of a sibling within the first year or fifteen months of life. Such children seem to have been robbed of their infancy and subjected to the torments of bodily discharged jealousy, before speech and locomotion have been securely established. They have been stimulated to precocities in the face of and partly by the constant, generally fruitless, regressive pulls, together with excessive external demands for progressive behaviour.

It is my opinion further that in all of these cases of increased narcissism, due to traumatic stimulations of the first year or two of life, the groundwork for later bisexual identification may be appreciably intensified by the constant exposure to siblings of the opposite sex, where the children are bathed and undressed together and otherwise constantly together. The baby of eight to ten months begins to recognize people individually and certainly responds to the face of the mother. It seems from reconstructions that the infant of this age or at least a little later also responds to the sight of the genitals of another child and does notice the absence or presence of external genitals at this same period if there is constant exposure and stimulation of this kind. I cannot unreservedly agree with the earlier belief (1) that the prephallic infant 'takes for granted the likeness of its own sexual organization to that of others and the genital is a matter of no greater concern than the other erogenous zones, notably the mouth,' and that the 'sex of the child is immaterial.' It seems pertinent to raise here certain questions regarding these assumptions. It is worth noting that ordinarily by the age of three the child knows its own sex (cf. the Binet test). This may be an acceptance of sexual identity due to observations concerning clothing and hair arrangements, but is likewise based on concern with the genitals if there has been any opportunity for comparisons. One may well question whether there is some primitive endogenously aroused body image which forms the foundation of sexual identity. That observation of anatomical differences occurs regularly at two to three years of age is the experience of nursery-school teachers and others in daily contact with young children. It is apparent in the almost universal attempts of young girls at this time to urinate as a boy, but with the definite realization in most instances that this cannot be accomplished. That the child may and frequently does go through a period of assumption that others' genital organization is like his own or that his is like others is more likely a narcissistic phenomenon following rather than preceding actual observation of the differences which may again be denied (2). It seems rather that what is important in the earlier stage is the degree of primary identification with others, the way in which this is influenced by early stresses promoting capacity for firmer body illusions, and its relation to later experiences which furnish reinforcements. It has also been my own direct observation that in some girl children awareness of sexual differences with the development of un-mistakable penis envy may make a strong and sharp impression if the child is already in a state of deprivation and narcissistic hurt.

Returning to the question of increased primary narcissism due to early repeated overstimulation of the infant, such in-crease implies a prolongation and greater intensity of the tendency to primary identification as noted and impairment of the developing sense of reality in combination with the in-creased capacity for body responsiveness and registration of stimulus. It may be that this latter is an important factor in the subsequent belief in magic, since the somatic elements in the identification give it greater force and semblance of reality. This may actually be observed in the peculiar recurrence some-times of highly specific physical symptoms, drawn from an early time in the patient's life and repeated in the course of an analytic situation which again favours their occurrence and their observation.

One such impressive example occurred in a patient of mine who had a younger sibling born when she was 27 months old. This child was badly damaged at birth, forceps injury pro-ducing severe head mutilation (later found to cause bilateral deafness). My patient had accompanied her mother to the distant city where this sibling was born and had stayed in a hotel with a nurse while the mother was in the hospital. On the trip home, my patient developed a severe mastoiditis which re-quired hospitalization and much traumatic dressing of the wound. The whole area became erotized, and the subsequent depressed scar was fingered by the little girl in an autoerotic fashion. Whether the injury of the baby had any effect on localizing the infection by any process of identification could not be definitely told later, but that the occurrence of this in-fection and its treatment caused a secondary identification with both mother and infant in which there was a strong somatic pull was clear in the content of the analysis. It was most strikingly reproduced when the patient's mother became ill with a gynecological condition requiring operation, thus simulating the early birth situation. The patient left the analysis to go to her mother who was some distance away, actually retracing the journey of her early childhood. Her return was delayed because, it was reported, she had contracted chickenpox. Her opening remark to me on her first subsequent hour was, 'What do you think of my catching a kid illness like that?' On further examination it developed, however, that she had not actually developed chickenpox but a localized eruption with small blebs, limited entirely to the old mastoid area, and clearly associated with the reactivated memory. (Other aspects of this case are given in Chapter II. Note also the case described in Chapter XIII.)

Such children may, therefore, become more than ordinarily prone to strong bisexual identifications reproduced with illusory body compliances. This means an unusual burden at the oedipal period, with evidences of particularly vivid and severe conflicts followed by an incomplete solution of the oedipus complex in boys and no solution at all in many girls. In severe cases the whole oepidal problem is then deferred until puberty, when the castration problems arise with extreme intensity, according to the bisexual identification, under impact with the genital and secondary sexual body changes, and especially influenced by the secondary narcissistic problems of group identifications of this period. In such situations it is glaringly apparent that the main focus is the unresolved oedipal incestuous attachment, but neither the intensity of this nor its stubbornness can be understood in terms alone of the specific family constellation and relationships, resting as it does on the nature of the pre-genital components and corresponding deformation of the ego development in its early stages. Without analysis of these elements, work with the oedipus complex as such may be unsuccessful.

It should be noted, however, that such malformation and intensification of the oedipus complex do not appear to be a precocity of the complex itself; that, in fact, the greatest contributing disturbance occurring in the first year of life increases and prolongs the introjective and projective mechanisms in which the incomplete differentiation of the infant from mother and surroundings must blur the identity perception but increase potentialities for further disturbance after the development of conceptual memory.

# REFERENCES

CHAPTER I

1. Cannon, Walter B., *The Wisdom of the Body*. New York, Norton, 1932. Chapt. XVI, 'Natural Defenses of the Organism,' p. 229.
2. Morgan, Clifford T., *Physiological Psychology*. New York & London, McGraw-Hill, 1943. P. 265.
3. DeLee, Joseph B., and Greenhill, J. P., *Principles and Practice of Obstetrics*. (8th ed). Philadelphia, W. B. Saunders, 1943. Introduction, p. xiii.
4. Wolff, Harold G., and Goodall, H., 'The Relation of Attitude and Suggestion to the Perception of and Reaction to Pain,' in *Pain*, Research Publication, Assoc. Nerv. & Ment. Dis., XXIII, pp. 434–448. Baltimore, Williams & Wilkins, 1943. This article gives a concise statement of easily demonstrated variations in perception of pain under laboratory conditions.
5. Menninger, Karl, *Love against Hate*. New York, Harcourt Brace, 1942. Pp. 97–98.
6. Jones, Ernest, 'Psychology and Childbirth,' *Lancet*, 1942, vol. 242, p. 695.
7. Ford, Frank R., Crothers, Bronson, and Putnam, Marion C., *Birth Injuries of the Central Nervous System*. Med. Monographs, XI, section on 'Cerebral Birth Injuries,' pp. 13–18. Baltimore, Williams & Wilkins, 1927.
8. Nevinny, H., 'On Lesions of the Central Nervous System by Birth Injury,' *Beilage zur Ztschr. f. Geburtshilfe u. Gynaekologie*, vol. 114, 1936.
9. Greenacre, Phyllis, 'The Predisposition to Anxiety, Part I,' *Psychoanalytic Quarterly*, X, 1941, pp. 66–94.
10. Freud, S., *The Problem of Anxiety*. New York, Norton, 1936. Pp. 96, 97, 102, 121–126.
11. Preyer, W., *Embryonic Motility and Sensitivity*. (Trans. from *Specielle Physiologie des Embryo*.) Monographs of the Society for Research in Child Development, National Research Council, pp. 42, 57. Washington, D.C., 1937.
12. Hooker, Davenport, 'Fetal Behavior,' in *Interrelations of Mind and Body*, Research Publication, Assoc. Nerv. & Ment. Dis., XIX, pp. 237–243. Baltimore, Williams & Wilkins, 1939.
13. Arey, Leslie B., *Developmental Anatomy*. (4th ed.) Philadelphia, W. B. Saunders, 1942. P. 423.
14. Kappers, C. W. A., 'Further Contributions on Neurobiotaxis,' *J. Comp. Neurol.*, XXVII, 1917, pp. 261–298.

15. Windle, W. F., 'Neurofibrillar Development in Central Nervous System of Cat Embryos,' *J. Comp. Neurol.*, LVIII, 1933, pp. 643, 723.

16. de Crinis, M., 'Die Entwicklung der Grosshirnrinde nach der Geburt in ihren Beziehungen zur intellektuellen Ausreifung des Kindes,' *Klinische Wochenschrift*, XL, 1932, pp. 1161–1165.

17. Conel, J. L., *The Postnatal Development of the Human Cerebral Cortex*. Vol. II. Cambridge, Mass., Harvard Univ. Press, 1942. Pp. 39–41.

18. Angulo y Gonzales, A. W., 'The Prenatal Development of Behavior in the Albino Rat,' *J. Comp. Neurol.*, LV, 1932, p. 395.

19. Hooker, Davenport, 'Early Fetal Activity in Mammals,' *Yale J. Biol. & Med.*, VIII, p. 579.

20. Coghill, G. E., *Anatomy and the Problem of Behavior*. New York. Macmillan, 1929.

21. Windle, W. F., O'Donnell, J. E., and Glasshagle, E. E., 'The Early Development of Spontaneous and Reflex Behavior in Cat Embryos and Fetuses,' *Physiol. Zool.*, VI, 1933, p. 521.

22. Carmichael, Leonard, 'Origin and Prenatal Growth of Behavior,' in *Handbook of Child Psychology*, Carl Murchison, Ed. (2nd ed.) Worcester, Mass., Clark Univ. Press, 1933. Pp. 31, 159.

23. Windle, W. F., *Physiology of the Fetus*. Philadelphia, W. B. Saunders, 1940. P. 141.

24. Irwin, O. C., and Weiss, A. P., 'A Note on Mass Activity in Newborn Infants,' *Pedog. Sem.*, XXXVIII, 1930, pp. 20–30.

25. Dusser de Barenne, J. G., 'Central Levels of Sensory Integration,' in *Sensation: Its Mechanisms and Disturbances*, Research Publication, Assoc. Nerv. & Ment. Dis., XV, pp. 274–288. Baltimore, Williams & Wilkins, 1935.

26. Minkowski, M., 'Neurobiologische Studien am menschlichen Fetus,' *Abderhaldens Handb. d. biol. Arbeitsmethoden*, 1928, pp. 511–618.

27. McGraw, M., *Neuromuscular Motivation of the Human Infant*. New York, Columbia Univ. Press, 1943. Pp. 7–10.

28. Gesell, A., Halverson *et al.*, *The First Five Years of Life*. New York, Harper, 1940. P. 18.

29. Bühler, Charlotte, *The First Year of Life*. New York, John Day, 1930. Pp. 21, 22, 29, 30, 35, 39, 111, 119.

30. Dewey, E., *Behavior Development in Infants*. New York, Columbia Univ. Press, 1935. P. 85. This contains an excellent summary of literature from 1920–1934.

31. Genzmer, A., *Untersuchungen über die Sinneswahrnehmungen des neugeborenen Menschen*. Halle, Niemeyer, 1882. Pp. 1–28.

32. Canestrini, S., *Uber das Sinnesleben des Neugeborenen*. Berlin, Springer, 1913. iv and 104 pp.

33. Koffka, K., *The Growth of the Mind*. (2nd ed.) New York, Harcourt Brace, 1931. Pp. 133, 135.
34. Sherman, M., and Sherman, I. C., 'Sensorimotor Responses in Infants,' *J. Comp. Psychol.*, V, 1925, pp. 53–68.
35. Langworthy, O. R., *Development of Behavior Patterns and Myelinization of the Nervous System in the Human Fetus and Infant*, Contributions to Embryology, XXIV, no. 139. Washington, D.C., Carnegie Institution, 1933.
36. Smith, J. R., 'The Electroencephalogram during Normal Infancy and Childhood; Rhythm Tendencies Present in the Neonate and Their Subsequent Development,' *J. Gen. Psychol.* LIII, 1938, pp. 455–469 and 471–482.
37. Stirnimann, F., 'Versuche über die Reaktionen neugeborener auf Wärme und Kältereize,' *Ztschr. f. Kinder-Psychiatrie*, V, 1939, pp. 143–150.
38. Wagner, I. F., 'Curves of Sleep Depth in Newborn Infants,' *J. Gen. Psychol.*, LV, 1939, pp. 121–135.
39. Freud, S., 'A Case of Paranoia,' in *Collected Papers*, III (2nd imp.) London, Hogarth Press, 1934. P. 446.
40. ————, 'On Narcissism,' in *Collected Papers*, IV. (2nd imp.) London, Hogarth Press, 1934. Pp. 30–59.
41. Rado, S., 'Fear of Castration in Women,' *Psychoanalytic Quarterly*, II, 1933, p. 449 footnote.
42. Chadwick, Mary, *Difficulties in Child Development*. New York, John Day, 1928. P. 28.
43. Bak, Robert C., 'Regression of Ego Orientation and Libido in Schizophrenia,' *Int. J. Psa.*, XX, Pt. I, 1939, pp. 1–8.
44. Jones, Ernest, 'Cold, Disease and Birth,' in *Collected Papers*. London, Baillière, Tindall & Cox, 1938. Chapt. XXII, pp. 460–4.

## CHAPTER II

### Part I

1. Freud, S., *The Problem of Anxiety*. (Trans. by H. A. Bunker.) New York, The Psychoanalytic Quarterly Press and Norton, 1936.
2. Sontag, L. W., and Wallace, R. F., 'The Response of the Human Foetus to Sound Stimuli,' *Child Development*, VI, 1935, pp. 253–258.
3. *Ibid.*
   Peiper, A., 'Sense Perception of the Prematurely Born,' *Jahrb. f. Kinderh.*, 1924, pp. 104–195; 1925, pp. 29, 236.
   Catel, W., 'Neurologic Investigations in Premature Children,' *Monatssch. f. Kinderh.*, 1928, pp. 38–303.
   Ray, W. S., 'Preliminary Report on a Study of Foetal Conditioning,' *Child Development*, III, 1932, p. 175.

Forbes, H. S., and Forbes, H. B., 'Fetal Sense Reactions: Hearing,'
    *J. Comp. Psychol.*, VII, 1927, pp. 353–355.
4. Ahlfeld, Friedrich, *Verh. d. deutsch. Gesellsch. f. Gynäk.*, II, 1888,
    p. 203.
5. Watson, John B., *Psychology from the Standpoint of a Behaviorist.*
    Philadelphia, Lippincott, 1919.
    .Streeter, G., 'On the Development of the Membranous Laby-
    rinth and the Acoustic and Facial Nerves in the Human
    Embryo,' *Am. J. Anat.*, VI, pp. 139–166.
7. Freud, S., *Three Contributions to the Theory of Sex.* (4th ed.) Ner-
    vous and Mental Disease Publishing Co., 1930. P. 62.
Köhler, W., *The Mentality of Apes.* (2nd ed.) New York, Harcourt
    Brace, 1927. P. 302.
8. Cannon, W., *Bodily Changes in Pain, Hunger, Fear and Rage.* (2nd
    ed.) New York, Appleton, 1929.
9. Blanton, M., 'The Behavior of the Human Infant during the
    First Thirty Days of Life,' *Psychol. Rev.*, XXIV, 1917, p. 456.
10. Halverson, H. M., 'Infant Sucking and Tensional Behavior,'
    *J. Gen. Psychol.*, 1938, LIII, pp. 365–430.
11. Ford, F. R., 'Cerebral Birth Injuries and Their Results,'
    *Medicine*, V, 1926, pp. 121–191.
12. Shirley, Mary, 'A Behavior Syndrome Characterizing Pre-
    maturely Born Children,' *Child Development*, X, No. 2, 1939.
13. Hess, Mohr, and Bartelme, *The Physical and Mental Growth of
    Prematurely Born Children.* Chicago, Univ. of Chicago Press,
    1934.
14. Gesell, Arnold, and Ilg, Frances L., *Feeding Behavior of Infants.*
    Philadelphia, Lippincott, 1937.
15. Freud, S., 'On Narcissism,' *Collected Papers*, IV, p. 31.
16. ———, 'Negation,' *Imago*, XI, 1925.
17. Ferenczi, Sandor, *Further Contributions to the Theory and Tech-
    nique of Psychoanalysis.* London, Institute of Psycho-Analysis
    and Hogarth Press, 1926. P. 367.
18. Wittels, F., 'Unconscious Phantoms in Neurotics,' *Psycho-
    analytic Quarterly*, VIII, No. 2, 1939; 'Psychology and Treat-
    ment of Depersonalization,' *Psa. Rev.*, XXVII, No. 1, 1940.


### Part II

1. Fromm-Reichmann, Frieda, 'Transference Problems in Schizo-
    phrenics,' *Psychoanalytic Quarterly*, VIII, 1939, p. 412.
2. Lorand, Sandor, 'Contribution to the Problem of Vaginal
    Orgasm,' *Int. J. Psa.*, XX, 1939, p. 438.
3. Bullard, Dexter, 'The Application of Psychoanalytic Psychiatry
    to the Psychoses,' *Psa. Rev.*, XXVI, No. 4, 1939.
4. Cohn, Franz, 'Practical Approach to the Problem of Narcissistic
    Neuroses,' *Psychoanalytic Quarterly*, IX, 1940, pp. 64–79.

5. Lorand, Sandor, 'Dynamics and Therapy of Depressive States,' *Psa. Rev.*, XXIV, No. 4, 1937.
6. Sullivan Harry, 'The Oral Complex,' *Psa. Rev.*, IX, No. 1, 1925; also, 'Affective Experience in Early Schizophrenia,' *Am. J. of Psychiat.*, VI, No. 3, 1927.
7. Thompson, Clara, 'Development and Awareness of Transference in a Markedly Detached Personality,' *Int. J. Psa.*, XIX, 1938, pp. 299–309.
8. Tidd, Charles W., 'Increasing Reality Acceptance by a Schizoid Personality during Analysis,' *Bull. of the Menninger Clinic*, I, 1937, pp. 176–183.

## CHAPTER III

1. Watson, John B., *Psychology from the Standpoint of the Behaviorist.* Philadelphia, Lippincott, 1919. P. 200.
2. Sherman, M., and Sherman, I. C., 'Sensorimotor Responses in Infants,' *J. Comp. Psychol.*, V, 1925, pp. 53–68.
3. Taylor, J. H., *Innate Emotional Responses in Infants.* Ohio State Univ. Studies, 12, 1934, pp. 69–81.
4. Pratt, K. C., Nelson, A. K., and Sun, K. H., *The Behavior of the Newborn Infant.* Contrib. Psychol., Ohio State Univ. Studies, X, 1930, pp. 1 and 237.
5. This material has been reviewed by Wayne Dennis, 'Infant Reaction to Restraint; an Evaluation of Watson's Theory,' *Transactions*, N.Y. Acad. of Sci., May, 1940, pp. 202–218.
6. Dennis, Wayne, *Infant Development under Conditions of Restricted Practice and Minimum Social Stimulation.* Genet. Psychol. Monogr., 23, 1941, pp. 143–189.
7. Kaila, E., 'Uber die Reaktionen des Sauglings auf das Menschliche Gesicht.,' *Psychology*, II, 1935, pp. 156–163.
8. Dennis, W., 'An Experimental Test of Two Theories of Social Smiling in Infants,' *J. Soc. Psychol.*, VI, 1935, pp. 214–223.
9. Bühler, C., *The First Year of Life.* New York, John Day, 1930. P. 55.
10. Gesell, A., and Thompson, H., *Infant Behavior.* New York, McGraw-Hill, 1934. Pp. 261, 282, 283, 287, 288.
11. *Encyclopaedia Britannica.* (Eleventh and Fourteenth Eds.) Article on 'Mutilations.'
12. Swan, J. G., *The Northwest Coast.* New York, Harper, 1857.
13. Gunther, E., *Klallam Ethnography.* Univ. of Wash. Pub. in Anthropology, I, 1920–1927, p. 236.
14. Dennis, W., and Dennis, M. G., 'The Effect of Cradling Practices upon the Onset of Walking in Hopi Children,' *J. Gen. Psychol.*, 56, 1940, pp. 77–80.
15. de Kok, Winifred, *Guiding Your Child through Formative Years.* New York, Emerson Books, 1935. Pp. 9–13.

16. Danziger, Lotte, and Frankl, Liselotte, 'Zum Problem der Funktionsreifung,' *Ztschr. f. Kinderforschung*, 43, 1934, pp. 219–255.
17. Cox, R., *Adventures on the Columbia River: a Residence of Six Years.* New York, Harper, 1832. P. 274.
18. Kane, Paul, *Wanderings of an Artist among the Indians of North America.* Toronto, The Radisson Society, 1925. P. 123.


CHAPTER IV

1. Freud, Anna, and Burlingham, Dorothy T., *War and Children.* New York, Medical War Books, 1945. P. 75.
2. Huschka, M., 'A Study of the Training in Voluntary Control of Urination in a Group of Problem Children,' *Psychosomatic Medicine*, V, No. 3, July, 1943, pp. 254–265.
3. McGinnis, John M., *Eye Movements and Optic Nystagmus in Early Infancy*, Genet. Psychol. Monogr., 1930, pp. 8, 4, 321–430; quoted by Gesell *et al.* in *The First Five Years of Life.* New York, Harper, 1940. *See also* Blanton, M., 'The Behavior of the Human Infant during the First Thirty Days of Life,' *Psychol. Rev.*, XXIV, 1917.
4. Gesell, A., Ilg. F., Learned, J., and Ames, L., *Infant and Child in the Culture of Today.* New York, Harper, 1943. P. 328.


CHAPTER V

1. Abraham, Karl, *Selected Papers on Psychoanalysis.* London, Hogarth Press, 1927. P. 483.
2. Lewin, Bertram D., 'The Body as Phallus,' *Psychoanalytic Quarterly*, II, 1933, pp. 24–48.
3. Zilboorg, Gregory, 'Some Observations on the Transformation of Instincts,' *Psychoanalytic Quarterly*, VII, 1938, pp. 1–24.
4. Ferenczi, S., *Further Contributions to the Theory and Technique of Psychoanalysis.* London, Hogarth Press, 1926. P. 317.
5. Addis, Miller, and Winnicott, 'Discussion of Enuresis,' *Proceedings*, Royal Society of Medicine, XXIX, No. 2, 1936, pp. 1515–1524.
6. van der Heide, Carel, 'A Case of Pollakiuria Nervosa,' *Psychoanalytic Quarterly*, X, 1941, p. 267.
7. French, Thomas M., Alexander, Franz *et al.*, *Psychogenic Factors in Bronchial Asthma*, Psychosomatic Med. Monograph, IV. Washington, D.C., National Research Council, 1941, Pp. 13–90.
8. Saul, Leon, and Bernstein, Clarence, *The Emotional Setting of Some Attacks of Urticaria*, Psychosomatic Med. Monograph, III. Washington, D.C., National Research Council, 1941. Pp. 349–369.

9. Best and Taylor, *Physiological Basis of Medical Practice*. (2nd ed.) Baltimore, Williams & Wilkins, 1940. P. 439.
10. Selye, Hans, 'Studies in Adaptation,' *Endocrinology*, XXI, 1937, pp. 169–188. *Also* Howlett and Browne, J. S. L., 'Studies on Water Balance in the Alarm Reaction,' *Amer. J. Physiol.*, CXXVIII, 1940, pp. 225–332.

CHAPTER VI

1. Mahler, Margaret S., 'Pseudoimbecility: A Magic Cap of Invisibility,' *Psychoanalytic Quarterly*, XI, 1942, pp. 149–164.
2. Jelliffe, Smith Ely, 'Two Morphine Colour Dreams,' *Psa. Rev.*, XXXI, 1944, pp. 128–132.
3. Freud, S., 'Psychoanalytic Notes upon an Autobiographical Account of a Case of Paranoia,' *Collected Papers*, III, p. 438.
4. Abraham, Karl, 'Restrictions and Transformations of Scoptophilia in Psychoneurotics with Remarks on Analogous Phenomena in Folk-Psychology,' *Selected Papers*. London, Hogarth Press, 1927. Pp. 168–235.
5. Bonaparte, Marie, 'Die Identifizierung einer Tochter mit ihrer verstorbenen Mutter,' *Int. Ztschr. f. Psa.*, XV, 1929.
6. ————,'Notes on the Analytic Discovery of a Primal Scene,' in *The Psychoanalytic Study of the Child*. Vol. 1. New York, International Universities Press, 1945.
7. Stragnell, Gregory, 'The Golden Phallus,' *Psa. Rev.*, XI, 1924, pp. 292–323.
8. Lashley, K. S., 'Patterns of Cerebral Integration Indicated by the Scotomas of Migraine,' *Arch. Neurol. and Psychiat.*, XLVI, 1941, pp. 331–339.

CHAPTER VII

1. Klein, M., *The Psychoanalysis of Children*. London, Hogarth Press, 1937. Pp. 179–200.
2. Sheldon, W. H., *The Varieties of Human Physique*. New York, Harper, 1940.
3. Sollenberger, R. T., 'Some Relationships between Urinary Excretion of Male Hormone by Maturing Boys and Their Expressed Interests and Attitudes,' *J. Psychol.*, IX, 1940, pp. 179–189.
4. Horney, K., 'On the Genesis of the Castration Complex in Women,' *Int. J. Psa.*, V, 1924.
5. Lewin, B. D., 'Smearing, Menstruation and the Feminine Superego,' *Int. Ztschr. f. Psa.*, XVI, 1930.
6. Carmichael, L., *Manual of Child Psychology*. New York, Wiley, 1946. Pp. 954–1000.

7. Hartshorn, H., and May, M. A., *Studies in Deceit.* New York, Macmillan, 1928.

8. Brunswick, R. M., *The Accepted Lie.* (Yearbook of Psychoanalysis, I.) New York, International Universities Press, 1945. Pp. 137–142.

9. Lehman, H. C., and Witty, P. A., *The Psychology of Play Activities.* New York, Barnes, 1927.

10. Foster, J. C., 'Play Activities in the First Six Grades,' *Child Development*, I, 1930, pp. 248–254.

11. Kimmens, C. W., *Children's Dreams*: an Unexplored Land. London, Allen and Unwin, 1937.

12. Abbott, M. A., 'A Study of the Motion Picture Preferences in the Horace Mann High School,' *Teachers' College Record*, XXVIII, 1927, pp. 819–835.

13. Leagol, M. V., 'The Child's Reaction to the Movies,' *J. Juv. Res.*, XV, 1931, pp. 169–180.

14. Hicks, J. A., and Hayes, M., 'Study of the Characteristics of 250 Junior High School Children,' *Child Development*, IX, 1938, pp. 219–242.

15. Blair, C. M., *Mentally Superior and Inferior Children in the Junior and Senior High School; Comparative Study of Their Backgrounds, Interests and Ambitions*, Columbia Univ. Teach. Coll. Contrib. Educ., No. 766.

16. Wyman, J. B., *Tests of Intellectual, Social and Activity Interests.* Stanford Univ. Press, Genetic Studies of Genius, No. 1, pp. 455–483.

17. Davis, E. A., 'The Form and Function of Children's Questions,' *Child Development*, III, 1932, pp. 57–74.

18. Jersild, A. T., Markey, F. V., and Jersild, C. L., *Children's Fears, Dreams, Wishes, Daydreams, Likes, Pleasant and Unpleasant Memories.* Child Development Monograph No. 12, 1933, pp. 1 and 172.

19. Terman, L. M., and Miles, C. C., *Sex and Personality Studies in Masculinity and Femininity.* New York, McGraw-Hill, 1936.

20. Searl, M. W., 'A Note on the Relation between Physical and Psychical Differences in Boys and Girls,' *Int. J. Psa.*, XIX, 1938, pp. 50–62.

21. Jordan, A. M., *Children's Interests in Reading*, Columbia Univ. Teach. Coll. Contr. Educ., No. 107.

22. Terman, L. M., and Lima, M., *Children's Readings.* New York. Appleton, 1926.

23. Johnson, B. L., 'Children's Reading Interests as Related to Sex and Grade in School,' *School Rev.*, XL, 1932, pp. 257–272.

24. Freud, S., 'Some Psychological Consequences of the Anatomical Distinction between the Sexes,' *Int. J. Psa.*, VIII, 1927, pp. 133–142.

25. Foster, S., 'A Study of the Personality Make-up and Social Settings of 50 Jealous (Pre-School) Children,' *Mental Hygiene*, II, 1927, pp. 53-57.
26. Sewell, M., *Two Studies in Sibling Rivalry*. Smith Coll. Stud. Soc. Work, I, 1930, pp. 6-22.
27. Smith, S., 'Age and Sex Differences in Children's Opinions Concerning Sex Differences,' *J. Gen. Psychol.*, 54, 1939, pp. 17-25.
28. Sachs, Hans, 'One of the Motive Factors in the Formation of the Superego in Women,' *Int. J. Psa.*, X, 1929, pp. 37-50.
29. Müller-Braunschweig, C., 'The Genesis of the Feminine Superego,' *Int. J. Psa.*, VII, 1926, pp. 359-362.
30. Jacobson, E., 'Development of the Feminine Supergo,' *Int. Ztschr. f. Psa.*, XXIII, 1937, pp. 402-412.
31. Lampl de Groot, J., 'The Evolution of the Oedipus Complex in Women,' *Int. J. Psa.*, IX, 1928, p. 322.
32. Brierley, M., 'Specific Determinants in Feminine Development,' *Int. J. Psa.*, XVII, 1936, pp. 163-180.
33. Gatewood, M. C., and Weiss, A. P., 'Race and Sex Differences in Newborn Infants,' *J. Gen. Psychol.*, XXXVIII, 1930, pp. 31-47.
34. Goodenough, F. L., *Anger in Young Children*. Inst. Child Welfare, Monograph No. 9. Minneapolis, Univ. Minn. Press, 1930. Pp. xiii and 278.
35. Hattwick, L. A., 'Sex Differences in Behaviour of Nursery School Children,' *Child Development*, VIII, 1937, pp. 343-355.
36. Caille, R. K., *Resistant Behaviour of Pre-School Children*. Child Development Monograph No. 11, 1933, pp. xvi and 142.
37. Berne, E. U. C., *An Experimental Investigation of Social Behavior Patterns in Young Children*. Univ. Iowa Stud. Child Welfare, No. 4, 1930, p. 3.

CHAPTER VIII

1. Levy, David M., 'Primary Affect Hunger,' *Am. J. Psychiat.*, Vol. 94, 1937, pp. 643-652.
2. Bender, Lauretta, and Yarnell, Helen, 'An Observation Nursery,' *Am. J. Psychiat.*, Vol. 97, 1941, p. 5.
3. Powdermaker, Florence, 'Psychopathology and Treatment of Delinquent Girls,' *Am. J. Orthopsychiat.*, VII, 1937.
4. Lowrey, Lawson G., 'Personality Distortion and Early Institutional Care,' *Am. J. Orthopsychiat.*, X, 1940, p. 3.
5. Goldfarb, William, 'Infant Rearing and Problem Behavior,' *Am. J. Orthopsychiat.*, XIII, 1943, p. 2.
6. Ford, C. A., 'Institutional Rearing as a Factor in Delinquency,' *Proceedings*, Fourth Conf. on Education and the Exceptional Child. Child Research Clinic of the Woods Schools, May 1938.

7. Healy, William, *Reconstructing Behavior in Youth*. New York, Knopf, 1929; Alexander, Franz, and Healy, William, *Roots of Crime*. New York, Knopf, 1935. Chapt. 8, 'Nobody's Son.'
8. Glueck, Sheldon, and Glueck, Eleanor T., *Five Hundred Delinquent Women*. New York, Knopf, 1934.
9. Dunn, William H., 'The Psychopath in the Armed Forces,' *Psychiatry*, IV, 1941, pp. 251–259.
10. Henderson, D. K., *Psychopathic States*. New York, Norton, 1939.
11. Cleckley, Hervey, *The Mask of Sanity*. Philadelphia, Mosby, 1941.
12. Lindner, Robert, *Rebel without a Cause*. New York, Grune & Stratton, 1944.
13. Reich, Wilhelm, 'Der triebhafte Charakter,' *Int. J. Psa.*, 1925, p. 132.
14. Klein, M., 'Early Development of Conscience,' *Psychoanalysis Today*, 1944, p. 66.
15. Deutsch, H., 'Some Forms of Emotional Disturbance and Their Relationship to Schizophrenia,' *Psychoanalytic Quarterly*, II, 1942, pp. 301–321.

CHAPTER IX

1. Deutsch, H., 'Ueber die pathologische Luege (Pseudologia phantastica),' *Int. Ztschr. f. Psa.*, VIII, 1922.
2. ————, *Psychoanalysis of the Neuroses*. London, Hogarth Press, 1933.
3. Fenichel, O., 'Zur oekonomischen Funktion der Deckerinnerungen,' *Int. Ztschr. f. Psa.*, XIII, 1927.
4. ————, 'The Inner Injunction to Make a Mental Note,' *Int. J. Psa.*, X, 1929, p. 447.
5. ————, 'Zur Oekonomik der Pseudologia Phantastica,' *Int. Ztschr. f. Psa.*, XXIV, 1939.
6. Freud, S., 'Ueber Deckerinnerungen,' *Ges. Schriften*, I, pp. 465–488; also *Monatsschrift f. Psych. u. Neur.*, 1899.
7. ————, *Psychopathology of Everyday Life*. New York, Macmillan, 1914. Chapter II.
8. ————, 'Recollection, Repetition, and Working Through,' in *Collected Papers*, II, p. 368.
9. ————, 'A Childhood Recollection from *Dichtung und Wahrheit*,' in *Collected Papers*, IV, p. 359.
10. Glover, E., 'The Screening Function of Traumatic Memories,' *Int. Ztschr. f. Psa.*, X, 1929, pp. 90–93.
11. Greenacre, P., 'Vision, Headache, and the Halo,' *Psychoanalytic Quarterly*, XVI, 1947, p. 177. *See* Chapter VI.
12. Jones, E., *Papers on Psychoanalysis*. London, Baillière, Tindall & Cox, 1938. P. 299.

13. Lewin, B. D., 'Sleep, the Mouth, and the Dream Screen,' *Psychoanalytic Quarterly*, XV, 1946, p. 419.
14. Mansfield, K., *The Dove's Nest and Other Stories*. New York, Knopf, 1930. P. 74.

CHAPTER X

1. Greenacre, Phyllis, 'A Contribution to the Study of Screen Memories,' in *The Psychoanalytic Study of the Child*. Vol. III–IV. New York, International Universities Press, 1949. *See* Chapter X.
2. Deutsch, H., *Psychology of Women*. Vol. I. New York, Grune & Stratton, 1944. Chapt. 1, pp. 1–24.
3. Stuart, Harold C., 'Normal Growth and Development during Adolescence,' *New England J. of Med.*, Vol. 234, 1946, pp. 666, 693, 732.

CHAPTER XI

1. Freud, S., *Psychopathology of Everyday Life*. London, Ernest Benn, 1914. Chapts. VIII, IX.
2. Fenichel, Otto, 'Neurotic Acting Out,' *Psa. Rev.*, XXXII, 1945, p. 197.
3. Freud. S., 'Further Recommendations in the Technique of Psychoanalysis: Recollection, Repetition and Working Through,' in *Collected Papers*, II, Chapt. 32.
4. Freud, Anna, *The Ego and the Mechanisms of Defense*. London, Hogarth Press, 1936. Chapt. II.
5. Greenacre, Phyllis, 'The Predisposition to Anxiety, Part II,' *Psychoanalytic Quarterly*, X, 1941. *See* Chapter II, Part II.

CHAPTER XII

1. Brierley, M., 'Specific Determinants in Feminine Development,' *Int. J. Psa.*, XVII, 1936.
2. Brunswick, R. M., 'The Preoedipal Phase of Libido Development,' *Psychoanalytic Quarterly*, IX, 1940.
3. Freud, S., *New Introductory Lectures on Psychoanalysis*. New York. Norton, 1933. Chapter 5.
4. ————, 'Female Sexuality,' in *Collected Papers*, V.
5. Gesell, A., and Ilg, F., *Infant and Child in the Culture of Today*. New York. Harper, 1943.
6. Greenacre, P. 'Predisposition to Anxiety, Part II,' *Psychoanalytic Quarterly*, X, 1941. *See* Chapter II, Part II.
7. Halverson H. M., 'Infant Sucking and Tensional Behaviour,' *J. Gen. Psychol.*, LIII, 1938.

8. Hendrick, I., 'Instinct and the Ego during Infancy,' *Psychoanalytic Quarterly*, XI, 1942.
9. Jacobson, E., 'Development of the Feminine Superego,' *Int. Ztschr. f. Psa.*, XXIII, 1937.
10. Jones, E. 'Early Female Sexuality,' in *Papers on Psychoanalysis*. London, Baillière, Tindall & Cox, 1938.
11. Klein, M., 'Early Stages in the Oedipus Conflict,' *Int. J. Psa.*, IX, 1928.
12. Lampl de Groot, J., 'The Evolution of the Oedipus Complex in Women,' *Int. J. Psa.*, IX, 1928.
13. Langworthy, O. R., *Development of Behavior Patterns and Myelinization of the Nervous System in the Human Fetus and Infant.* Contributions to Embryology, Vol. XXIV, No. 139. Washington, D.C., Carnegie Institution, 1933.
14. Müller-Braunschweig, C., 'The Genesis of the Feminine Superego,' *Int. J. Psa.*, VII, 1926.
15. Payne, S. M., 'A Conception of Femininity,' *Brit. J. Med. Psychol.*, 1936.
16. Sachs, H., 'One of the Motive Factors in the Formation of the Superego in Women,' *Int. J. Psa*, X, 1929.

### CHAPTER XIII

1. Rank, O., *Der Doppelgänger*. Int. Psychoanalyticher Verlag, Leipzig, Wien, Zurich, 1925. Pp. 7–117.
2. Freud, S., 'A Case of Paranoia Running Counter to the Psychoanalytical Theory of the Disease,' in *Collected Papers*, III, London, Hogarth Press, 1925. Pp. 150–161.
3. Jones, E., *On the Nightmare*. London, Hogarth Press, 1931. Pp. 7–350.
4. —————, 'The Nature of Autosuggestion,' in *Psychoanalysis*. (4th ed.) London, Baillière, Tindall & Cox, 1938. Pp. 356, 361.
5. Freud, S., 'The Uncanny,' in *Collected Papers*, IV. London, Hogarth Press, 1925. P. 387.
6. Fenichel, O., 'Ueber Respiratorische Introjektion,' *Int. Ztschr. f. Psa*, XVII, 1931.
7. —————, *The Psychoanalytic Theory of Neurosis*. New York, Norton, 1945. Pp. 250–252.
8. Harnik, J., 'One Component of Fear of Death in Early Infancy,' *Int. J. Psa.*, XI, Pt. 4, 1930, pp. 485–491.
9. Klein, M., *The Psychoanalysis of Children*. London, Hogarth Press, 1932. Pp. 281–282.
10. Chadwick, M., *Difficulties in Child Development*. New York, John Day, 1928, P. 142.

## CHAPTER XIV

1. Brunswick, Ruth Mack, 'Preoedipal Phase of the Libido Development,' *Psychoanalytic Quarterly*, IX, No. 2, 1940, pp. 292–319.
2. Jones, Ernest, 'The Phallic Phase,' in *Papers on Psychoanalysis*. (4th ed.) London, Baillière, Tindall, & Cox, 1938. Pp. 571–604.

# INDEX

Abbott, M. A., 144, *290*
Abraham, Karl, 119-120, 135, *288, 289*
Abreaction, and sense of reality, 47
Acting out, 208-219
  analyst's reaction to, 219
  defined, 208-209
  distortions of language, 211
  infancy of patients, 213
  narcissism in, 217-218
  preverbal period, 218
  primal scene influence in, 214
  repetition of past events, 214-215
  special problems, 209-210
  speech and action in, 211-212,
    techniques for, 215-219      [214
  transference relationships, 215
  traumata, 210
Addis, Miller, and Winnicott, 120,
    *288*
Aggression, 123; *see also* Rage, Tem-
    per tantrums
  associated with restraint, 78-98
  childbirth and, 150
  infantile, 156, 169
  muscular, and superego, 151
  narcissism and primitive aggres-
    sion, 19
  need for separation from mother,
    169
Aggressive defence, 93, 121
  edema, 130
  urination and, 110
Ahlfeld, Friedrich, 29, *286*
Aichorn, 159n
Albania, infant swaddling, 91-94;
    *see also* Restraint
Alcoholism, in psychopaths, 153,
    165-168
Alexander, Franz, Thomas M.
    French *et al.*, 120, *288*
Allen, Edward B., and James H.
    Wall, 159n
*American Journal of Orthopsychiatry*,
    78n, 99n, 100n, 138n, 151n
*American Journal of Psychiatry*, 55n,
    61n

Ames, L., 101n
Ames, L., F. Ilg, J. Learned, and
    A. Gesell, 102, *288*
Anesthesia, effects of early, 75-76
Anal phase, overlapping phallic
    phase, 244
  defecation and urination, common
    word for, 105
  defecation patterns of infancy, 104
Anal stimulation, 224-225, 231
Analysis
  excess narcissism and anxiety, 48
  practical considerations of treat-
    ment, 50-63
    education of the narcissism, 56,
      57, 58, 63, 76
    of the essential neurosis, 58-62
    handling of overload of anxiety,
      51-58
    management of the residue of
      blind, unanalysable anxiety,
      51, 57, 62
  of severe neuroses in adults, 25
Analyst, attitudes of, 55-56, 57
Anatomical structure
  influence of, on superego forma-
    tion, 140
  superego development and, 138-
    152
Angulo y Gonzales, A. W., 10, *284*
Anxiety
  anxious expectation, 19
  basic
    patient learns to manage, 62
    problems of, 25, 32
  blind, free-floating, unanalysable,
    32, 51, 57, 62
  cardiorespiratory symptoms, 29
  definition of, 7, 25
  Freud's views of, 25-30
  headaches and, 23
  hysteria, 69
  infantile, 42
  pattern, 40
  preanxiety, 28, 32, 43
  predisposition to, 6, 25-77
    clinical studies, 63-76

Anxiety—*cont.*
process of birth and, 7, 18, 25–77
reactions, birth trauma and, 28–29, 40
responses
beginnings of, 49–50
infantile, to maternal anxiety, 75, 79–80
somatic pattern of, 7, 18–19
secondary, 51, 54
sensory-motor tension level and, 18
urination and weeping, in relation to, 99
Appearances, overvaluation of external, 158
Appersonation, maternal, 159, 195,
Arey, Leslie B., 10, *283*
As-if behaviour, in psychopaths, 155, 171
Asthma, 125n
weeping and, 120–121
Aurora, screen memories and, 175–179
visual shock and, 122
Authority
conflict of parental attitudes towards, 158–159
fear of, 157
Autoerotic discharge, 64
Autoerotic response, 43
Autoerotism, 142
Autogenous behaviour, 89

Bak, Robert C., 23, *285*
Ball throwing, relation of sex difference in, 145
Bartelme, Hess, and Mohr, 40, *286*
Basic anxiety; *see* Anxiety, basic
Behaviour
antisocial, of psychopaths, 153
autogenous, 89
developmental locomotor, 87
infants, 30–38
premature, 40–44
Bender, Lauretta, and Helen Yarnell, 171, *291*
Benedek, Therese, 75n
Berne, E. U. C., 150, *291*
Bernstein, Clarence, and Leon Saul, 121, *288*
Best and Taylor, 121, *289*

Birth
biological economy of, 3–24
castration problem of mother with birth, 5
cerebral injury, 38–40
cortex and, 10–13, 15–16
defence activities of infant, 7
distribution of presentations at, 15n
dry labour and body phallus, 22–23
effect of
clinical studies, 63–76
on infant, 3–24
energy patterning by birth, 8
erection in male babies immediately after, 33–34, 35–37
fatigue to infant, 12–13
hearing at, 31
hiatus of, 13–14
myelinization and, 14–15
organization of primary narcissism by, 3
prematurity, 40–42
process of, influences on child, 3–24, 32–33
psychology of, 15
Rank's theories of birth trauma, 15, 26–27
relation of, to anxiety, 6
sensory stimulation at, 17
stimulation to infant during, 13
symbolism of, 29
thermal orientation and, 23
trauma of, 6, 26–28
clinical studies on, and predisposition to anxiety, 63–76
pathologicoanatomic evidences of, 38–40
variations in sleep of infant after, 18
Bisexuality
bisexual identification, 228, 280
in psychopaths, 161
Blair, C. M., 144, *290*
Blanton, M., 34, 102n, *286*
Body image, 142, 152, 225, 228, 263
confused, 148–149
Body language, 214
Body phallus
dry labour and, 22
with pathological weeping, 117

Bonaparte, Marie, 135, *289*
Breast and oral envy, 229, 234
Brierley, M., 147, 151, 237, *291*,
    *293*
Brill, A. A., 55n
Browne, J. S. L., and Howlett, 121,
    *289*
Brunswick, R. M., 144, 239, 273,
    *290*, *293*, *295*
Bühler, Charlotte, 12, 75n, 86, 102n,
    *285*, *287*
Bullard, Dr. Dexter, 54n, 77, *286*
*Bulletin of the Menninger Clinic*,
    121n
Burlingham, Dorothy T., and Anna
    Freud, 97, *288*


Caille, R. K., 150, *291*
Canestrini, S., 12, *284*
Cannon, Walter B., 4, 33, *283*
Carmichael, Leonard, 11, 12n, 144,
    *284*, *289*
Case studies
    cosmic identifications, 242-244
    effect of birth on predisposition
        to anxiety, 63-76
    phallic phase, 246-264, 267
    prepuberty trauma in girls, 192-
        200
    psychopaths, 162-163
    reaction to restraint, 79-82
    screen memories, 179-188
    shower type weeping, 112-115
    stream type weeping, 115-119
    superego formation, 123-134
Castration problems, 119, 145, 146,
    147, 148, 190, 199-200, 227,
    230, 242
    anxiety, 22, 65
    early female sexual development
        and, 228, 233-235
    mutilations related to, 94-96
Catatonia, angry ambulant, 81
Catel, W., 29, *285*
*Cerebral Birth Injuries* (S. Freud),
    38n
Cerebral cortex, birth and, 10-13
Cerebral injury, resulting from
    birth, 38-40
Cerebrum, birth stimulates, 24
Chadwick, Mary, 23, 270, *285*, *294*

Character formation, disturbances
    to, 157-158
Child Development Center, Har-
    vard School of Public Health,
    40
Children; *see also* Infants
    discovery of organs of opposite
        sex, 145-147
    ideals of, 152
    premature stimulation, 274-275
    sexual identity, 278
    skeletal development, 149-150
    stimulation of organs, 141-143,
        274-276
    superego influenced, 140
    visual shocks, 246-262
China, foot-binding in, 91; *see also*
    Restraint
Clairvoyant quality, of severe neu-
    rotics, 46
Claustrophobia, 115, 247
Cleckley, Hervey, 172, *292*
Clinical studies
    on the effect of birth on predis-
        position to anxiety, 63-76
    of the effect of restraint, 79-82
Clitoris, early female sexual develop-
    ment, 142, 220, 226-228, 232
Coghill, G. E., 11, *284*
Cohn, Franz, 77, *286*
Colours, in dreams, 130-132, 136
Concentration, 98
Condensation, screen memories and,
    175, 192
Conel, J. L., 10, *284*
Conscience; *see also* Superego
    controls, internalized, 169-170
    development of, 156-157, 168
        fear of punishment, 157
    distorted sense of reality and, 154
    fear of authority and, 157
    oedipus complex and, 155-156
    in the psychopath, 153-173
    sense of guilt and, 168-170
Constitutional factors, Freud's view,
    28, 28n
Cortex, fetal life and, 15-16
Cox, R., 194, *288*
Crothers, Bronson, Marion C. Put-
    nam, and Frank R. Ford, 6,
    *283*
Cry, of newborn infant, 101-102

Crying, sobbing, and weeping, 100n
Cultural patterns, sexual differences, 138

Danziger, Lotte, and Liselotte Frankl, 91-92, *288*
Darwin, Erasmus, 14n
Davis, E. A., 144, *290*
Daydreams, 192
Death, child's preoccupation with, 244
de Crinis, M., 10, *284*
de Kok, Winifred, 91, *287*
DeLee, Joseph B., and J. P. Greenhill, 5, *283*
Dennis, Wayne, 84, *287*
Dennis, Wayne, and M. G. Dennis, 91, *288*
Deutsch, H., 171, 175, 189, 190, *292*
Dewey, E., 12, *284*
Discipline, 195-196
Displacement, screen memories and, 175, 177, 187
Dreams
    analysis and, 228
    male genital, 128-131
    phallic phase, 251, 252, 253-254, 258, 260, 261, 265-266
    screen memories and, 174, 188
    urination-weeping problems, 111-114
Drives, pregenital and genital, 195-196
Drug addiction, of psychopaths, 151
Dunn, William H., 171, *292*
Dusser de Barenne, J. G., 11, *284*

Eadie, Dr. George S., 142n
Ego
    development, 197, 230
    strengthening of, for acting out, 216
*Ego and the Mechanisms of Defense, The* (A. Freud), 209n
Embryo; *see* Fetus
Emotion, extreme excitation, 33
Emotional behaviour responses, infants, 82-84, 87-88
Emotional deprivation, 171-172

Emotional disturbances, case study, 191-206
*Encyclopaedia Britannica*, 91, *287*
Enema situations, 196, 197-201, 237
Enuresis
    army camps, 97
    'evacuated' children, 97
    induced weeping, 120
    nocturnal, 80, 166
    premature children, 41
Environment, development and, 197
Erection, of male babies after birth, 33-34, 35-38
Erogenization, 22
Erotization, 190
    of skin at birth, 22-23
    of thinking, 22
Exhibitionism, 101, 159, 165
    tendency to, 54

Fantasies, 199, 245
Fantasy
    and sex differences, 193
    withdrawal from reality, 193
Father, identification with, 191
Fear
    birth experiences and, 14n
    reciprocal, 90
    response in infants, 30-31
Feeding training, character development and, 157
Female genitals, 131, 144
Female sexual development
    review of literature on, 235-239
    special problems of early, 220-239
Feminine identification, 228
Fenichel, Otto, 175, 208, 212, 269, *292, 293*
Ferenczi, Sandor, 43, 47, 108n, 120, *286, 288*
Fetishism, 179, 250, 257
Fetus
    oral reflex, 44n
    preanxiety response of, 43
    reaction to external stimuli, 29-30
    sensory-motor state of, 7-9
*First Year of Life, The*, 102n
Flatus, significance in childhood, 241

Folk customs, of restraint, 90–96
Foot-binding, restraint and, 91
Foot-penis symbolism, 63–65
Forbes, H. B., and H. S. Forbes, 29, 286
Forcefulness, lack of, 123
Ford, C. A., 71, 291
Ford, Franklin R., 38, 38n, 286
Ford, Franklin R., Crothers, Bronson, and Marion C. Putnam, 6, 283
Foster, J. C., 144, 290
Foster, S., 145, 291
Frankl, Liselotte, and Lotte Danziger, 91–92, 288
French, Thomas M., Franz Alexander et al., 120, 288
Freud, Anna, 209n, 215, 293
    observations on acting out, 215
Freud, Anna, and Dorothy T. Burlingham, 197, 288
Freud, Sigmund, 7, 19, 20, 25, 26, 33, 44, 45, 135, 146, 174, 208, 215, 220, 221, 222, 236, 259, 269, 283, 285, 286, 289, 290, 292, 293, 294
    on acting out, 208
    on anxiety, 25–30
    biological foundation of psychoanalysis, 273
    on birth and anxiety reaction, 6–7
    on birth trauma, 26–28
    Cerebral Birth Injuries, 38n
    on conscience, 156
    on discovery of organs of opposite sex, 145–146
    on early sexual development of women, 220–222, 230
    on narcissism, 19–20
    on 'Negation,' 47
    on The Problem of Anxiety, 25–30, 30n
    on screen memories, 174–175
    on the sun, 135
    technique in acting out, 215
Frigidity, vaginal, 230, 232
Fromm-Reichmann, Frieda, 60, 76, 286
Frustration, negative reactions of, 85

Gatewood, M. C., and A. P. Weiss, 150, 291

Genital and pregenital organization, 272–281
Genital drives, nature of, 195–196
Genital stimulation, 52–53, 65, 221
Genzmer, A., 12n, 284
Gesell, A., 44n, 101n, 102, 104, 105, 107, 109n, 156n
Gesell, A., H. M. Halverson et al., 12, 284
Gesell, A., and F. Ilg., 44n, 231, 286, 293
Gesell, A., F. Ilg., J. Learned, and L. Ames, 102, 288
Gesell, A., and H. Thompson, 86, 287
Ghosts, air, and flatus, 245
Girls, prepuberty trauma in, 189–206
Glasshagle, E. E., W. F. Windle, and J. E. O'Donnell, 11, 284
Glover, E., 175, 292
Glueck, Eleanor T., and Sheldon Glueck, 171, 292
Goals
    of achievement, 158
    patient needs satisfactory, 58
Goldfarb, William, 171, 291
Goodenough, F. L., 150, 291
Goodhall, H., and Harold G. Wolff, 5, 283
Greenacre, Phyllis, 6, 175, 189, 217, 224, 283, 293
Greenhill, J. P., and Joseph B. DeLee, 5, 283
Guilt, feeling of, in psychopaths, 157, 168–170
Gunther, E., 91, 287

Hallucinations, phallic, 229–230
Halo
    development of, 122, 123, 137
    screen memories and, 175–179
Halverson, H. M., 35, 225, 286, 293
Halverson, H. M., A. Gesell et al., 12, 284
Harnik, J., 269, 294
Hartshorn, H., and M. A. May, 144, 290
Harvard School of Public Health, 40
Hattwick, L. A., 150, 291

Hayes, M., and J. A. Hicks, 144, 290
Headaches, 122, 136
  process of birth and, 11n, 23
Head-binding, restraint and, 90–91, 94–96
Healy, William, 71, 292
Hearing, in newborn infants, 31
Heaver, W. Lynwood, 159n
Henderson, D. K., 172, 292
Hendrick, I., 239, 294
Hess, Mohr, and Bartelme, 40, 286
Hicks, J. A., and M. Hayes, 144, 290
Homosexual panic, 132–133
Homosexual tendencies, in psychopaths, 151, 161, 162–165
Hooker, Davenport, 10, 11, 289
Horney, K., 141, 289
Howlett and J. S. L. Browne, 121, 289
Humiliation, 193
Huschka, M., 99, 100n, 288
Hydrocephalus, 39
Hysteria
  anxiety, 69
  symptoms of, 63

Ideals; see also Superego
  based on parental images, 155
  of children, 152
  loftiness and visual stress, 122
  projection of ideals, 122
  of psychopaths, 160, 171
  sex differences and, 152
Identification with father, 191
Ilg, F., 44n, 101n
Ilg, F., L. Ames, J. Learned, and A. Gesell, 102, 288
Ilg, F., and A. Gesell, 231, 286, 293
Imaginary companions, 156n
Imago, 47, 286
Imbeciles, moral, 153
Impulsiveness, in psychopaths, 153
Independence, parental attitude towards, 158
Indians, swaddling practices of, 91
Individuation, sense of, 159

Infant and Child in the Culture of Today (Gesell et al.), 101n, 109n, 156n, 288
Infants; see also Children
  behaviour of newborn, 12–13, 30–38, 46–47
  crying at birth, 101–102
  developing adaptation to surroundings, 46–47
  effect of swaddling, 90–96
  fetal deaths, 150
  focusing eye, 86, 102, 109
  oral trauma, 213
  pain sensitivity, 13
  premature, clinical observations of, 40–44
  process of birth and, 3–24
  rage-like behaviour, 31–32, 82–86, 89–90
  reactions to restraint, 78–97
  reflect attitude of those around them, 46, 86, 89–90
  relations between weeping, vision, and urination, 101–110
  sexuality, 190
  sleep of newborn, 17–18
  tears first appear, 102, 109
  types of emotional reaction in, 30–44, 82–85
  urination, 101–107, 109
  vision, 101–103
  Watson's observations, 82–86
Inhibitions, case study, 191–206
Instincts, testing for, 8
Intellectual impairment, relation between restraint and, 78, 97–98
Interpretation
  for management of acting out, 215, 216, 217
  premature, 59–60
Intrauterine life, 6, 28–29, 31, 32, 39, 45, 91, 96
Introjection, 46–47
Introjection-projection mechanism, 156
  superego development, 139
Irwin, O. C., and A. P. Weiss, 11, 284

Jacobson, Dr. Edith, 135, 147, 148, 237, 291, 294

Jealousy, 233
Jelliffe, Smith Ely, 131, *289*
Jersild, A. T., C. L. Jersild, and
    F. V. Markey, 144, *290*
Johnson, B. L., 145, *290*
Jones, Ernest, 5, 23, 188, 238, 268,
    278, *283, 285*, 292, *294, 295*
Jordan, A. M., 145, *290*

Kaila, E., 86, *287*
Kane, Paul, 94-95, *288*
Kappers, C. W. A., 10n, *283*
Katan, Dr. Anna, 214
Kimmens, C. W., 144, *290*
Kinesthetic erotism, 195
Klang associations, 211
Klein, M., 140, 156, 157, 238, 270,
    *289, 292, 294*
Koffka, K., 13, *285*
Kohler, W., 33, *286*
Kris, Dr. Ernst, 137, 175

LaMar, Dr. N. C., 125n
Lampl de Groot, J., 148, 237, *291*,
    *294*
Langworthy, O. R., 13, 222, *285*,
    *294*
Lashley, K. S., 137, *289*
Latency period, 161n, 199, 226
    prepuberty trauma and, 189-190,
    200
Laughing and urination, 104, 107
Leagol, M. V., 144, *290*
Learned, J., 101n
Learned, J., F. Ilg, L. Ames, and A.
    Gesell, 132, *288*
Learning, effect of deprivation of
    practice situation, 86
Lehman, H. C., and P. A. Witty,
    144, *290*
Levy, Dr. David M., 61n, 103n, 171,
    *291*
Lewin, Bertram D., 120, 144, 188,
    *288, 289, 293*
Libido, 49, 244, 272, 273, 274, 298
    narcissistic, 44-45
    stage of, 177, 187
Lima, M., and K. M. Terman, 145,
    *290*
Lindner, Robert, 172, *292*
Locomotor development, 87-90

Lorand, Sandor, 77, *287*
Love
    development of impulse, 159, 160,
    168
    response in infants, 32
Lowrey, Lawson G., 171, *291*

McGinnis, John M., 102, *288*
McGraw, M., 12, *284*
Magic, belief in
    elements in conscience, 173
    in psychopath, 173
    and the supernatural, 246
    of words, 45, 46
Mahler, Margaret S., 131, *289*
Malapropisms, 211
Mansfield, Katherine, 177, *293*
Markey, F. V., C. L. Jersild, and
    A. T. Jersild, 144, *290*
Masculinity complex, 191, 205, 206,
    207, 220, 227, 228-229
    early female sexual development
    and, 228, 229, 231
Masochism, 199, 274
    economy of, 96
Mastering body urges, in superego
    development, 139
Masturbation, 53, 54, 65, 67-68,
    124, 126, 127, 142, 147, 151,
    193, 194, 198, 226, 228, 229,
    243, 248, 253
    early female sexual development
    and, 220, 227, 228, 232
Maturation processes, 21
May, M. A., and H. Hartshorn, 144,
    *290*
Mechanical skill and masturbation,
    151
Medea complex, 233-235
Memory
    in phallic phase, 244-245
    pictures, 9
    screen, 174-188
        brightness of, 174, 176-179
        case study, 179-188
        central theme of the neurosis
        and, 176
        deflection of focus, 176
        dreams and, 174, 175
        forces lending pressure and in-
        tensity to, 176-179, 195

Memory—*cont.*
  screen—*cont.*
    Freud on, 174–175
    halo or aurora, 175–179
    sexual trauma and, 189
    shocking childhood experiences,
      176
    structure of, 176
    traces, 7, 23
Menninger, Karl. 5, *283*
Menstruation, 120, 199, 200
Meyer, Dr. Adolf, 67
Michaels, Dr. J. J., 100n
Miles, C. C., and L. M. Terman,
    144, *290*
Miller, Addis, and Winnicott, 120,
    *288*
Minkowski, M., 11, *284*
Mirroring reaction, 45–46, 50, 60
Mohr, Hess, and Bartelme, 40, *286*
Monsters, 11, 17
Moral imbeciles, 153
Morgan, Clifford T., 4, *283*
Motility in acting out, 209, 212
Motion, restraint of, in infants, 82–90
Motor activities, embryonic develop-
    ment of, 8–11
Müller-Braunschweig, C., 147, 237,
    *291, 294*
Muscular ambivalence in males, 151
Mutilations, castration and, 96
Myelinization, 13–15, 17, 22
Myopia, 134

Narcissism, 217, 218, 279
  antenatal, 3
  definition of, 19–20, 44–45
  education away from, 56, 57, 58,
    63, 76
  excess, 48, 50
  fetal, characteristics of, 20, 44–45
  identification, 47
  mirroring, 46, 50
  parents, 158–159
  postnatal, attributes of, 45–48
  predisposition to anxiety and, 25–
    77
Negativism, chronic, 98
Nelson, A. K., K. H. Sun, and K. C.
    Pratt, 83, *287*
Nephritis, 124

Nervous system, birth and, 13
Neurobiotaxis, 10n
Neuroses
  compulsive, 52
  depressive obsessional, 187
  essential, analysis of, 58–59
  predisposition to anxiety and, 48
  severe, analysis of, 25
  traumatic, 175, 179
Neurotics, constitutional, tension-
    discharging symptoms, 99–
    100
Neurotic scoptophilia, 173
Nevinny, H., 6, *283*
Nightmares, 199, 268

O'Donnell, J. E., E. E. Glasshagle,
    and W. F. Windle, 11, *284*
Oedipus complex, 190–191, 229,
    272, 281
  conscience and, 155–156
  early female sexual development,
    228
  prepuberty trauma and, 196–200,
    206–207
  in psychopaths, 161
  traumata, 207
Omnipotence, sense of, 50
Oral-anal-vaginal stimulation, 229,
    231, 233
Oral erotism, 212, 225
Orality, 212
Oralization, premature, 43
Orgasm, 194, 199, 224
Overconscientiousness, 123
Overstimulation
  at birth, 21–22
  suffusion of, 52, 275, 276
  vaginal stimulation, 142
  visual situations of, 131

Pain, 3–5, 12–13, 153
  comparison with anxiety, 4
  implications of, 3–4
  question of pain to infant in birth,
    3
Panic states, 54
Parent-child relationships, 195
  psychopaths and, 157–162, 165,
    168, 170, 172
Parents, aggression against, 159

Pathological sexual development, 221

Patients, treatment of, 50–63

Patterning
anxiety reaction, 19
sensory-motor tension level, 18

Payne, S. M., 237, *294*

Peiper, A., 29, *285*

Penis envy, 117, 119, 127, 146, 148, 149, 191, 199, 205, 227–229, 264, 279
early female sexual development and, 220, 227, 228–229, 231
feminine weeping and, 101
masculine urination and, 108, 109

Perversions, 175, 179

Phallic phase and respiratory incorporation, 240–271
anal and genital phases, 243–245
clitoral stimulation, 227–228
dreams, 251, 252, 253, 254, 258, 260, 261, 265–266
early female sexual development and, 221, 231
genital stimulation, 221, 226
hallucinations, 229–230, 244–245
memory and thought, 245
superego and, 243

Phobias, 69, 187, 191

Play acting, 199, 208–219; *see also* Acting out

Polymorphous perverse tendencies
early discharge of, 43–44, 53
clinical description, 66
overstimulation and, 276
psychopaths, 154

Powdermaker, Florence, 171, *291*

Pratt, K. C., A. K. Nelson, and K. H. Sun, 83, *287*

Preanxiety response, 32, 43

Precocity, stimulation to, 275, 277

Pregenital drives, 190, 196–200

Premature children, clinical observations, 40–44

Prepuberty, 190

Prepuberty trauma in girls, 189–207

Pressures, psychological, 7

Preyer, W., 8, *283*

Pride, parent-child relationship, 158

Primal scene, 130, 131, 173, 196, 214

Pseudoaphasias, 211

Pseudoimbecility, 131

Pseudologia, 199 (including lying)
feminine, 147
psychopath, 153

Pseudologia phantastica, 175

Psychic paralysis, state of, 54

Psychic traumata, 176

*Psychoanalytic Quarterly, The,* 50n, 53n, 56n, 75n, 86n, 100n, 111n, 122n, 189n, 208n

*Psychoanalytic Study of the Child, The,* 174n, 220n, 240n

Psychopathic personalities, 153

*Psychopathology of Everyday Life* (S. Freud), 208

Psychopaths
case studies, 162–168
characteristics of, 153, 160, 173
conscience in, 153–173
constitutional, 153
criminal, 172–173
defective character of, 154–155
homosexual tendencies of, 153, 161, 162–165
identification problems, 156, 160
irresponsible behaviour of, 154–155
oedipus period, 160–161
parent-child relationship, 158–162, 165, 168, 170, 172
psychiatric treatment of, 154
recent writings on, 171–173

Psychotic patients, 111–119, 223

Puberty
masculinity complex, 229
prepuberty trauma and, 190

Punishment, 157, 188

Putnam, Marion C., F. R. Ford, Bronson, and Crothers, 6, *283*

Rado, S., 22, *285*

Rage, response in infants, 31–32, 82–85, 89–90
Watson's theory, 82–85

Rank, O., 225, *294*

Ray, W. S., 29, *285*

Reality
degradation of the sense of, 160
developing sense of, 228
disturbed sense of, 47, 50
problems of, 57
psychopath, 154
testing, 159, 188

Reassurance, role of, in analysis, 55–56
Rectal stimulation, 224–225, 226–227
Reich, Wilhelm, 173, 292
Religiosity, 246
Renunciation, in superego development, 139
Repression, screen memories and, 174, 175
Respiratory incorporation, 245, 268–271
Responses, emotional, of infants, 82–84, 88
Restraint, 197
　aggression and, 97–98
　child's need for protective, 197
　clinical observations of, in psychiatric patients, 79–82
　customs of, in folk groups, 79, 90–96
　definition of, 78
　Dennis' experiment-deprivation of stimulus, 87–89
　effects of, 78–79
　elimination of practice situations, 82, 96–97
　emotional attitude of the restrainer and, 86, 89–90
　experimental work in, 82–90
　infants' reactions to, 78–97
　intellectual impairment and prolonged, 78, 97–98
　motor retardation and, 89, 93
　positive and negative, 97
　punishment, 85
　rage and, 89
　sado-masochism and, 98
　social responses and, 88, 89, 93–94
　swaddling, 91-93
　types of, 97
Retardation, restraint and, 97–98

Sachs, Hans, 147, 257, 291, 294
Sado-masochistic character structure, 96, 98, 178, 188, 205, 206–207
Saul, Leon, and Clarence Bernstein, 121, 288
'Scab-picking,' 56–57
Schizophrenics, development of, 157

Schreber case
　narcissism described, 19
　sun symbolism, 135
Scoptophilia, 123, 128, 173
Screen memories, 174–188
Searl, M. W., 145, 290
Self-critique, method of, 63
Selye, Hans, 121, 289
Semantic dementia, 172
Senn, Dr. Milton J. E., 15n
Sensation, embryonic development of, 8–11
Senses
　kinesthetic, 34
　smell, 245
Sensitivity, physiological, 50
Sensory fatigue, in newborn infants, 13, 17, 24
Sensory-motor balance, 7–10
　levels of tension and, 7–11
　relation to anxiety, 18
　restraint and, 78–79
Sensory-motor tension level, in infants, 18
Sensory stimulation, 8, 17
Separateness, sense of, 159, 161
Sewell, M., 147, 291
Sexual development, female, special problems of, 220–239
　Medea complex, 233–235
　review of the literature on, 235–239
Sexual difference, cultural patterns and, 138
Sexual drives, 190
Sexual identity, 278
Sexual investigations, among young girls, 190, 199, 229
Sexuality
　infantile, 190
　prepuberty trauma and, 206
Sexual perversions, of psychopaths, 153
Sexual trauma, 184
Shadows, child's interest in, 246
Shame, 105, 158
Sheldon, W. H., 141, 289
Sherman, I. C., and M. Sherman, 13, 83, 285, 287
Shinn, Millicent, 34
Shirley, Mary, 40, 286
Shocks, visual in children, 123, 134, 136, 137, 177, 246–262

Silberpfennig, Dr. Judith, 173n
Skin, erotization, 22–23, 279
  sensitivity of, 39
Sleep, in newborn infants, 7–18
Slips of the tongue, 175
Smell, sense of, 245
Smith, J. R., 17, 285
Smith, S., 147, 291
Snake-worshipping cults, 142n
Sobbing, weeping, and crying, 100n
Social development, 93–94
Social influences, in superego development, 140–141
Sollenberger, R. T., 141, 289
Somato-instinctive urges, 140
Sontag, L. W., and R. F. Wallace, 29, 285, 286
Sound, reaction to, 29, 31
Spacing of siblings, 277
Speech development, 45–46, 212–214
  oral trauma and, 213, 214
Sphincter control, 213, 225
Spitting, relation to urination, 145
Spoonerisms, 74, 211
Stein, Gertrude, 212
Stimulation
  birth, 21–22
  experiments with twins, 87–90
  premature, 274–276
  thermal, and newborn babies, 17–18, 23
Stirnimann, F., 17, 285
Stragnell, Gregory, 136, 289
Streeter, G., 31, 286
Stuart, Harold C., 206, 293
Stubbornness, 98
Sucking, thumb, 29, 35, 41, 44n, 79, 99
Suffering, organic stamp of, 50
Sullivan, Harry, 76, 287
Sun, K. H., A. K. Nelson, and K. C. Pratt, 83, 287
Superego, 122–23, 134, 135, 248, 250
  constitution and, 140
  development, 178, 186, 188
    anatomical structure and, 138–
    genital organs and, 140  [152
    headache and, 122
    muscular development and, 140
    stages in, 138–140
    visual stress and superego, 122–137

Swaddling infants, custom of, 79, 90–98
Swan, J. G., 91, 287
Symbolization, screen memories and, 174–175

Tact
  feminine, 143
  in psychopaths, 160
Taylor, J. H., 83, 287
Taylor and Best, 121, 289
Telepathy, 246
Temper tantrums, 80, 99, 195
Tempo, slow, 81, 97
Tension-discharging functions, 99
Tensions
  erotic, 61
  excessive chronic, birth and, 6
  infantile, 170
  level of, 7–8
  patterning of the sensory-motor, 18
  relaxation of, 43
Terman, L. M., and M. Lima, 145, 290
Terman, L. M., and C. C. Miles, 144, 290
Testicle-breast comparison, 233–235
Tetany, 151
Thompson, Clara, 77, 287
Thompson, H., and A. Gesell, 86, 287
Three Contributions to the Sexual Theory, The (S. Freud), 147
Thumb sucking, 29, 35, 41, 44n, 79, 99
Tics and tremors, 99
Tidd, Charles W., 76, 287
Toilet training, 106, 157, 186, 187, 195, 198
Tonsillectomy, 124, 265
Transference, 60–62, 215
Trauma
  birth, and the predisposition to anxiety, 63–76
  effect of, 273–274
  oral, 213
  postnatal life and, 48
  prepuberty, in girls, 189–207
  sexual, screen memories and, 189

Traumata
  anxiety patterns and, 19
  oepidal, 206
  psychic, 176
Traumatic neuroses, 175, 179
Treatment; *see also* Analysis
  practical consideration of, 50–63
Tremors, 99
Twins, experiments on the effect of
  restraint, 84, 87–90


Urination and weeping, 98–110,
    113, 116–117, 118–119
  babies, 101–110
  constitutional neurotics, 99–100
  control, 105–107
  dreams, 112–115, 117
  'evacuated' children, 99
  interrelations, 99
  psychotic patients, 111–119
  sex differences, 103–107
  social attitudes to, 107
  tension-discharging activity, 99
Urticaria, weeping and, 121


Vagina
  conditions of dominance of, 230–
    232
  discharge from, 225
  early female sexual development
    and, 220, 221
  indications and conditions of early
    sensations, 223–225
  oral-anal stimulation, 229, 231,
    233
  situations in which a bipolarity
    develops, 228–230
  stimulation, 142–143, 144, 147–
    148, 204, 221–222
  tic, 71
van der Heide, Carel, 120, *288*
*Vertebrate Eye and Its Adaptive Radia-
  tion, The* (Walls), 102n
Vision, focusing of eye, in infants,
    46, 102,
  related to urination and weeping,
    109
  in relation to male urination, 107

Visual incorporation, 278–279
Visual shock,  123,  134,  135–136,
    157, 246–262
Voyeurism, 179


Wagner, I. F., 17, *285*
Wall, James H., 159n
Wallace, R. F., and L. W. Sontag,
    29, *285*
Walls, G. L., 102n
Watson, John B., 30–31, 82–83, *286*,
    *287*
Weeping; *see also* Urination and
    weeping
  exhibitionism in, 100–101
  pathological, 111–121
    shower type, 100, 109, 111–115
    stream type, 100, 109, 111, 112,
      115–119
  social attitude toward, 107–108
Weiss, A. P., and M. C. Gatewood,
    150, *291*
Weiss, A. P., and O. C. Irwin, 11,
    *284*
Whistling and urination, 145
Wind and air erotism, 245–246
Windle, W. F., 8, 11, *284*
Windle, W. F., J. E. O'Donnell, and
    E. E. Glasshagle, 11, *284*
Winnicott, Addis, and Miller, 120,
    *288*
Wittels, F., 47, 161n, *286*
Witty, P. A., and H. C. Lehman,
    144, *290*
Wolff, Harold G., and H. Goodall,
    5, *283*
Women, early sexual development
    of, 220–239
Word sounds, 212
*World is Round, The* (Stein), 212
Wyman, J. B., 144, *290*


Yarnell, Helen, and Lauretta Ben-
    der, 171, *291*


Zilboorg, Gregory, 55n, 120, *288*